In The Name Of Liberty

By

Owen Johnson

IN THE NAME OF LIBERTY

I

IN SEARCH OF THE REVOLUTION

In the month of August of the year 1792 the Rue Maugout was a distorted cleft in the gray mass of the Faubourg St. Antoine, apart from the ceaseless cry of life of the thoroughfare, but animated by a sprinkling of shops and taverns. No. 38, like its neighbors, was a twisted, settled mass of stone and timber that had somehow held together from the time of Henry II. The entrance was low, pinched, and dank. On one side a twisted staircase zig-zagged into the gloom. On the other a squat door with a grating in the center, like a blind eye, led into the cellar which la Mère Corniche, the concierge, let out at two sous a night to travelers in search of an economical resting-place. Beyond this rat-hole a murky glass served as a peep-hole, whence her flattened nose and little eyes could dimly be distinguished at all hours of the day. This tenebrous entrance, after plunging onward some forty feet, fell against a wall of gray light, where the visitor, making an abrupt angle, passed into the purer air of a narrow court. Opposite, the passage took up its interrupted way to a farther court, more spacious, where a dirt-colored maple offered a ragged shelter and a few parched vines gripped the yellow walls. The tiled roofs were shrunk, the ridges warped, the walls cracking and bulging about the distorted windows. Along the roofs the dust and dirt had gradually accumulated and given birth to a few blades of gray-green plants. Nature had slipped in and assimilated the work of man, until the building, yielding to the weight of time and the elements, appeared as a hollow sunk in fantastic cliffs, where, from narrow, misshapen slits, the dwellers peered forth. About the maple swarmed a troop of children, grimy, bare, and voluble. In the branches and in the ivy a horde of sparrows shrilled and fought, keeping warily out of reach of the lank cats that slunk in ambush.

In front of No. 38, each morning, prompt as the sun, which she often anticipated, la Mère Corniche appeared with her broom. She was one of those strange old women in whom the appearances of youth and age are incongruously blended. Seen from behind, her short, erect stature (she was an equal four feet), her skirt stopping half-way below the knees to reveal a pair of man's boots, gave the effect of a child of twelve. When she turned, the shock of the empty gums, the skin hanging in pockets on the cheeks, the eyes showing from their pouches like cold lanterns, caused her to seem like a being who had never known youth.

She had thrown open the doors on this August morning and was conducting a resolute campaign with her broom when she perceived a young man, who even at that early hour, from the evidence of dust, had just completed an arduous journey. A bulging handkerchief swinging from a staff across his shoulder evidently contained all his baggage, and proclaimed the definite purpose of the immigrant. The concierge regarded him with some curiosity. He was too old to be a truant scholar, and too much at ease to be of the far provinces. Besides, his dress showed familiarity with the city modes. He seemed rather the young adventurer running to Paris in the first flush of that enthusiasm and attraction which the Revolution in its influx had awakened.

The dress itself proclaimed, not without a touch of humor, the preparation of the zealous devotee approaching the Mecca of his ambitions. His cocked hat, of a largeness which suggested another owner, was new and worn jauntily, with the gay assurance of youth in its destiny. A brilliant red neck-cloth was arranged with the abandon of pardonable vanity. A clear blue redingote, a cloth-of-gold vest, and a pair of drab knickerbockers completed a costume that had drawn many a smile. For while the coat was so long that the sleeves hid the wrist, the vest was bursting its buttons, and though the knickerbockers pinched, the hat continued to wobble in dumb accusation; so that two generations at least must have contributed to the wardrobe of the young buccaneer.

At the moment the concierge discovered the youthful adventurer, he was engrossed in the task of slapping the dust from his garments, while his eyes, wandering along the streets, were searching to some purpose.

Curiosity being stronger than need, it was la Mère Corniche who put the first question.

"Well, citoyen, you seek some one in this street?"

"The answer should be apparent," the young fellow answered frankly. "I seek a lodging. Have you a room to let?"

"H'm!" La Mère Corniche eyed him unfavorably. "Maybe I have, and maybe I haven't; I take no aristocrats."

The young man, seeing that his clothes were in disfavor, began to laugh.

"In as far, citoyenne," he said, with a sweep of his hand, "as it concerns these, I plead guilty: my clothes are aristocrats. But hear me," as his listener began to scowl. "They were; but aristocrats being traitors, I confiscated them; and," he added slyly, "I come to deliver them to the State."

"And to denounce the traitors, citoyen," the concierge exclaimed fiercely, "even were they your father and mother."

"Even that—if I had a family," he added cautiously. "And now, citoyenne, what can you do for me?"

With this direct question, the fanatic light in her face died away. The little woman withdrew a step and ran her eyes over the prospective tenant. She made him repeat the question, and finally said, with a sigh, as though regretting the price she had fixed in her mind, "How long?"

"A year—two years—indefinitely."

"There are two rooms and a parlor on the second," she began tentatively.

"That suits me."

"The price will be for you—" la Mère Corniche hastened to increase the sum, "thirty francs a month."

"Good."

"Payable in advance."

The young fellow shrugged his shoulders, and with a comical grin turned his pockets inside out.

"What!" la Mère Corniche shrieked in her astonishment. "You swindler! You have taken an apartment at thirty francs a month without a sou in your pocket."

"At present."

"Get off, you, who'd rob a poor old woman."

"We'll renounce the apartment, then," he cried, with a laugh. "One room, citoyenne; give me one room if you are a patriot."

"Patriot—robber! Be off or I'll denounce you!"

The young fellow, seeing his case hopeless, prepared to depart.

"Good-by, then, mother," he said. "And thanks for your patriotic reception. Only direct me to the house of Marat and I'm done with you."

"What have you to do with the Citoyen Marat?" cried the old woman, startled into speech at that name.

"That is my affair."

"You know him?"

"I have a letter to him."

La Mère Corniche looked at him in indecision. An emissary to Marat was a very different matter. She struggled silently between her avarice and the one adoration of her life, until her listener, mistaking her silence, turned impatiently on his heel.

"Here, come back," the concierge cried, thus brought to decision. "Let me see your letter."

The young fellow shrugged his shoulders good-humoredly and produced a large envelope, on which the curious eye of his listener beheld the magic words, "To Jean Paul Marat." But if she had hoped to find on it some clue to its sender, she was disappointed. She turned the letter over and handed it reluctantly back.

"Private business, hey?"

"Particularly private," he said. Then, seeing his advantage and following up his good fortune, he added: "Now, citoyenne, don't you think you could tuck me away somewhere until I make a fortune?"

The old woman hesitated a moment longer, whereupon he fell to scanning pensively the address, and mumbling over "Jean Paul Marat, a great man that."

"Damn, I'll do it!" la Mère Corniche suddenly cried, and with a crook of her thumb she bade him follow her. But immediately she halted and asked:

"Citoyen—?"

"Citoyen Barabant—Eugène Armand Barabant."

"Of—?"

"Of 38 Rue Maugout," he said laconically, then, with a smile, modified his step to follow the painful progress of his guide.

At the dark entrance a raven came hopping to meet them, filling the gloom with his raucous cry. Barabant halted.

"It's only Jean Paul," explained the old woman. "He brings good luck."

She placed him, flapping his wings, on her shoulder and continued. At the first court, by the stairs that led to the vacant apartment on the second floor, she hesitated, but the indecision was momentary. Into the second court Barabant followed with an air of interest that showed that, though perhaps familiar with the streets of Paris, he had never delved into its secret places. Twice more la Mère Corniche halted before possible lodgings, until at last, having vanquished each temptation, she began to clamber up the shaky flights that led to the attic.

Barabant had perceived each mental struggle with great enjoyment. He was young, adventurous, entering life through strange gates. So when at length they reached the end of their climb, and his guide, after much tugging, accompanied by occasional kicks, had forced open the reluctant door, the dingy attic appeared to him a haven of splendor.

La Mère Corniche watched him curiously from the doorway, rubbing her chin. "Eh, Citoyen Barabant? Well, does it suit you?"

"Perfect."

He cast a careless glance at the impoverished room and craned out of the window. In his survey of the court, his eye rested a moment on the window below, where, through the careless folds of a half-curtain, he had caught the gleam of a white arm.

"And what is the price of this?" he asked; but his thoughts were elsewhere.

"Nothing."

La Mère Corniche sighed heroically, and hastened on as though distrusting her generosity. "Only, when you see Citoyen Marat, tell him that I, Citoyenne Corniche, have done this to one who is his friend."

Barabant remained one moment motionless, as though confounded at this remnant of human feeling in the sibyl. But the door had hardly closed when, without a glance at his new quarters, he was again at the window. The truth was that, without hesitating to reflect on the insufficiency of the evidence, he had already built a romance on the sight of a white arm seen two stories below through the folds of a curtain. So when he returned eagerly to his scrutiny, what was his disenchantment to perceive below a very buxom matron, who was regarding him with equal attentiveness.

Barabant, with a laugh at his own discomfiture, began to search more cautiously. And as one deception in youth is sufficient to make a skeptic for an hour, when in turn he began to explore the window opposite he received, with indifference, the view of another arm, though it was equally white and well modeled.

But this time, as though Fate were determined to rebuke him for scorning her gifts, there appeared at the window the figure of a young girl, whose early toilet allowed to be seen a throat and arm of sufficient whiteness to dazzle the young romanticist.

Youth and natural coquetry fortunately are stronger than the indifference of poverty. Had Barabant been fifty the girl would have continued her inspection undisturbed; but perceiving him to be in the twenties, and with a certain air of distinction, she hastily withdrew, covering her throat with an instinctive motion of her hand, and leaving Barabant, forgetful of his first disenchantment, to gallop through the delightful fields of a new romance.

II

A RESCUE FROM ARISTOCRATS

After a moment of vain expectation, Barabant withdrew to the inspection of his new possessions. In one corner stood a bed that bore the marks of many restorations. Each leg was of a different shape, rudely fastened to the main body, which, despite threatening fissures, had still survived by the aid of several hitches of stout rope that encouraged the joints. One pillow and two coverings, one chair and a chest of drawers, that answered to much tugging, completed the installation. The floor was of tiles; the ceiling, responding to the sagging of the roof, bulged and cracked, while in one spot it had even receded so far that a ray of the sun squeezed through and fell in a dusty flight to the floor.

Barabant's survey was completed in an instant. Returning to the bed, he paused doubtfully and cautiously tried its strength with a shake. Then he seated himself and slowly drew up both legs. The bed still remaining intact, he turned over, threw the covers over him, and, worn out with the journey, fell asleep.

It was almost ten when he stirred, and the August sun was pouring through the gabled window. A mouse scampered hurriedly home as he started up; a couple of sparrows, hovering undecidedly on the sill, fluttered off. He sat up, rubbing his eyes with the confusion of one who awakens at an unaccustomed hour, and then sprang to the floor so impetuously that the bed protested with a warning creak. His first movement was to the window, where an eager glance showed the opposite room vacant. More leisurely he turned to a survey of his horizon, where in the distance the roofs, of an equal height, rolled away in high, sloping billows of brown tile dotted with flashes of green or the white fleck of linen. The air was warm, but still alive with the freshness of the morning, inviting him to be out and seeing. He left his bundle carelessly on the chair, brushed his clothes, arranged his neck-cloth by means of a pocket-mirror, preparing himself with solicitude for his appearance in the streets.

He descended the stairs alertly, listening for any sound of his neighbors; but the stairways, as well as the courts, were silent and empty, for at that period all Paris hastened daily to the streets, expectant of great events.

Through the ugly, tortuous streets of the Faubourg St. Antoine Barabant plunged eagerly to the boulevard, where the crowd, circulating slowly, lingered from corner to corner, drifting to every knot of discussion, avaricious for every crumb of rumor. Hawkers of ballads and pamphlets sought to slip their wares into the young fellow's hand with a show of mystery and fear of detection. One whispered his "Midnight Diversions of the Austrian Veto"; another showed him furtively the title, "Capet Exposed by his Valet."

Refusing all these, Barabant halted at every shop-window, before numberless engravings representing the Fall of the Bastille, the Oath in the Tennis-court, and the Section-halls.

The gloomy, disheveled figures of the Marseillais were abroad, stalking melodramatically through the crowds or filling the cafés to thunder out their denunciations of tyrants and aristocrats. Fishwives and washerwomen retailed to all comers the latest alarms.

"The aristocrats are burning the grain-fields!"

"A plot has been unearthed to exterminate the patriots by grinding glass in their flour."

"The Faubourg St. Antoine is to be destroyed by fire."

Venders of relics offered the manacles of the Bastille and the rope-ladder of Latude; fortune-tellers prophesied, for a consideration, the fall of Capet and the advent of the Republic; an exhibitor of trick-dogs advertised a burlesque on the return of the royal family from Versailles. At a marionette theater the dolls represented public personages, and the king and the queen (Veto and the Austrian) were battered and humiliated to the applause of the crowds.

At points on Barabant's progress he listened to young fellows from tables or chairs reading to the illiterate from the newspapers, quoting from witty Camille Desmoulins or sullen, headlong Marat. Barabant was amazed at the response from the audience, at their sudden movements to laughter or anger. Swayed by the infection, his lips moved involuntarily with a hundred impetuous thoughts. In this era that promised so much to youth, which demanded its ardor, its enthusiasm, and its faith, he longed to emerge from obscurity. For youth is the period of large resolutions, ardent convictions, and the championship of desperate causes. In that season, when the world is new, the mind, fascinated by its unfolding strength, leaps over decisions, doubts nothing, nor hesitates. In revolutions it is the generation that dares that leads.

From the young and daring Faubourg St. Antoine Barabant emerged, inspired, elated, and meditative. Barabant, disciple of the Revolution of Ideas, was bewildered by the might of this torrent. It excited his vision, but it terrified him. It was immense, but it might erupt through a dozen forced openings.

In the Rue St. Honoré, where the discussions grew more abstract, he was startled at the contrast. Great events were struggling to the surface, yet here in the cafés men discussed charmingly on theory and principle; nor could he fancy, fresh from the vigor of the people, the sacred Revolution among these gay colors, immaculate wigs, and well-fed and thirsty orators.

But this first impression, acute with the shock of contrast, was soon succeeded by a feeling of stimulation. Attracted, as is natural in youth, by the beautiful and the luxurious, and led by his imagination and his ambition, he forgot his emotions. Whereas in the mob he had felt himself equal to the martyr, he now breathed an air that aroused his powers. They discussed the freedom of the individual, the liberty of the press, and the abolishment of the penalty of death, with grace and with unfailing, agile wit, and debated the Republic with the airs of the court.

Barabant, who wished to see everything at once, made a rapid excursion to the Tuileries, to the Place de la Grève, the Place de la Revolution, the Markets, and the famous Hall of the Jacobins.

Toward evening, as the dusk invaded the streets, and the lanterns, from their brackets on the walls, set up their empire over the fleeting day, an indefinable melancholy descended over him: the melancholy of the city that affects the young and the stranger. Barabant's spirits, quick to soar, momentarily succumbed to that feeling of loneliness and aloofness that attacks the individual in the solitudes of nature and in that wilderness of men, the city.

He was leaning against a pillar in the Rue St. Honoré, in this ruminative mood watching the unfamiliar crowd, when his glance was stopped by the figure of a flower-girl. She was tall, dark, and lithe, and, though without any particular charm of form, she had such an unusual grace in her movements that he fell curiously to speculating on her face. But the turning proving a disappointment, he laughed at his haste, and his glance wandered elsewhere.

"Citoyen, buy my cockade?"

Barabant turned quickly; the flower-girl was at his side, smiling mischievously up at him. He was conscious of a sudden embarrassment—a solicitude for his bearing before the frank amusement of the girl. This time he did not turn away so carelessly. The face was attractive despite its irregularity, full of force in the free span of the forehead and of sudden passions in the high, starting eyebrows. The eyes alone seemed cold and sardonic, without emotion or change.

"Come, citoyen, a cockade."

Barabant shrugged his shoulders, and diving into his purse, at length produced a few coppers.

"A patriot's dinner is more my need, citoyenne, than a cockade."

The girl, who had been watching with amusement this search after the elusive coins, ignoring his answer, asked curiously:

"From the provinces?"

Barabant, resenting the patronizing tone, said stiffly:

"No."

"But not quite Parisian," the flower-girl returned, with a smile, and her glance traveled inquiringly over the incongruous make-up.

Barabant laughed. "Parisian by a day only."

The girl smiled again, and, suddenly fastening a cockade on his lapel, said: "You are a good-looking chap; keep your sous; when your purse is fuller, remember me." And thrusting back his proffered money, she took up her basket and nodded gaily to him. "Good luck to you, citoyen. Vive la jeunesse!"

The accidental meeting quite restored him to his eager zest again. The one greeting converted the wilderness into a familiar land. He started on his walk, seeking a humble bill of fare within the range of his modest resources. He chose one where the dinner consisted of a thick soup the filling qualities of which he knew—a purée of beans and a piece of cheese. It was still somewhat earlier than the dinner-hour, and he finished his meal silently watched by the waiter with suspicious eyes. Thence he wandered through brighter streets, pausing at times on the skirts of the crowd that invaded the cafés, which now began to grow noisy with impromptu oratory.

The Palais Royal with its flaring halls drew him to its tumultuous life. He wandered through the gambling-rooms, through fakers' exhibitions, heedless of siren voices, watching the play of pickpockets and dupes, until suddenly in the crowd a figure of unusual oddity caught his attention: a tall, military man with a cocked hat, shifted very much over one ear, and a nose thrown back so far that it seemed to be scouting in the air, fearful lest its owner should miss a single rumor.

Without purpose in his wanderings, Barabant unconsciously fell to following this new character. The body was lank, the legs long,—out of all proportion, and so thin that they seemed rather a pair of pliable stilts,—while the arms hung or moved in loose jerks as though dependent from the joints of a manikin.

Oblivious to the banter and the scrutiny of the throng, the wanderer pursued his inquisitive way. From time to time he stopped, craning his neck and remaining absorbed in the contemplation of a chance display of tricolor or a group of shrill orators sounding their eloquence to the eager mass. The inspection ended, a guttural exclamation or a whistle escaping the lips showed that the impression had been registered behind the keen, laughing countenance. Gradually the crowd, inclined at first to jeer, perceiving him utterly unconscious of their interest, turned to banter; but there too they were met with the utmost complacency.

"Hey, Daddy Long-legs!"

"Beware you keep out of their reach, my friend."

"Citizen Scissors!"

"Citizen Stilts!"

"Citizen Pique la bise!"

At this last allusion to the manner in which his nose might be said to cut the breeze, he opened wide a gaping mouth and roared "Touché!" so heartily that the crowd, who never laugh long at those who laugh with them, returned to their occupation with grunts of approval. Still there remained to be revealed the complexion of his political belief: whether it was a patriot that thus paraded the steadfast Palais Royal, or a hireling of a tyrant aristocracy.

Here again the visitor puzzled all conjectures. Arrived opposite the café, "To the Fall of the Bastille," his glance no sooner seized the inscription than he snatched off his hat with so hearty a "Bravo!" that his neighbors echoed the infectious acclamation; but at the very next turn, perceiving a mountebank's counter presided over by a pretty citizeness, he paused and repeated the salute with equal vigor. Now, though the tribute to a pretty face could not justly distinguish the parties, yet the inspiration and the manner had the taint of aristocracy. So that those who had listened looked dubious, then scratched their heads, and finally retired, laughing over their own mystification.

With a gluttonous chuckle the stranger turned suddenly into a neighboring passage. Barabant followed, in time to see the lean figure mount a chance staircase, ascending which on the humor of the moment, he emerged in turn into a café of unusual magnificence.

Having no money with which to pay a consommation at the tables, Barabant remained among the spectators. The tall stranger had joined a group in the middle of the room, whence a florid Chevalier de St. Louis cried bombastically:

"Citizen Bottle-opener, send me the Citizen Table-wiper!"

"And bring the Citizen Broom," took up another, "to expel this Citizen Dog!"

"Let the Citizen Crier," added another, with careless scorn, "call the Citizen My Carriage!"

Amid this persiflage Barabant remained, chafing and angry, realizing that he had stumbled into that abomination of patriots, a den of aristocrats.

The purport of all table-to-table addresses was the incompetency of the National Assembly and the state of anarchy existing since the royal power had been defied. Although the café was not accessible to the mob, and was evidently of a certain clientèle, there was a smattering of unaccustomed guests, who manifested their disapproval of these remarks by grumbling and even threats.

Barabant at length, losing control of his temper, sprang upon a chair.

"A government," he cried—"yes, a government is what we need. Let us be frank: the present condition of affairs is an anomaly. It cannot exist. The Revolution is to-day a farce."

"Anarchy!" "Chaos!" "Bravo!" "Continue!"

"And why?" he went on. "Because it has not gone far enough. Either king or revolution: the two cannot exist. What we need is the Republic, the Republic, the Republic!"

The words fell on the room like offal thrown in the midst of ravenous wolves. A hideous upheaval, a hoarse shout, a multitude of scrambling forms, and the listeners who had mistaken the drift of his first words rose in fury. Some one pulled the table from under him. There were shouts and blows, a confusion of bodies before his eyes, and babel let loose. In the midst of it he felt himself suddenly enveloped in a pair of wiry arms and dragged through the mêlée. He struggled, but the grip that held him was not to be shaken. Leaving behind the shouting, they passed out into the turning of a corridor, then through another into quiet and a garden. There his captor, setting him on his feet, drew back with a smile. Barabant, glancing up, beheld the lank military figure of an hour before, with his nose tipped in the air in impudent enjoyment.

"Well, my knight-errant," he said quizzically, "the next time you preach the Republic, select a Sans-Culotte audience and not a Royalist café, or there may not be a Dossonville to rescue you."

Barabant smoothed out his clothes, crestfallen, but resumed his dignity.

"From the country!" his rescuer continued, and the amusement gave place to one of reflectiveness. "Dame! are they already crying for the Republic outside of Paris?"

"They are. That is," Barabant added, "the masses are done with the king. The Girondins are not so radical."

"H'm!" Dossonville said for all answer. He stood silent a moment, wrapped in his own thoughts, before he again questioned him: "And the Revolution: do you hear such opinions as you heard to-night in the provinces? Is there no sign of a reaction?"

"No; everything is for more radical measures."

With this answer, Dossonville seemed to dismiss the matter from his mind. He looked him over again, and a twinkle showing in his eyes, he asked:

"More enthusiasm than friends, hey?"

Barabant laughed. "True."

"And what are you counting upon doing?"

Barabant remained silent.

"Good—discretion!"

Barabant, determined to shift the inquiry, demanded point-blank:

"What were you doing in a café of aristocrats?"

"What were you?" Dossonville retorted. "There are many ways to serve the Revolution besides proclaiming it from the tops of tables. Leave me my ways. Do you think if I were an aristocrat I'd have taken the pains to save you? Come, young man, don't turn your back on opportunities. Swallow your pride and confess that there are not many more meals in sight."

"I am but a day in Paris," Barabant answered; and then, lest he should seem to have relented: "there are a hundred ways to find a living."

"Can you write? Have you written pamphlets?" Dossonville persisted. "What would you say to a chance to see that fine eloquence caught in black and white and circulating in the streets?"

Barabant's face flushed with such a sudden delight that the other laughingly drew his arm into his and exclaimed:

"Come, I see how it is. Camille Desmoulins is only twenty-nine. It is the age for the youngsters. Only—" He stopped suddenly. "There are many degrees of Republicans nowadays.Does your eloquence run in the line of our valiant radical Marat, or Danton and Desmoulins, or are we of the school of Condorcet and Roland?"

"I am Girondin," Barabant answered.

"Good." He reflected a moment. "Just the place!"

He started on, and then suddenly stopped, as by habit of caution. "No, not to-night. Where do you live?"

"Eugène Barabant, Rue Maugout, No. 38." He drew out two letters. "I have a word of introduction to Roland."

"And the other?"

"To Marat."

"Ah, Marat," Dossonville said, with a sudden cooling. "A strong man that, and very patriotic."

"I do not intend to present it," Barabant said, seeing the change. He hesitated a moment, as though to reveal a confidence, while a smile struggled to his lips. But in the end, resisting the desire, he said evasively, "It is a measure of protection, in case of danger."

Dossonville scrutinized him sharply, and then, as though reassured by the frank visage, he said: "Very well; I'll be around to-morrow night. Try your hand at a polemic or two. Have you a knack of poetry? Satires are more powerful than arguments. A laugh can trip up a colossus."

"I have done a little verse."

"Who hasn't?" He paused. "You will be discreet? Au revoir!"

He turned on his heel, but immediately returned.

"I forgot. One word of advice."

"Well?"

"Revolutions strike only among the steeples. Take my advice: renounce publicity and remain obscure."

"But I had rather die in this age than live through another."

"Well, my duty's done," Dossonville answered, shrugging his shoulders. Then repeating to himself Barabant's last response, he added, "That sounds well; food for the mob; put it down."

And without more ado, he left him as delighted as though he had just been elected to the National Convention.

III

CITOYENNE NICOLE

Toward six o'clock the next morning, when la Mère Corniche and her broom alone were stirring, there appeared at a gabled window that broke through the crust of the roofs, the figure of a young girl, who, after a glance down at the quiet courtyard and the windows void of life, remained to give the final touches to a scattering of golden hair.

The air was still young, and in the skies the multifarious tints of the dawn had not quite faded as the burly sun bobbed up among the distant chimney-tops. She ensconced herself in the window, running her hands with indolent movements through the meshes as though reluctant to leave the flash and play of the sun amid its lusters. She was young and pretty, and she knew it, and, with a frank enjoyment, she let the long locks slip through her fingers or brought them caressingly against her cheek.

Though from her figure she could not have been more than eighteen, yet in the poise of her head and in the subtile smile, full of grace and piquancy, there showed the coquetry of the woman who plans to please the masculine eye.

Suddenly she sprang back, leaving the window vacant. A moment later there emerged opposite the thoughtful face of Barabant. Unaware of her proximity, he swept the courtyard with an indifferent look, and drawing from his pocket the three sous that alone remained to him, he fell into a deep meditation.

Presently the sprightly eyes and mischievous profile of the girl returned, cautiously, as though awaiting a challenge. Then, as in the abstraction of his mood he continued to be oblivious to her presence, she advanced to fuller view.

Gradually her curiosity became excited by an evident conflict in his moods. At one moment he pulled a long, somber face, and at the next he lapsed into laughter. As human nature cannot endure in silence the spectacle of someone laughing to himself, the girl, unable longer to restrain her interest, called to him with that melody which is natural to the voice of a maiden:

"Well, citoyen, are you going to laugh or cry?"

At her banter, Barabant started up so suddenly that one of the sous which he had been regarding meditatively slipped from his fingers, bounded on the roof, rolled along the gutter, and disappeared in the water-hole.

"Diable! there goes my dinner!"

"How so?" the girl said, repressing her laugh at his long face.

"I had three; one for lunch, one for dinner, and one for some purchases I intend to make."

"Dame! citoyen, three are not many sous."

Barabant drew himself up proudly. "Plenty, after to-night."

"When your banker returns?"

"Exactly."

"And I have made you lose your dinner: a bad beginning for neighbors, Citoyen—?"

"Citoyen Eugène Barabant. Citoyenne—?"

"Nicole."

"Nicole—?"

"Heavens, isn't Nicole enough? One name is all we need; besides, it would take me too long to find out the other."

As she said this, she smiled so unaffectedly that Barabant, forgetting the pangs of hunger, looked on admiringly.

"You are a philosopher, Nicole. And what do you do—if it is not indiscreet to ask?"

She understood perfectly the hesitancy, but laughed without a trace of disconcertion.

"Oh, I work hard; I am a bouquetière. Which reminds me, I must be off to the flower-market."

However, she lingered a moment. "And you, citoyen?"

"Traveler," Barabant said, with a superb wave of his hand, and then exploded in laughter at the thought. "Citoyenne, tell me something."

"Speak."

"Have you ever fasted a day?"

"Hundreds of times."

"If you have but one meal in sight, when is the best time to take it?"

"In the middle of the day; something may happen before dinner."

Barabant made a wry face.

"Seriously, how much have you?"

He held up the two sous.

"Two sous, and you speak of buying a meal,—a crumb of bread!"

"Perhaps," Barabant admitted, "meal is an exaggeration."

"Come, you are a good fellow," Nicole said, nodding approvingly. "You have the right spirit. I have made you lose one dinner; it is only right that I should make reparation. Will you lunch with me?"

To her amusement, he drew up proudly at the thought of accepting a favor from her. She smiled at this show of pride, liking it, but trusting in the bloom and charm of her youth to defeat it. She did not trust in vain. After a brief conflict which showed clearly the weak surrender, he ended by smiling in turn.

"Only," he cried, "I accept it as a loan."

"Heavens! but I didn't intend to pay, myself," she protested, well pleased with her victory. "If you think dinners are to be had only for pay you are not a Parisian yet."

"In that case, I accept."

"Meet me, then, at eleven o'clock, Place de la République, Citoyen Barabant."

"I shall be there an hour ahead!"

At the door of the next room she called, "Louison!" drumming quietly with her fingers. Receiving no answer, she entered. The bed was vacant, undisturbed. Without surprise, and with even a certain satisfaction at being freed from the company of her friend, she passed down and out into the streets on her way to the Marché des Fleurs.

As she went, with many an energetic toss of her head interspersed with pensive smiles, she turned over in her mind the impressions of her first encounter, with the confidence of the woman who at the first exchange of glances feels her power. He had shown his admiration without timidity, which would have been vexatious, or forwardness, which would have been unendurable. She liked his show of pride, and more that he had yielded before the temptation of her eyes. That tribute sent her straying into the thousand and one pleasurable paths with which her ardent imagination filled the future.

At the flower-markets her preoccupation was so evident that she was compelled to run the fire of banter. She bore the ordeal with equanimity, hurrying away with buoyant step and eyes alert, impatient for the morning to pass.

She passed along the boulevards, disposing of her cockades among regular customers, until at length she arrived at her destination, the Café Procopé. There, mounted on a chair, a short, roly-poly ragamuffin, with bloated, pouter cheeks and squinting, almond eyes, was reading the morning bulletins in such thunderous tones that one readily divined the crier of carriages, whose voice had been trained in the battle of street sounds.

Among those assembled at the tables, she directed her way to where a gruff, gaunt man, sunk in a capacious redingote, was heralding her approach with a look of welcome.

"Good morning, Papa Goursac," she said, slipping into a waiting seat. "Here's your cockade,—the best, as usual!"

"There, take your drink," he answered, showing her the glass. He roused himself from his attitude of whimsical inspection, turning to her a look that belied the stern voice. "Well, and what luck to-day?"

"The best," she said, showing him her lightly laden basket.

"Of course you did not notice the new lodger," said Goursac, scornfully. His bushy eyebrows and looming beak seemed so grim that Nicole with difficulty suppressed a laugh.

"Indeed," she said, pretending ignorance to plague him, "is there a new lodger?"

"Yes, but he's a doctor, old as I am, so he'll not interest you."

"What a bad humor you are in," she said, enjoying his wrath. "As though you did not interest me!"

"You know what I mean."

Aware of his suspicious scrutiny, she continued. "What a pity! Why couldn't he have been a young fellow? Ah, mon Dieu, what time is it?"

"Why do you want to know?" growled Goursac. "Whom are you going to meet?"

"The old doctor, of course," she answered, laughing as she escaped.

As she passed in front, the ragamuffin was still roaring the news.

"Heavens, Jambony," she cried, "there is no need to let the foreigners know what is taking place!"

"Citoyenne, you exaggerate," the carriage-crier answered; "I am only whispering."

"Then, my dear Jambony, just think your thoughts. I am sure they will be loud enough!"

In great good humor, she began to work her way in the direction of the wrecked Bastille, and perhaps from the very elevation of her spirits, good luck quickly emptied her basket. Thus freed, she lapsed into the spectator, flattening her nose against the shop-windows or drifting lazily from knot to knot of discussion.

All at once, when she was wandering from the thoroughfares among a tangle of silent, murky alleys, a child's scream brought her to an attentive halt. The cries redoubled. Without a thought of personal danger, she plunged recklessly down the alley in the direction of the appeals. Under the bulging shadow of a balcony a girl was struggling in the clutches of a mountebank, while, from a box on the ground, a monkey was adding its shrill chatter to the broil.

At Nicole's charge the man released the girl with an oath and sprang back against the wall. At the sight of the shriveled-parchment face and the familiar leer Nicole burst out, in astonishment:

"Ah, Cramoisin, I might have known it was you!" She replaced in her belt the knife she had drawn, facing him with the whips of her scorn.

"Women are too strong for you, then! You must match your strength with children. Bravo! my brave fellow, you are the victor at last. Wait until I sing your praises. You shall become famous, tamer of children!"

"Vixen!" shrieked the mountebank, stung to words by her gadding. He shook a lean fist at her, crying, "Thy turn'll come!"

"And I who thought you were pining away for love of me!" she continued mercilessly. "Fickle Cramoisin! There, be off, be off, do you hear, or I shall be tempted to chastise you!"

Cramoisin, not disdaining the offer of retreat, slung his mountebank's box on his back and scurried off, the ape on his shoulder chattering back at them with communicated fear.

Nicole turned. A slip of a girl, half child, half savage, was regarding her from round, wolfish eyes, shrinking against the wall. "There, there, ma petite," she said, "there is nothing tocry about. That Cramoisin is as weak as a leaf; you could have pushed him over with a finger. And your knife?"

The girl, still sobbing, shook her head.

"Heavens! child, you are not fit to be abroad. There, stop crying, I tell you. I do not like to hear it." But perceiving that the girl was thoroughly unnerved, she abandoned her note of command, and, enveloping her with her arm, said gently: "Come, mon enfant, I promise you there is nothing more to fear. Cramoisin is as much afraid of me as the fat Louis of the

Citoyen Marat. I'll take you under my protection. You are nothing but a child; no wonder the brute has frightened you. Come, what's your name?"

"Geneviève."

"How old?"

"Fifteen."

"But that is almost a woman! Why, I am but eighteen. One must be gay, that is all, and have a bit of a temper."

Seeing that the girl was recovering, she continued for a while her light tone. "And where do you live?"

"38 Rue Maugout."

"Impossible! Since when?"

"Two months."

"How curious! And I have never noticed you."

"I am not very big."

"Bah, you are big enough and old enough, only you need some hints. See there!" With a deft hand she drew in the dress over the hips and loosened it at the throat. "You have really a good figure, but you don't know it. You must be coquette before you can be a woman. In future I'll keep an eye on you. Where do you sleep?"

"In the cellar."

"I thought so. Sleep with me to-night, then; there's room enough. All right now? I must be going."

Geneviève caught her hand and covered it with kisses.

"There, kiss my cheek," Nicole said, affected by her display of gratitude. "What a baby! You shall stay with me. Until to-night, then."

All at once she remembered her engagement, and on the moment, forgetting the new partnership so lightly contracted, she hurried away, with such good will that she arrived exactly on time. As this was not to her liking, she screened herself in the crowd, seeking Barabant. She found him soon, approaching, still immersed in his projected article and betraying his preoccupation by such scowls and sudden gestures that the passers-by would have taken him for demented had not the spectacle been one familiar to their eyes.

"Ah, mon Dieu!" Nicole said to herself, "I thought I'd found a man, and he turns out a philosopher. Also, he does not seem very much occupied in looking for me!"

She stepped forward to meet him, saying mischievously: "Well, have you settled the affairs of the nation? What furor on an empty stomach, Citoyen Eugène!"

Barabant returned to earth quickly, not a little ashamed at the flights of his imagination, and his laugh betrayed his discomfiture as he said:

"It helps one to forget the vacancy."

Nicole leading the way, they hurried through the thronged streets, scenting at every step the inviting odor of soups and stews, until they arrived at a large tavern, or brasserie, around which was a thick crowd struggling for admission.

"Have you heard of Santerre?" Nicole said. "A very wise man who has discovered that the seat of popularity lies in the stomach."

"The Romans placed all the affections there."

"Ah, you've had an education," Nicole said, with a new respect. "There's Santerre."

Before the entrance a huge mass of a man, boisterous in his hospitality and his laughter, was distributing enormous hand-shakes.

Nicole saluted him with evident familiarity.

"I have brought you a patriot to dinner, citoyen!"

Santerre winced a bit and grumbled:

"Eh, Nicole, and you have brought yourself along."

"Vive Santerre!" the girl cried, with a laugh. "Citoyen Barabant has just arrived, and the first thing he asked was to see the famous leader of the Faubourg St. Antoine."

"At lunch-time, of course," said Santerre, with a shrug. "Pass in and eat."

Nicole seized Barabant by the hand and entered the restaurant, already crowded with the self-invited guests of the leader's ready hospitality. They found a corner table and settled down to a quiet inspection of the noisy room.

Masons, carters, and laborers preponderated, while a smattering of young lawyers and journalists circulated from table to table, with ready hand-shakes, to take up the conversation or clink a glass in toasts to the dozen subjects most in favor. Above the din of plates and cutlery, cutting the hum of voices, the toasts emerged sharply.

"To the Bonnets Rouges!"

"To the good Sans-Culottes!"

"À bas les Tyrans!"

"Vive la Constitution!"

"Vive Santerre!"

"Long life to our host!"

At times the Carmagnole, at times some popular ballad of the day, would start from a corner, and gathering headway, would gradually run through the noise of the room until, absorbing all other sounds, it ended in a gale. Whereupon there would be a clatter of knives and glass, shouts of "Bravo!" laughter, and more drinking.

Barabant was too susceptible a nature not to respond to the magnetism of such surroundings. His look regained all its ardor of the morning, until Nicole regarded him with a new interest. He had the long, narrow forehead of the period, marked with thoughtfulness and curiosity. The nose was high-bridged, the nostrils were sensitive and dilating with emotion. The gray eyes were shrewd, kind, gay, and noting, with the mobility and charm of the enthusiast, but, in their repose, without that impress of authority and earnestness of purpose which give to the man of imagination the genius of leadership.

"Come, citoyen," Nicole said, at the end of her inspection, "tell me something about yourself. I am filled with curiosity."

"Ma foi, Nicole," Barabant answered, "it's not much. I was at Fontainebleau; I'm now in Paris. I had an uncle who disapproved of my ideas; he showed me the door, I declared his goods confiscate, and here I am, not a bit depressed,—with but one debt," he added as an afterthought.

"Debts are aristocratic; renounce them."

"The trouble is, I can't rid myself of the creditor, though I pay him over and over."

Nicole raised her glance in surprise, but Barabant added, smiling, "It is my stomach, and a persistent creditor he is."

Nicole laughed gaily. "There, touch hands," she cried. "You are the philosopher." Persisting in her inquiry, she continued encouragingly: "You have a father?"

Barabant smiled. "And a mother, too. And now no more questions, Nicole, for I shall refuse them."

She drew back with a little movement of pique, but yielding to her natural moods, she lifted her eyebrows and, with her charming smile, said with frankness:

"Ah, you are legitimate, then. I have only a mother; that is to say, I had. She is dead now. I don't remember her. God rest her soul."

A little movement of superstition passed over her face and she crossed herself. "My father was a sergeant of the line, so they tell me." She threw out the palms of her hands. "Who knows? It might as well be a rag-picker, or a prince, for all the good it does me."

"Diable!" Barabant exclaimed, regarding her more closely. "You don't seem to be cast down."

"Oh, no; it's only this year I've been by myself. I was brought up by my aunt—Aunt Berthe. What a woman!" She shook her head grimly. "When I came in late she beat me,—oh, but solidly, firmly." She grimaced and, with the instinct of acting that is of the people, drew her hand across her shoulder, as though still smarting under the sting. "And do you know how it ended?"

"Well, how?"

"It ended by my taking the cane from her one night and laying it over her. Oh, such a beating! I was striking for old scores. Aïe! aïe! After that, you understand, I couldn't return."

"I understand."

"So I took a room next to Louison."

Barabant raised his eyebrows in question.

"Louison? She's a comrade. You will see her." She stopped. "We are good friends, only I—well—I don't know." Nicole, who conversed abundantly with her shoulders, raised them again. "When you're rich you can choose; but with us, we take what's nearest. We must have some one to gossip with, to weep with, to laugh with, to confide a little in, and so we take what we can get. That's how it is." Suddenly she halted suspiciously. "Are you a patriot?" she asked point-blank.

"You'd have thought so last night." Barabant, remembering the drubbing he had escaped the night before, grinned and nodded. At his description of the café Nicole showed great interest.

"You said that, and escaped with your life from that den of aristocrats!" she exclaimed, in horror, for she had the popular idea that aristocrats were ogres and inhuman monsters. At the first words descriptive of his rescue she cried:

"Dossonville; beyond a doubt, Dossonville!"

"What, do you know him?" said Barabant. "Who and what is he?"

"Now you have asked me a question. What is Dossonville?" Suddenly she became serious. "He is a mystery to me and to more than me. Frankly, I do not know his party, and don't believe any one else does. He is here and there, with the patriots one moment and the court the next; but whether he is acting for one side or for neither, no one knows. And he rescued you!" She meditated a moment. "That sounds like a patriot; but then, what was he doing in such a place?"

The crowd became more boisterous as the wine-jugs grew lighter; seeing which, Nicole rose and made a sign to him to follow. In the front room she stopped before a vat on which, his huge body astride, Santerre was bandying jests with the crowd. Nicole, approaching, whispered:

"Is it for to-night?"

The brewer affected not to understand her.

"Look here, my big fellow," she said, with the familiarity of the day, "do you want me to cry it from the housetops? Will you understand me now?"

"I don't know when it is to be, or if it will ever be." He sank his voice. "The leaders are wavering; only the tocsin can tell."

"We assemble by sections?"

Santerre nodded.

Nicole, only half satisfied, turned away.

Barabant, who had overheard enough to form a conjecture, kept his counsel; but Nicole, approving his discretion, imparted the information.

"They say we are to storm the Tuileries. But every one hangs back. They are in a panic at the last moment."

"Why, it is folly; think of the National Guard!" Barabant exclaimed.

"I see well you have just arrived. The National Guard, indeed! We are the National Guard. It is only the Swiss we have to fear."

They had gained the right bank of the Seine, and paused from time to time to watch the water-carriers filling their casks in the river, and the loiterers angling sleepily in the shadow of the boats.

Barabant, despite the fires of patriotic fervor, had for some time forgotten his mission in the contemplation of the fresh cheeks and the free carriage of his companion, more and more beguiled from his task of righting the wrongs of the nation by this gipsy of the streets who traversed the rough paths of fortune with such perfect bonhomie.

Nicole, happening to look up, met an unmistakable fixture of gaze, and divined the workings of his mind. She withdrew slightly and said reprovingly: "Not too fast, Citoyen Barabant; we are not in the provinces."

Barabant defended himself.

"My dear Nicole, I have committed no offense. I have done nothing but wish. Judge my acts; my thoughts are not offenses."

"You are not slow at an answer, citoyen," said Nicole, amused. "There, take my hand if you wish. Only, not too fast."

He took her hand, and together they went joyfully through Paris, laughing like two children of the people.

"Barabant, I like you," she said from time to time. "You are a good fellow." Once she added naïvely, "You know, all the same, it is lonely at times." Then, with a laugh, "Allons, comrade!"

She led him through the boulevards, pointing out celebrities at every step, showing him the cafés, Feuillantes or Jacobin. They were constantly halted by the sudden assembly of a crowd to listen to some singer perched on a chair above their shoulders, intoning his ballads.

Presently Nicole said: "Barabant, do you not feel something in the atmosphere—something extraordinary?"

He sharpened his wits and gradually began to distinguish currents in the crowd, and it seemed to him that there was some subtle communication by furtive glances of inquiry and nods of intelligence.

"I believe it will be for to-night," she whispered.

He felt in her hand something nervous and exalted.

"Were you at the taking of the Bastille?" he asked.

"Yes. Wait till you see the women of Paris!" Her eyes grew large as they lost themselves in recollection. Then suddenly she added: "But you haven't seen the gardens of the Palais Royal, and the tree of the green cockades from which Desmoulins called us to arms!"

Leading him into the historic garden, she showed him the chestnut-tree surrounded by a crowd of curious seekers, many of whom snatched up the leaves for mementos.

Everywhere were swarms of children, shrieking high, shrill notes, running and leaping, dodging in and out of the most sedate groups, and stopping occasionally to mimic the swollen front and bombastic arm of the hundred and one orators about whom swirled a hundred and one eddies. Newsboys, racing ahead of their competitors, cried hoarsely the latest bulletins; while in their wake improvised orators mounted on tables and announced the news amid a gale of comments. Through the throng a score of flower-girls twisted their way, calling their patriotic cockades, nodding familiarly to Nicole, who from all sides received salutations of deputies and orators.

"You are well known," said Barabant, surprised at the range of her acquaintance.

"Pardi, I should hope so," she answered, with a proud toss of her head. "Bouquetières are useful. We go everywhere, see everything. We are the scouts of the Republic. I have influence, Barabant; I'll push you ahead," she added, with a determined nod. "Can you speak from the tribune?"

"I have done so."

"Good. You must go to the club. Speak out. Do not be afraid. I adore fire and spirit!" She looked at him critically. "You have the eyes and the lips of the orator. Yes, I'm sure you can speak."

Barabant thrilled at the inspiration in her eyes, and some of the fierce, exulting spirit, the unconquerable gaiety and daring of this gamine, passed swiftly into his soul. Filled with the bombastic daring and sublime confidence of the patriot, he cried: "Give me the chance; give but the chance! They shall hear me—and listen!"

Nicole had a wild impulse to embrace him, but, restraining her enthusiasm, she contented herself with passing from his hand to his arm.

"How old are you?" she asked all at once.

"I am twenty-four," Barabant said, with importance.

"Why, you are a child."

"Camille Desmoulins is not thirty."

"True."

"And what is six years?"

"I hadn't thought of it," admitted Nicole. "I am eighteen; but in Paris at eighteen there is not much unlearned. Allons, les enfants." She drew up to his side, hanging a little on his arm. "Barabant, you are a lucky fellow," she said mischievously.

Barabant, who perfectly understood her allusion to mean lucky in meeting her, drew her closer as they elbowed their way out of the throng. He bent his head to scrutinize her, while Nicole not too consciously accepted the gaze, confident in herself: she was young and she was a Parisian. Her features were rather saucy than regular; her figure, though full and graceful, was perhaps too perfect for eighteen, when a certain slenderness is a future guaranty. But the eyes of the young man do not look into the future. Barabant saw only—giving color to her cheeks, a glow to the eye, and a spring to the foot—that bloom which is of youth and which speaks of eagerness and impatience to embrace life.

Suddenly Nicole, seeking an interruption to this scrutiny, which, though delightful, had become embarrassing, exclaimed, "There's Louison now." She made a movement as though to free her arm, immediately checking it.

Barabant, looking up, beheld the high eyebrows, the starting eyes, and the curious, thin smile of the flower-girl who had spoken to him the night before.

She sent Nicole a greeting from her fingertips, and then perceiving Barabant, she accosted him with a smile of tolerant amusement.

"Why, it's my little man from the country!" Nodding, she passed, with the exclamation, "Bien vrai, you don't lose any time!"

"What, you have already met her?" Nicole exclaimed, disengaging her arm, suddenly quieted and sobered.

"In the Rue St. Honoré, last night."

A frown, swift as a thunderbolt, passed over Nicole's forehead. She stopped, extended her hand, and said curtly, "I must go; good day."

Barabant looked at her in dismay.

"What has happened? What have I done?"

She shook her head, and without further explanation disappeared.

IV

BREWINGS OF THE STORM

When Barabant had groped his way up the tortuous ascent, he was surprised to find his door open, sending a feeble glow over the remainder of his journey. He crossed the threshold on tiptoe, and, to his amazement, beheld a man, in the uniform of the National Guard, stretched out upon his bed, and two lank legs that, over-lapping, were perched on the footboards. He came forward, advanced another step, and recognized Dossonville.

Barabant, believing him to be shamming, went softly to the farther corner and installed himself to wait. But the steady, tranquil breathing of the sleeper soon convinced him. With a sudden inspiration, he stole to the threshold, grasping the handle of the door. The next moment there thundered upon the slumberer the cry:

"Arrest him! The aristocrat!"

As though propelled from a catapult, the lank form in one bound shot over the end of the bed, threw two chairs in front of him as a rampart, snatched out his sword, and beheld, in this bellicose posture, no horrid band of Jacobins, but the lithe figure of Barabant, laughing silently, with folded arms.

"Tonnerre de Dieu! Why did you do that?"

Dossonville returned the sword to the scabbard, pushed aside the rampart, and extended his hand, saying, "I was asleep; serves me right; but you have a rude manner of jesting."

"I did not suspect your conscience was so uneasy," Barabant said, retaining the quizzical smile.

"Oho!"

With his lips in this startled oval, Dossonville halted. His eyes contracted into slits as he said dryly, "So that was a ruse."

"If you like."

"Hello! it was well conceived. Tiens, tiens, tiens!" His eyes continued their scrutiny. "I have, perhaps, not done justice to your acumen. My compliments and my excuses."

He swung his bonnet in a long, awkward, trailing swoop across his feet. Barabant executed a bow of equal assurance.

Dossonville returned to uprightness with a snap of his heels, and a certain asperity rang in the next question.

"And why did you deem the experiment necessary?"

"Before intrusting my safety I prefer to reassure myself."

"You saw that at the cry of 'aristocrats' I sprang to my guard."

"I said 'the aristocrat.'"

"I understood, 'Arrest him, aristocrats!'"

The two men, Dossonville cool, Barabant amused, measured looks, until, dismissing the subject with a motion of his arm, Dossonville seated himself.

"Well, what do they say of me?"

Barabant, who did not intend to surrender his vantage, straddled his chair, rested his arms on the back, and, looking him magisterially in countenance, answered:

"Citoyen Dossonville, you seem to be a mystery. No one knows where to place you. You consort with patriots and traitors alike."

Dossonville, facing this accusation, appeared to reflect a moment.

"That's true. I do not hide it—from patriots." His voice gave a meaning inflection to the ending; then he added, irritably: "There are more ways than one of serving the nation. I repeat, leave me mine." He broke off. "Have you written anything? Give it to me."

Barabant extended the precious manuscript. He took it, but before spreading it upon his knee, he said: "After all, you are right. I have a way to convince you. You shall see. But first for this."

He began to read, with approval. "Good—good"; "very good"; "excellent."

At the end he brought his hand down upon his knee with a slap. "Tonnerre de Dieu, that is well put!"

Barabant, who was soaring in the seventh heaven, made a superhuman effort and forced back a smile. Dossonville, much amused, tapped him on the shoulder.

"Come, it is not a crime to be pleased with one's self."

"You think it will do?" Barabant stammered.

"Splendid! And now to convince this suspicious republican." He eyed him a moment, enjoying the surprise his next words would cause. "Suppose you return with me to Santerre."

Barabant, astounded at this acquaintance with his doings, dropped his jaw.

"So, do you think I would employ you without some knowledge of your actions?" He enjoyed for a moment Barabant's embarrassment. "Come, and Santerre shall reassure you." At the door he paused, cast a rapid glance at the impoverished fittings, and drew out his purse. "Republican or not, the essential thing is to dine." Then evading the young fellow's thanks, he led the way into the city.

It was now toward twilight. The streets were choked with laborers returning home. In the air was an unwonted stir, a muttering, defiant and eager, as the crowd discussed openly, with impassioned questions, the prospective attack on the Tuileries.

"It is for to-night, sure?"

"For to-night, yes, at the tocsin."

"It's true, is it, the National Guards are coming over?"

"They've armed the Marseillais."

"Who?"

"Pétion."

"Vive Pétion!"

Hundreds of National Guards fraternized with the crowd, reassuring them. Occasionally was to be seen the glimmer of a weapon, a scythe, a cutlass, or a half-concealed dagger. Questioners stopped them from time to time.

"Is it true, we are to attack to-night?"

Dossonville shrugged his shoulders.

"If the tocsin sounds you are. That is all I know."

From time to time there were new accessions in the streets; until, as the two approached the Rue St. Antoine, they were forced to beg their way at every step.

Dossonville, his head flung back, reviewed the throng from his great height.

"What a people! Is there anything they will not dare?" he exclaimed. "Brave people! Sublime people!"

They passed through a side street, deserted except for some straggler hastening toward the human torrent. Dossonville, in a burst of confidence, laid his hand on his companion's shoulder.

"That was good to see. I, Citoyen Barabant—I take nothing seriously. Men, individuals, are but blind little animals wriggling for a day or so. I have seen too much of selfishness, of wickedness, of deceits and hypocrisy, to be moved by human motives. Nothing really matters, nothing is serious. But when I see such a sight as that, a whole people rising with one accord, ah, then that thrills me; yes, I am moved!"

Barabant was silent, more perplexed concerning his companion than ever, and in this reflective mood he persevered, resolving to be on his watch for artifices and tricks. About the brasserie of the famous brewer the throng was massed so tightly that the two companions would have stuck thirty feet away, unable to turn, had not Santerre, from an upper window, perceived the lanky form of Dossonville. The moment his eye fell upon that appealing figure, he started up, as though awaiting him, and hurrying down-stairs, appeared at the entrance, where, by dint of command and abuse, he managed to open a passage, through which the crowd disgorged them.

Barabant, at a nod from Dossonville, remained in an anteroom listening to the compressed rumble of the crowd, that reached him through the open window on the warm, suffocating air. He did not have long to wait. Santerre soon reappeared, excited and red with the emotion communicated to his fleshy head. Dossonville, more tranquil, called him to them.

"I must take a message to the Bonnet Rouge," he said. "It is urgent. So I must leave you—only, I do not forget." He glanced at him, adding slyly: "Is there anything you care to ask of the Citoyen Santerre?"

Barabant, gulping down his confusion, cried: "Nothing."

"Good. Then you are no longer afraid you are dealing with an agent of the perfidious Pitt?"

Barabant seized the occasion to vanish through the side exit, carrying with him the memory of a chuckle.

Nicole no sooner had dismissed Barabant than she regretted the act. Her intuition had warned her that caprice was necessary to counteract her bonhomie, which might have produced in the young man an assurance of facile conquest. But, left to her own devices, to her astonishment she found the solitude oppressive. She made an effort to dispel the ennui by seeking Goursac; but no sooner had she perceived him than, apprehending the banter in which he was privileged to indulge, she halted and then turned away.Toward evening, according to her custom, she joined Louison in search of supper.

"What have you done with your companion?" the girl asked at once.

"I dismissed him long ago," Nicole answered carelessly: from that quarter she welcomed attack. "A man interferes with the business."

"How did you meet him?"

"Why, I thought you knew! He has taken the room across from us!"

"Ah, indeed. He seems interesting." She took her companion's arm and said abruptly, "I have taken a fancy to him, so garde à toi!"

Nicole, not certain whether she spoke in jest or in earnest, abandoned uneasily the conversation, saying, "Where do we dine to-night?"

"At the Bonnet Rouge."

"Why there?"

"It is the rendezvous for the Marseillais. If there is to be an attack, we'll have the news."

"Do you think it will be for to-night?"

"Yes; there is something in the air that makes me think so."

Their way soon involved them in a network of dusky, gaping streets. On each side somber walls, peopled with dim, curious flecks of headgear, strained upward and back in a bulging effort to draw down a little more of the allotted strip of sky. The windows of taverns, on the ground floor, were beginning to redden and to cast faint streaks across the black, oozing streets; but the frugal inhabitants of upper stories, in deference to the price of candles, still hung on the sills, causing the evening to resound with the nervous chatter of window-to-window speculation.

At times the tension of conjecture and discussion would be broken by the bass voice of a passing laborer thundering forth,

"Ça ira! Ça ira! Ça ira!"

Above the soprano of women's voices and the thin piping of children responded feverishly:

"La liberté s'établira:Malgré les tyrans tout réussira!"

They found the cabaret beginning to fill up by twos and threes—workingmen for the most part: water-carriers divesting themselves of their barrels at the door with a sigh of contentment; wood-carriers, with relaxed limbs, slipping gratefully into the hard wooden benches; women of the markets, corpulent, quick-tongued, smelling of onion and garlic; erstwhile actors still with the strut of the stage; an occasional bourgeois in misfortune; a handful of gamins, impudent and witty—all discussing feverishly the projected attack.

The two girls, perceiving the congestion in the outer room, elbowed their way to where, by an inner door, a waiter of exceptional but broken height was scanning the crowd with an eye to orders.

"Well, Citoyen Boudgoust, what news?"

At Louison's question, he showed the palms of his hands, finally volunteering:

"Santerre is to send us word."

"There's room beyond?"

"You are going to eat?"

"Of course," Louison said impatiently, as he barred the way. "Besides, mon ami, don't you think we know what's going on?"

He allowed them to pass, grumbling, "Every one comes to talk; no one to eat."

In the farther hall the crowd was thinner and composed mostly of Marseillais and the National Guard, who looked up furtively, until half a dozen greetings removed their suspicions.

"Good evening, Citoyenne Nicole."

In her astonishment, she turned to find Geneviève.

"What are you doing here, child?" she cried.

"I am listening."

"You are no longer afraid?"

"We are to attack," the girl said proudly, and her eyes snapped with defiant ardor.

"Bravo, little one!" laughed Nicole. "Sit with us, then."

She turned to Louison in explanation.

"She is my protégée who is coming to me for lessons."

Louison nodded without surprise and turned her slow, restrained gaze on the room, while the eyes of Nicole, full of enthusiasm, leaped from group to group in rapid, eager scrutiny, resting finally on a knot of Marseillais near by. One man dominated these uncouth, bristling, living arsenals—a squat figure, sprawling under the grotesque shadows of the lamp, which further distorted his huge bulk and bullet head. One ungainly, crooked hand leaned in ponderous support upon the table; the other was flourished above him in frantic gestures, magnetic, absurd, comic, and terrible, as he harangued his comrades, who acclaimed his exhortations with shouts that burst above the ceaseless roar of the room.

"They are not very coquette," Nicole said critically, "and not very clean."

"Ah, but think how they have marched, all the way from Marseilles!" Geneviève cried, in protest.

"You know them, then?" Nicole asked, astonished at this side of the girl.

"Yes."

"And that bear of a man in the center, do you know his name?"

"Yes," she answered, with a slight disconcertion. "He is the Citoyen Javogues."

"He looks like an ogre."

"Wait till you hear him."

"Really!" answered Nicole, with a smile which threw the girl into confusion.

At this moment a rumble reached them from the outer room. Boudgoust, profoundly dejected, appeared, followed by the insouciant figure of Dossonville. Instantly the room was filled with cries.

"What news?"

"What news from Santerre?"

"We attack?"

"For to-night?"

Dossonville, facing the eager, breathless gallery, shrugged his shoulders, uttering but one word:

"Postponed."

A roar of rage and disappointment drowned his voice.

"Citoyens!" he cried, "I am but announcing the decision; I did not make it. The tyrants are intrenched. Mandat is in ambush at the Pont Neuf and the Arcade St. Jean. The leaders have decided the moment is unfavorable."

The storm of protests increased.

"More delay! Enough of waiting!"

"Mon Dieu, we are not cowards!"

"And the Prussians?"

"Hé, yes, are we to wait for the foreign bandits?"

"Javogues! Javogues!"

"Javogues, lead us!"

"Lead us, Javogues!"

Nicole felt through the child at her side a sudden trembling and drawing of breath. Then into the center of the suddenly quiet room lurched the squat figure, bareheaded, bare-armed, bare-chested but for a tattered shirt. He seemed rooted to the floor, like a mound transformed to human shape, quivering in the primeval mold and passions.

"Well, yes, I'll lead you!" The huge fist, describing a circle, crashed upon a table. "We're here to fight. We'll wait no longer. Hesitate and bandy words and deliberate whoever wants—we are not such! We have suffered and ached. We have been crushed to the ground, saddled to the earth,—we, human beings, like cattle, and we remember our wrongs. Fear? Neither God nor men do we fear. We came here, we, marching from Marseilles,—all the way from Marseilles,—to wipe out the accursed tyrants, to make things go faster, and, by God, they shall go!"

Nicole saw the hideous face transformed, lighted up with the glow of martyrdom. From lungs of leather there burst a welcoming response. Dossonville, facing the fanatic without a change of position, waited imperturbably the lull. Geneviève was breathing hard, in her excitement seizing the hand of her protectress.

"Bravo, patriot, you are eloquent!" came at last the calm answer of Dossonville. "But what can you do? March and be made into beefsteaks? The people, it is true, are hungry, but not a step will the sections move without Santerre. Will you march alone? What say you?"

"I say they are traitors who would halt us!" burst forth Javogues, glancing at the man who dared to jest with him.

"Meaning Santerre?"

"Meaning those who bear false messages. I don't like these manners. Who are you?"

"My friend," Dossonville said, with cool scorn of the threatening throng, "you are curious."

"Aristocrat!"

"Am I?"

"I say you are!"

"Indeed!"

"You will not answer?"

"Certainly! Citoyen Dossonville, at present lieutenant of the Section des Bonnes Nouvelles, in the past soldier, sailor, actor, innkeeper, a bit of everything except the law and the church. Citoyen Boudgoust," he continued, shifting his head just enough to bring into range the apathetic waiter, "before this fire-eater is at my throat, come, vouch for me!"

The hang-down head wabbled a moment on the bent shoulders.

"Yes, yes, a good patriot, Citoyen Javogues, and an eater of little aristocrats."

"As all good patriots should be!" retorted Dossonville, gravely. "There, citoyen, good patriots should not quarrel when there are so many tyrants to be digested. There is my hand—touch!"

Javogues stared at the proffered hand a moment stolidly, drunkenly, then deliberately folded his arms. A murmur of dissent gathered volume.

"Comrade, you are wrong!"

"Give him your hand!"

"Aye, touch together!"

Above the outburst the voice of Dossonville rose acridly.

"Dame! mon ami, you bring strange manners from Marseilles."

"I bring something else."

"And that is— "

"The way to tell a traitor."

"And that is— "

"By the look in his eyes!" Raising his fist, the Marseillais lurched forward with the angry shout of "Spy!"

A dozen men rushed to separate them, while the Marseillais, echoing the accusation of their leader, surged furiously forward. Louison and Nicole, with a common impulse, seized Dossonville, and in the confusion drew him into the hall and out by a rear entrance into the cool of the night.

"Thanks, my dears!" he cried, once free of the turmoil, nonchalant and flippant as ever. "It is always difficult to find the right word on which to retreat with dignity. You saved me the trouble. What! it is you, Louison and Nicole? Diable! if it were only one I could offer my eternal devotion—for a week."

"Citoyen," cried Nicole, reprovingly, "you were wrong to bait him. You have gained an enemy."

"On the contrary," Louison interposed, and strangely on her cold face there was a flash of admiration. "Citoyen Dossonville, you were splendid!"

"No, I was a fool," he said. "It is very stupid that some men must be at each other's throats from the first glance. Diable! I have a feeling this fellow will bother me some day. However, it will add a little interest to these quiet times. Au revoir—I must be off. If I stay I shall be falling in love with both of you. What good would that do? Thanks, and good night!"

In the distance his footsteps grew faint, while for a time the gay chorus of the Carmagnole told of his passage.

Nicole, leaving Louison, sought Geneviève, and, with a desire to reconnoiter, struck out through the now quiet Faubourg toward the Hôtel de Ville. There, all was animation with the arrival of the delegates from the forty-eight sections, assembling to deliberate upon a plan of action, while from time to time messengers passed like streaks down the steps and across the crowd, leaving the disturbance of their trail on the surface.

They passed along the Seine, where the river, as though, too, at the end of the day it sought its rest, lay still and black, shot across with faint reflections. They arrived at the Tuileries only to be barred passage by a patrol. Everywhere as they made the rounds they found the palace guarded and prepared; while a hundred other scouts passed ceaselessly to and fro, examining the frowning walls, grim in the shadow of night.

A dozen rumors were current: the palace was filled with Swiss and Chevaliers du Poignard; there were cannons masked at every point; the windows were protected with screens of oak; the court were dancing inside, drinking to the white cockades, as they had done at Versailles. Others affirmed that the city was to be set on fire from the four quarters; that the king had fled; that the National Assembly was to be arrested. Nicole, her curiosity satisfied and wearying of these wild rumors, returned home. At the Faubourg St. Antoine they found everything tranquil, and retired for the night. It was then half-past ten.

In their room Geneviève hazarded the question for which Nicole had waited with amused patience.

"Tell me, Nicole, what did you think of him?"

"Of whom?"

"Of the Citoyen Javogues. Was I not right?"

"He frightens me," Nicole said frankly. "He had the air of a butcher—a madman. Well, how shall I express it? He made me tremble, almost with a premonition of danger."

"Ah, you cannot understand him," Geneviève protested. "To me he is heroic!"

"What a little Jacobin!" Nicole said, with a smile. Without attaching further importance to what she considered the whim of a child, she added: "Well, mon enfant, here is your room. The half of it is yours for as long as you want it."

She passed to the window, casting a longing glance at the dark window opposite. Surprised at Geneviève's silence, she turned, a little provoked. The child was crying.

"Dear Geneviève!" she cried, springing to her side and taking her in her arms. "Don't try to thank me; I understand."

But the girl, through her sobs, murmured again and again, "Thank you, ah, thank you!"

"But it is I who am thankful," Nicole protested. "You bring me something to love and to care for. I was getting used to solitude, which is dangerous."

Checking her thanks, she snuffed the candle, stretching out upon the bed beside the girl.

"Yes, it is bad for one to be always alone," she said.

Geneviève timidly covered her hands with kisses.

"No, no, kiss me on the cheek," Nicole said. "And now, if you are going to obey, go right to sleep."

The child nestled closer, drawing Nicole's arm about her. The embrace seemed strange to Nicole, and, without quite understanding why, she sought to draw her arm away.

V

THE TAKING OF THE TUILERIES

Boom! Boom!

All at once Nicole and Geneviève found themselves on their feet in the middle of the dark room. Through the open window there fell upon their ears a wild metal shriek, hoarse, furious, angry, that spoke of fire and of the dungeon—the boom of the tocsin.

Boom! Boom! Boom! Boom!

Nicole bounded to the window. Below she beheld startled heads in white night-caps scattered down the length of the walls. As one dog wakes the pack, another and another bell took up the call, till from every point of the horizon broke forth the jangle and clang of the iron throats of Paris.

Below, a few tiny cries rose through the murmur. Across the roofs came the thin shrieks of a woman. Lights began to appear, forms clad in night-dress. Suddenly across the court tore into the night Barabant's frenzied voice.

"To arms! to arms!"

As though awaiting the signal, there burst upon the ear the rumbling of drums, the scattered popping of firearms, calls and answering calls flung from roof to roof.

"To arms, citoyens, to arms!"

A frenzy passed over Nicole. She leaned far out, and gathering her voice, echoed:

"To arms!"

She bounded back into the room, knocking over the chair, snatched up her cloak, bounded to the window to cry "To arms!" crashed down the stairs, dragging Geneviève, flung out of the blind passage, bumping and bruising her shoulders, down and out into the streets.

From every doorway figures shot forth and passed, running toward the north. The two girls, at top speed, joined the crowd. They passed a woman with a torch, whose hair stood out in long streams against the racing; la

Mère Corniche hobbling along as fast as her old legs would take her; families of five and six running in packs, panting and silent, while beneath, above, about, from disgorging cellars, from loud-flung open windows, from every bell the city writhed in nightmare.

Distancing their companions, they arrived among the first before the brasserie of Santerre, where the Quinze-Vingts were assembling, forming quickly into ranks. From one window Jambony, the crier, in an enormous red cap, was feeding pikes to a hundred outstretched hands. The arrival of fresh torches caused the walls to loom up like lurid cliffs, sparkling in spots where a window-pane blazed back the reflection. From the windows flattened faces with black-encircled eyes looked down,—children too young, men and women too old, to survive in the press below: unhuman faces of unhuman beings, like a multitude of rats driven to shelter by the influx of a torrent.

Below, the black mass surged in, spattered, under the glow of the torches, with the red of the liberty-caps, while two banners hung like huge blurs above the tossing surface of pikes and weapons. The noise was deafening, the confusion beyond control. Men rushed in and out, their arms flung wide and high, bellowing:

"Death to the tyrants!"

"Death to the fat Louis!"

A slip of a girl, clinging on a window-sill, harangued the mob; a fishwife, astride her husband, comic and furious, beat the air and screamed to the crowd to dye the Seine red. Hags with threatening fists shrieked themselves into a frenzy:

"To the Tuileries! To the Tuileries!"

Some, foaming, overcome with their passions, collapsed on the ground. The anger of the mob against the queen gathered at times in bursts and shouts:

"Death to Mme. Veto!"

"Death to the Austrian!"

Unthinkable obscenities were coupled with her name and tossed from eddy to eddy. The Marseillais, gathering in a body, dominated the tumult with the swelling chords of their battle hymn that on their voices became a chant of carnage and a thing of terror.

It was more than a mob: it was the populace in eruption. All the human passions and emotions were there, the basest and the noblest. There were the scum—the lepers, the beggars, and the criminals diffused among the zealots, the fanatics, and the idealists. There were the frankly curious and the adventurous, and those with hatred and vengeance in their hearts. There was youth, warm-blooded and chivalrous, stirred by visions, and old age impatient to see the dawn—all hoarse and all clamorous to march.

The order did not come. For an hour they waited, trembling for the word. The uproar subsided a little. The torches began to drop out: there were moments of darkness when one could hardly distinguish the faces about. The cries to advance changed to inquiries. Boudgoust brought back the report that Pétion, the mayor, was a captive, held as a hostage in the Tuileries.

Santerre, the Goliath, passed among them, distributing hand-shakes, reassuring them, counseling patience. The Assembly would meet and summon Pétion to its bar and the court would not dare detain him. Some listened, half satisfied; others, the Marseillais specially, cried out for action. They waited still another hour and a half. The first outburst had seemingly exhausted the populace: they remained quietly, awed at the immensity of their daring. Many, tiring of the long vigil on foot, imitated Nicole and Geneviève and stretched out upon the pavements, forming little shallows throughout the length of the street. A few melted away to seek sleep or food. No more torches were lighted. The few that spluttered on became pale and effaced before the drab of the morning. An ashen glow stole over the street. Then the army that had huddled through the night roused itself, shook itself, gathered spirit and anger and again clamored to advance.

Santerre, besieged by the eager, hesitated. He sent off a band of pikemen and then the Marseillais, but the rest he held irresolutely.

Suddenly a cry started up from the outskirts of the crowd. A tall man was seen running toward them with outstretched hands, trying to pierce the crowd that closed around him. A great shout went up:

"The news! The news!"

On the outskirts a hundred hands were flung up, then a thousand. The sound of a mighty cry could be heard indistinguishable, rumbling, gathering volume, sweeping over the crowd.

"Pétion is free!"

"Pétion is at the Hôtel de Ville!"

Santerre hesitated no longer. He descended from his brasserie and gave the signal. The enormous mass started, moving swiftly, consuming its way like a glacier. A scullion, with the sudden converging impulse toward comradeship that now permeated the throng, sought anxiously for a familiar face.

A pikeman from a group, seeing his trouble, called out:

"Hé, comrade, you seek friends. We are your brothers. March with us."

In measure, as they swarmed toward the Tuileries, fresh reports came back. Mandat had been summoned. The artillery at the Pont Neuf had been withdrawn. Mandat was at the Hôtel de Ville. Mandat had fallen before the vengeance of the crowd.

They hastened forward and rolled into the Place de la Grève. It was then seven o'clock in the morning. There, where they expected the order to attack, they were compelled again to wait. When they clamored they were told that they were delaying for the Faubourg St. Marceau, which was to join them at the Pont Neuf. Then these hordes, who had passed the night in suspense, in the midst of rumors and counterrumors, sent up a great shout of anger:

"Treachery!"

The populace that could dare anything could not stand suspense. A panic was imminent; but firmer spirits began to exhort them. On all sides knots of men flung one of their number into the air, where, from the shoulders of a comrade, witty, brilliant, and magnetic, he calmed the crowd with laughter.

Nicole and Geneviève, circulating from group to group, were halted by a familiar voice, and beheld, aloft the giant shoulders of Javogues, the ardent figure of Barabant addressing the throng.

"Peace, good, kind, gentle, loyal citizens," he was saying mockingly, "you will disturb the royal slumbers. Why such impatience? The Austrian cannot see you at such an hour. You are forgetting etiquette!" A roar of laughter showed him his ground. "I assure you, aristocrats will not fight before breakfast, before they are shaved and powdered and dressed. Patience, my Sans-Culottes; we do not want to stab them in their beds; give them time to sleep and breakfast, that we may show them how Sans-Culottes can fight. They are not Sans-Culottes; only Sans-Culottes can fight with empty stomachs!

"For shame, citizens; one does not grumble in the face of danger. Look about you. The moment is sublime. You who have felled the Bastille, you who brought Capet back from Versailles—you are now to strike the great blow for freedom, and you grumble. What matters it if we have waited twenty hours or twenty days, if we may see such an event? Who would not rather die at such a moment than live in any age or in any condition the world has ever known? Citizens, the moment is sublime; be ye also sublime!"

He slid to the ground, amid uproarious approval, satisfied and elate. Javogues, the Atlas, bellowed out, "That's the way to talk; he is right! Vive la Nation!"

"Vive le Citoyen Barabant!"

Barabant, recognizing the voice of Nicole, turned, while the crowd, eagerly catching up his name, saluted it with cheers.

"Bravo the Parisian!"

The second voice was Louison's. The two girls, each armed with a cutlass, sent him their applause over the crowd. But, while the frank enthusiasm of Nicole inspired him, there was something in the tolerant smile of Louison that seemed to mock his elation. Before he could reach them, the crowd, abandoning the cries of treachery, exploded in anger at the Faubourg St. Marceau.

"Fine patriots!"

"What the devil are they doing?"

"We do not need them; to the Tuileries without them!"

"Give us news of them!"

"Citoyens, I'll bring you news," Barabant retorted. "A little patience and you shall know of the Faubourg St. Marceau."

He returned through the chafing multitude, and departed down the Rue St. Honoré as fast as his legs could carry him. At the Place du Carrousel the mob was besieging the entrance to the Tuileries, clamoring for admittance. As he hesitated, the gate was flung open and the mass, with the quickness of gunpowder seeking an outlet, crashed in. Barabant, all else forgotten, hurled himself forward in a blind endeavor to reach the court. He tripped and fell, and before he could gain his feet the mob had passed him.

There had been not a moment of hesitation. They rushed into the trap, heeding neither the windows, bristling with muskets, that confronted them nor the walls that hemmed them in. Leaping and shouting, they ran to the vestibule at the end. There they saw a mass of red that colored it from top to bottom—a mass perfectly ordered. It was the Swiss, drawn up line by line on every step, their muskets at aim, awaiting the word.

The first assailants stopped irresolutely, but the impetus of those behind swept them on, until the vestibule was consumed and the first ranks looked into the threatening barrels. Still no sound. The two forces, the machine and the monster, looked into each other's eyes, noting little details. The populace, gaining confidence, began to jest, saluting the soldiers with friendly greetings, inviting them to join them.

Some one in the mob, extending a long crook, hooked a Swiss and drew him into the vortex, amid shouts of laughter. They clapped their hands, laughing like children, and set to work at this new game. A second, a third, five Swiss, were thus fished out of the ranks without resisting.

All at once, from the balcony above, a voice cried:

"Fire!"

As the sea with an immense impulse recoils from an earthquake, there was a vast recoil in the mob, an exact explosion from the machine. The smoke, rushing down the vestibule, swirled into the air and lifted. The officer leaned curiously over the balcony and gave the order to advance. The red ranks moved down and over the inanimate mound; of all those who a moment before had laughed incredulously not one survived.

Outside, the mob broke and fled up the Place du Carrousel, recoiling from the horrid vestibule, where suddenly there formed a bubble of red, that grew larger and trickled over the garden, widening and assuming mass and shape. At times across the red, like a diamond meeting the sun, there ran a brilliant flash. At every flash men stumbled in their flight and pitched forward. Pell-mell into the Rue St. Honoré they ran, routed, but full of anger and enthusiasm.

At this moment the sections of the Marais swept in, gathered them up, and, burning with vengeance at the sight of their wounds, rushed on to the attack. Barabant, who had received a flesh-wound in the hand, had barely time to bind it up before he was swept again into the Carrousel.

Then a vast hurrah burst from them, a shout of relief and of battle. From the quais the guerrilla band of the Marseillais were rolling forward, formidable, grim, and unleashed. Suddenly their ranks parted and two tongues of fire lashed out; in the solid bank of the Swiss two gaps appeared. A frenzy possessed the assaulting mass. It flung itself forward, without method, attacking only with its anger. The Swiss reëntered the vestibule, issuing forth from time to time to deliver a volley.

Barabant, in the midst of the swirl, lost consciousness of his acts, swayed by sudden, unreasoning passion. He fired fast and faster, caught by the infection of his comrades, cursing, exhorting wildly, laughing; but his bullets, without objective, flattened themselves against the death-dealing walls. At times he saw, through the thick smoke, Javogues and his comrades dragging a cannon forward toward the barracks. At another moment there suddenly emerged out of the mêlée the figure of the two bouquetières.

Amid the swirl of smoke, Nicole appeared to Barabant's excited senses as a goddess exhorting them to battle. Her hair had tumbled, rioting, her dress was torn open at the throat, her bare arms were stained with powder and red with the contact of the wounded; and yet, as she loaded a musket, or presented it to a volunteer, or showed him the flashing walls, she laughed one of those laughs sublime with the indifference to danger and the joy of heroism that inflame the souls of those who hear it, and transform the wavering with the frenzy of sacrifice.

On the contrary, Louison, among all the confusion and the tumult, moved quietly, gathering the bullets from the fallen and returning them to her friend. Her face was calm, cold; her eyes sought everything and showed nothing; and though she moved incessantly on her quests, she was apart from all—a spectator.

Barabant, unable to join them, was carried step by step toward the barracks. Once he slipped in a pool of blood and went down, his companion falling across him. He called to him to rise, but the man was dead. A woman of the halles freed him.

A series of explosions almost hurled him back; the next moment the barracks, rent in gaps, were swept with a sheet of flame. The assailants, with a cry of triumph, hurled themselves into the palace, while the Swiss, forced up the staircase, broke and fled, pursued and shot down by the victors.

Through the apartments, shattering doors, overturning furniture, howling along the empty corridors, the mob crashed in, as the first victorious blast of a tempest, shrieking:

"À la mort! À la mort!"

One by one the flying Swiss were overtaken. Packs of the invaders leaped upon them, burying them from view, until, stabbed with a dozen useless thrusts, their bodies were flung with exulting cries from the windows; while as the foremost stopped to enjoy their prey, the herd swept to the front with hungry arms and the ever-rising shout:

"Death to all! Death to all!"

Barabant, racing ahead to save the women, soon found himself in front, running beside a Marseillais, who cried to him with the voice of Javogues:

"Keep with me, citoyen, keep with me! Leave the curs to the others!"

A Swiss, hearing them at his back, fell on his knees, shrieking for mercy.

"Leave him. Don't stop!" Javogues panted. Seizing Barabant's arm, he bore him down a side gallery, shouting:

"There he is! There he is!"

At the end of the corridor Barabant beheld a tall form disappearing at the head of a narrow stairway.

Up this they rushed, into the single outlet, a guard-room, only to find it empty. Javogues threw himself furiously against the walls.

"I saw him, I saw him; he is here somewhere!"

"Who?"

"Dossonville! He was among the Swiss. I saw him." He ran around the room, assailing it with his huge fists. All at once he gave a cry, and lifting the hatchet he bore, he sent a secret door crashing in.

"He is here!"

He hacked his way through and disappeared, thundering down the passage. Barabant, only half comprehending what had happened, remained a moment in perplexity. But the sound of women's cries startled him again to activity. He darted back into the current of the mob and gained the women's apartments. At the foot of the staircase an officer of the National Guard was crying:

"We don't kill women!"

"Spare the women!" Barabant echoed.

A dozen others took up the cry.

"The Republic does not make war on women!"

The mob, balked of half its vengeance by the firmness of a dozen officers, turned to desecration and pillage. Troops of women, like furies, swarmed through the royal apartments, tearing the beds to pieces, exulting, foul and crazed.

Barabant, sickening at the sight of unnamable excesses, retraced his way down the strewn galleries, heaped with overturned furniture, and tapestries pulled from the wall, spattered with blood and dirt. Heedless of the shouts above him, he passed down the vestibule and over the mountain of slain, suffocated by the stench and the horror of wide-mouthed corpses. Now that the crisis was over, his inflammable nature recoiled before the ugliness of the triumph.

While Louison and Geneviève had been drawn into the frantic mob which swept the palace, Nicole had remained outside, joining the hundreds of women who visited the wounded or sought, in agony, among the dead. She also, with a new anxiety, sped among the slain with a sinking dread before each upturned face.All at once a familiar voice cried at her side:

"Help! help!"

The cry came from beneath the body of a Marseillais. With the aid of a fishwife she pulled away the corpse, discovering the shaken, limp form of the mountebank Cramoisin.

"Ah, mon Dieu," she cried, forgetting the rancor of the woman in the patriot, "are you wounded?"

"I—I think so."

"Where?"

"I don't know," he stammered, rising weakly to his feet. "Is it ended?"

"In thy stomach, I guess, my brave fellow!" the fishwife cried with rough scorn. "It seems to have failed thee!"

"You do not know him: he is a hero!" Nicole cried, ironically. "Wait a moment; we'll find the wound!"

With a laugh, the two sought to seize him; but Cramoisin, having recovered the use of his legs, escaped in a ludicrous, snarling flight.

Suddenly Nicole beheld Barabant stumbling forth from the vestibule. All coquetry forgot, she sprang to him with the cry:

"Barabant, you are wounded!"

He looked at his arm and saw it was covered with blood. He passed his hand over his face; a scalp-wound trickled a red stream down his forehead. He sat down while she hurriedly washed the wounds and bandaged them. When he essayed to rise, a dizziness made his step so unsteady that Nicole drew his arm over her shoulder, laughing at his feeble resistance.

"Allons, this is the hour of the women. I'll bring you back. Don't be afraid to lean on me!"

She put her arm about his waist and impelled him gently. He resisted no longer, and together slowly they moved homeward over the stricken field, amid the groaning and the silent.

He had a misty recollection of a phantasmagoric passage, of rapidly moving figures hideous with blood, of heads dancing on pikes above him, of stretchers bearing inanimate things, of rushing, floating women, of the sudden rumbling of drums, of companies swinging past him, of interminable streets, and of cliffs, mountains high, that gave forth shrieks of triumph. Then in the city, delirious with joy and sorrow, delirium, too, rushed through his brain, his head fell heavily upon Nicole's bare shoulder, and the will deserting his limbs, he slipped from her arms heavily to the ground.

VI

THE HEART OF A WOMAN

When at last Nicole had brought Barabant to his room, she was very tired. Goursac, whom she had summoned to help her, knelt by the bed to examine the unconscious form. Every now and then he turned a questioning look upon the girl, as though to penetrate the indifferent attitude she maintained.

"Why don't you say something?" Nicole cried at last, her anxiety mastering her prudence. "Is it so serious?"

"A mere scratch," he grumbled; "nothing to make such a fuss over. If he hadn't been as weak as a woman — "

Nicole, reassured, smiled at his ill-humor, knowing the mood of old. Goursac, furious at such a reception of his sarcasm, turned on her angrily.

"You are like all the rest—just as stupid. Because a young fellow gets a scratch and you pilot him home, you call that a romance. You know well enough what that leads to!"

"That may be true; why shouldn't I have my romance as well as another?"

"You say that to plague me. You know that is not so!" he said impatiently. "Now give me a bandage."

Stooping, Nicole seized her petticoat; but finding it stained with traces of the combat, she dropped it, and calling to him to wait, passed through the window and across the gutter, swaying lithely against the roof. In a moment she returned with half of a sheet, which they quickly tore into bandages.

"There; with a little rest—a chance to recover some blood—the fever will abate!" Preparing a sling, Goursac jerked his head toward the bed and demanded: "You are not going to watch?"

"Certainly I am!"

"Then say at once," he cried point-blank, "that you imagine you are in love!"

"Goursac, my friend, you are ridiculous with your ideas," Nicole answered impatiently. "You know that the Citoyen Barabant arrived only yesterday. We are good comrades. That's all!"

"Yes, yes, yes!"

He wrinkled his lips in scornful unbelief, raised his shoulders to his ears, and disappeared, heavily, down the stairs, grumbling ironically, "A man lies to deceive others; a woman lies to deceive herself!"

A moment later he called back:

"Hé, above there!"

Nicole went to the landing.

"Is that you, the comrade?"

"Yes, old cynic."

"If you need me, stamp twice on the floor."

"Agreed."

"Return now to your—acquaintance."

Nicole, laughing, returned to the bedside. She placed her hand on the heated forehead, frowned, smoothed down the covers, arranged the discarded clothes, and, after a moment's reflection, departed over the roof to her room.

When she again appeared, she had removed all traces of the battle. She pulled a chair near the bed, loosened her hair, scattering it over her shoulders, and began to comb it out, unraveling the tangle with many grimaces and an oft-wrung "Aïe! aïe!"

Occasionally she consulted a pocket-mirror, then resumed the combing, humming to herself. Barabant, his forehead enveloped in white, his arm in a sling, lay with his head turned toward her, one arm escaping bare above the covers. She regarded approvingly the lithe muscles suggested under the soft skin, and, ceasing her humming, pronounced:

"He is well made!"

She leaned over the bed and opened the collar of his shirt, revealing the full throat.

"Tiens, he's as white as a woman."

She withdrew, and resumed her humming.

"But, Dieu merci, it's not a woman." She was taking up another strand when the stairs cried out and Louison entered. Nicole frowned and said curtly:

"Ah, it's you, is it? Who told you?"

"La Mère Corniche. How goes it?" she asked, indicating Barabant.

"Well."

"Are you coming to eat something?"

"No, I'm staying here."

"Is it so serious?"

"I don't know," she said, continuing her combing. "He pleases me."

Louison stood at the bed, looking down. "Not bad; he's interesting. I noticed he had good eyes."

Nicole stopped her combing, and a frown gathered above the childish cheeks, as she cried impetuously:

"Louison, no interference, do you hear? Or— "

"Or what?" The dark eyebrows arched slightly, but the deep eyes remained cold. Nicole did not answer. Louison returned to the contemplation of the young man a moment longer, then reluctantly rousing herself from her reverie, turned on her heel. Her eye, falling on Nicole, regarded her with a trace of amusement.

"Child!" she said, standing in the doorway, her face relaxing into a smile. "You have chosen the best moment, my dear: you are adorable!"

Nicole listened, immovable, until the last footstep had grown silent. Then drawing her lips together, she seized her knees with her hands, and thus curbed, her eyes fixed themselves in intense contemplation, while several times a sudden anger knit her features before she shook off the disagreeable emotions and sought the cool of the window.

At a rustling from the bed she returned quickly. Barabant had stirred slightly, but so as to throw his weight upon the wounded arm. She slipped her arm under him and moved him to a more comfortable position. This maternal solicitude, slight as it was, awakened a new emotion in her. She arranged his hair, and seeking hungrily for any further service, began to bathe the hot eyelids.

Barabant, under the gentle stroking, opened his eyes. The confines appeared to him vast and silent, the window far removed and small. The long August twilight invaded the room with the delicious promise of a quieter night, while from without the distant, scattered sounds of rejoicing reached his ears, through the corridors of insensibility, like the tinkle of soft music. He sighed contentedly and closed his eyes again.

Presently he said, turning his head a trifle, but without opening his eyes:

"Thou art really there, Nicole?"

The accent and the caress pierced to the depths the heart of the young girl, already stirred by the maternal impulse of the woman.

"Really here, yes."

But almost immediately, as though regretting the softness of the response, she added, in remonstrance:

"I have not given you permission to call me thou!"

"It is my gratitude that—that permits me."

"Ah, that is nice." She smiled with pleasure. "That was very prettily said."

"Nicole?"

"Yes."

"Place your ear to my lips; I cannot talk so far."

The girl, with a smile, divining the ruse, leaned over him. But Barabant making no sound, she withdrew, scrutinizing anxiously the hot face.

"Nicole."

"I am here."

Again she stooped, and this time so close that her hair swept his forehead.

"You are there?"

"Yes."

"I love you," he said drowsily.

"Oh, oh!" Nicole started back, blushing and amused; but looking down, she saw he had dropped again into the wanderings of delirium.

"He does not know what he says," she said, shaking her head. "Poor fellow!"

She watched him in his helplessness, and all at once she sighed; but it was a sigh that rose from the soul, and while it filled her heart, it passed on and awakened in her a famine of tenderness, leaving a longing for tears.

Motionless and perplexed, she stood staring down at the dim bed, her lips parted, her breast filling with deep breaths, until at last she turned reluctantly and sought the window, still uncertain, nor comprehending what was germinating within her.

The night was beginning; in the clear heavens the high moon was strengthening in luster at every moment. Across the stretch of window lights the sounds of revelry and rejoicing persisted faintly to her ears. The courtyard, deserted by the men, was hushed with the silence of fatigue. The laugh of a girl mounted at times, clear and playful, mingling with the deeper, good-humored protests of her companion. From a window a hag, chin in hand, followed the lovers with due interest. In another room a weary mother had fallen asleep with her baby still feeding at her breast. At other windows the women waited patiently the return of the men, bending mechanically over their knitting or crooning to the sleepy children. There, under the enduring, tedious night, Nicole stayed from minute to minute, pressing her clenched hand tensely against her lips; while within her breast beat tumult and a revolt against the slavery of women. She returned to the bedside, rebelling against this helpless man who drew her irresistibly from her independence.

"Nicole— "

It was Goursac calling, and she sprang furiously to the landing, rebuking him with a low: "Silence! he is asleep. What do you want?"

"If you are tired, I'll watch."

"No, no!" she answered angrily. The cry seemed to burst from her heart, threatened by the very thought of such exile.

She knelt at the bed hungrily, waiting jealously for an opportunity to ease the restless body, her revolt forgotten in the defense of her right to soothe and minister. She slipped her arm under his body, and drew his head upon her shoulder. A sigh of contentment rewarded her. He grew more quiet, breathing gentle breaths that disturbed her hair and fanned her throat. In the half-darkness she remained, with aching shoulder, holding him in her arms as though to defend him from all who would separate them. Several times, in an access of tenderness, she approached her lips to the unconscious forehead, but each time instinctively drew back from the surrender. She had a desire for tears, for laughter, for swift anger, that he should wake at last. She would have kept him there forever, weak and helpless, turning to her in trust and necessity. At times, with a sudden alarm, she asked herself what had happened, what could be these new emotions, until at last, in the disturbance and bewilderment of her soul, she saw the utter loneliness of her life, and the cry went up from her:

"Ah, mon Dieu, how unhappy I am!"

The full sun was beating into the room when Barabant awoke. His forehead was cold, his senses were sharp; but his memory struggled in vain to reconstruct the events of the afternoon. His arm confined in a sling brought back his wound, and Nicole, and the beginning of the tedious journey; beyond that a black wall rose up and shut out all vision. He turned over, calculating his strength, when, his eye traveling over the bedside, what was his stupefaction to behold Nicole stretched upon the floor. Her hands were pillowed under her cheek, where the long eyelashes showed sharply against the heightened color. She slept easily, the lips slightly parted as though smiling under happy dreams. Barabant watched her breathlessly, jealously putting off the awakening. But at this moment, as though aware of the intensity of his gaze, the girl opened her eyes, met the enraptured glance of Barabant a moment only, then sprang to her feet with a confusion which she sought to cover with a laughing "Good morning!"

"You have been here all night?" Barabant said, in astonishment.

"Why not?" Nicole noticed that he did not address her as "thou." She rearranged her dress and said with forced naturalness, "Do you think that is much to do for a patriot who is wounded?"

Barabant, displeased with the answer, made no reply.

"So you have decided to return to this world, citoyen?"

"Have I been delirious?"

"Do you remember nothing?"

"Nothing since—since the Place de la Grève." As this answer seemed to plunge Nicole into silence, he asked, "How did you get me here?"

"It wasn't difficult," she began more gaily. "I begged your way from block to block. Let me see; two water-carriers brought you half-way, then a coachman a block on his route, then another block on a litter, and finally a fishwife helped me to the end."

"You carried me?"

"Indeed, I am not a weakling; look at that." She extended her arms, laughing. "They are solid."

"And this?" Barabant touched the sling.

"Oh, that was the Citoyen Goursac."

"Who?"

"Your neighbor below, a brown man who buries his chin like this, and scowls. That reminds me, it is time he should see you."

"Nicole!"

"Well, what?"

"Not now; not just yet."

"Why not?"

"I wish to talk with you."

"The idea, as though I had nothing to do!" She raised her foot and stamped twice. "I have a desire to dine to-night, thank you."

"Where are you going?"

"I'm going to work." She picked up her possessions and made for the window, while Barabant cried excitedly:

"Nicole, I have not thanked you. Wait, let me thank you."

"Why?" She shrugged her shoulders. "I'd do that for any one."

Barabant raised himself on his elbow and threatened, half angrily: "Nicole, if you go, I'll follow you. I swear I'll follow you. I will. Look at me. I swear I will!"

"What good will it do you? I'll be gone."

She shook her head, and, deaf to his entreaties, disappeared; while Barabant, furious, fell back, baffled and perplexed, little suspecting the awakening that was taking place in Nicole.

VII

THE FEAR OF HAPPINESS

When Nicole reached her room, she found Geneviève up and waiting.

"What are you doing, child?" she cried sharply, to cover her confusion. "Why are you here?"

"I—I am waiting," Geneviève stammered, "to see if I could do anything for you."

"There is nothing. I am going out now myself."

"What!" cried the child, opening her eyes wide. "You are not going to stay with the poor fellow?"

"There is no need. He is well."

"But I thought—" She stopped, in confusion, and then clumsily beat a retreat to the door. "I'll go now. I—I only wanted to be of service."

Nicole waited only long enough to be sure of Geneviève's departure before descending in turn. Her little room was too narrow; it choked her. She had need of the open span of the sky to think over the new emotions.

After an hour of unprofitable solitude, feeling the need of a confidence which would lessen the tension of her thoughts, she sought Goursac, beginning timidly with the question:

"And the Citoyen Barabant, how is he?"

"Why, he is still alive, clamoring for you like a lost child for his mother."

"Goursac, my old friend," she said, taking his arm, "be serious and gentle for once. I am unhappy, and I want to talk with you."

"Ah, you love him," he said bitterly.

"Yes," she said slowly, as though the revelation had just come, "I love him."

"Then why do you avoid him?"

"I am afraid."

"Of what?"

"Of loving him too much."

"I don't understand."

She tried to tell him a little of her emotions at the bedside—the wonder and the swift, acute joy of ministering, the longing to tend and own. Goursac, with a few questions, led her on. They were now in the Tuileries, a little apart from the quick throng, the swish of skirts, the laughter and the hum. At last he said:

"My little Nicole, listen. Love is not something that comes to us from the outside: it is a need within ourselves. We each have our functions in this world and our needs. At the bottom, what is strongest and best in woman is the maternal instinct. Listen to me! You fall in love when the need within you becomes too insistent. Any one of a hundred men can appeal to you. It is the moment and not the man. You knew the maternal instinct for the first time when you had in your keeping the Citoyen Barabant. You think that it is he that has awakened you. Not at all; all these emotions have been in you, dormant; it is they, not he, which enchant you. Voyons—you do not listen—Nicole!"

"That's true," she said, rousing herself from her reverie. Her eyes had been deep in the bright to and fro of the promenaders, but she saw only the room under the attic, and felt only the hot head on her aching shoulder.

"After all, you are thinking only of him, and I am a fool," he said. "Nothing that I can say will make any difference. You will learn, as others have learned, on the steps of experience. Out of some curious twist within you, in some strange way of reasoning you will decide for yourself."

"I suppose so," she said drearily. "But I wanted to talk it out; you are kind to me."

"I," he said calmly—"I adore you."

"Be serious."

"That is serious."

"Truly?"

"You know it."

"Why?" she said meditatively, but half believing him.

"You are young," he answered, looking steadfastly at the charming profile. "And to see you is good for the eyes. You are youth, and I have not been old long enough to be reconciled to age. But you don't believe me."

"Yes."

"No; at least, you do not understand."

She did not return home until nightfall, and then did not cross Barabant's window-sill, but contented herself with an inquiry as to his condition; nor could artifice and entreaty retain her longer. The next day she did not appear at all.Barabant, who saw in her absence nothing but coquetry, was furious with her, with himself, with all that kept him to his bed. The lagging, still hours seemed doubly lagging and still with the memory of the charm which the presence of the girl had brought to the bare walls. Time and time his eyes sought the empty floor where he had surprised her asleep; and, conjuring up that delightful picture, he accused himself in his unreasoning irritation for not having simulated insensibility throughout the day.

Why did she thus avoid him? He remembered their first encounter with Louison. Was she jealous of her comrade, or was it simply calculation? That Nicole should think of playing the coquette annoyed him exceedingly. He had yielded to the fascination of this gipsy from the moment she had taken his arm in the gardens of the Palais Royal with the mischievous "Barabant, you are a lucky fellow," with which she had opened their comradeship. But this easy, pleasurable interest had been fanned into a passionate flame at the storming of the Tuileries, where, by her fire, her tempestuous beauty, and her careless laughter, she had impressed herself imperishably on his imagination; and later the thought of her bearing him home, of her nursing, and of her tenderness had invaded his heart.

With the rapture of the first unfolding romance he abandoned himself utterly to the thought of her, while retaining in his deeper consciousness, as undebatable, that limit of common sense which must separate the man of education and promise from a daughter of the people.

The thought was a part of his intuitions rather than his consciousness; for in his simplicity he believed himself utterly unselfish in seeking her, and was at a loss to understand why she should have changed.

Neither the afternoon nor the evening brought any sign of Nicole, nor during the next day could he obtain more than one glimpse of her, as she departed toward the flower-market. Recovered from his exhaustion, he set forth on the following morning, piqued and angry, resolved to find her and force an explanation.

He searched the Palais Royal and the Tuileries without success, and it was only after luncheon that, passing down the left bank of the Seine, he found her near the Conciergerie.

She was a little apart from the throng, strolling meditatively by the river, into whose swift flood her look was plunged. The half-depleted basket, overrun with flowers, dangled from her arm, while in her fingers she was turning a cockade without purpose. Against the hot August foliage and the buildings weltering under the sun there was something about her inexpressibly cool and refreshing to the eye.

The meditative abandon of her pose suggested all at once to Barabant a reason for her absence, and with this pleasing thought his anger yielded to the zest of the eager and confident lover.

So serious was her reverie that she was unaware of his approach until his greeting startled her.

"Am I so terrible, Nicole," Barabant asked, smiling at her confusion, "that you find it necessary to avoid me?"

She rallied quickly, and simulating indecision, exclaimed:

"Why, it is the Citoyen Barabant!"

Barabant brought his brows together and said, with a return of his exasperation: "Nicole, why do you avoid me?"

She shook her head.

"I don't avoid you; I do not seek you out."

"Nicole, you are playing with me."

She again shook her head.

Barabant, taking her wrist, repeated the assertion.

"Barabant, I do not play with you," Nicole answered earnestly.

"Then why have you avoided me?"

He waited for her answer, but she said firmly: "I cannot tell you."

"Assuredly she is beginning to love me," thought Barabant, and, well content, did not press the question. They strayed a little from the Conciergerie, and leaning over the bank, contemplated the river scenes below, following the fortunes of the languid fishermen, the antics of a kitten that romped over the flat decks herded together, and the glistening backs of boys splashing near the shore.

"Of whom were you thinking so seriously before I came?" Barabant asked, secure in his new confidence. He sought her face, hoping to surprise some trace of confusion.

"I was wondering how it would seem to have a mother," Nicole answered. She crumbled a flower and scattered the petals on the wafting stir of the air before she turned. "But then we might not agree. Perhaps I am lucky. What do you think?"

"Such reverie for a mother?"

"Oh, there are moments when one has such moods."

"I had hoped you were thinking of me."

"Really?" She lifted her eyebrows slightly. "And why?"

Her composure routed his agreeable theories and plunged him into perplexities. So, abandoning his confident attitude, he exclaimed vehemently:

"Nicole, what has happened? What is there—a misunderstanding, or what? Surely you will not tell me that it is natural for you to shun me so persistently. I will be answered!"

"I don't; I don't. I will not have you saying that!" She seized the opportunity of a passing party of muscadins—the dandies of the day—to offer her cockades. On her return, Barabant said more quietly:

"Listen to me, Nicole. You misunderstand me; I do not upbraid you. I want to thank you. I owe you much, and you give me no opportunity to tell you of my gratitude. That is what vexes me. Voyons, Nicole, we had begun so well!" He leaned closer and said mischievously: "Oh, if I had known you would leave, I would have remained unconscious all the day. I've cursed myself ever since."

He laughed, and growing bolder as he perceived she listened without displeasure, he poured into her ear, in one breath daring, in another shy, a thousand and one of those vague, delightful half-confidences which in the imagination of the lover awaken as naturally as the flowers open to the sun.

Nicole could not but listen. She assembled a bouquet and pressed her face against it to screen her pleasure from his avid scrutiny. From time to time she turned, and looking him full in the face, sought to read there the true value of his words. But almost immediately she would turn with a wistful smile of unbelief. At length she checked him, saying, with reluctant gentleness:

"Enough, Barabant. Your imagination runs away with you. You do not know your own feelings."

Barabant, borne on by the ardor of his emotions, retorted point-blank:

"And you, do you know yours?"

At this sudden challenge, Nicole had a moment of confusion, during which she answered at random:

"I?" But immediately regaining her composure, she added, "Perfectly."

"You evade my question."

"If you begin like that, I warn you I will not listen. Besides, I am neglecting my cockades."

She unslung her basket and again accosted the crowd. Barabant, after the first outburst of expostulation, waited moodily, leaning against a tree, his gaze lost in the current. The moment Nicole was assured of his abstraction, she hesitated no longer, but slipping through the throng, quickly gained her liberty among distant streets.

She knew that the evasion was unwise, exposing her to his judgment either as a coquette or as fearing to betray her true feelings—opinions which she did not wish him to entertain. She had fled, but not by calculation. She had again avoided him, and yet she scarcely understood why. New emotions had awakened in her a commotion that disturbed her whole theory of life.Before, with happy tolerance, she had passed along the weary road of poverty, shrugging her shoulders at hunger, meeting adversity with a smile, expecting two or three attachments, not deep; delightful while lasting, sharp and saddening when broken; but, sad or sweet, not to be regarded too seriously,—the lot of life.

She had, therefore, welcomed the coming of Barabant with the pleasurable anticipation of a delightful comradeship. That she could retain him, or, in all probability, would care to retain him, beyond a certain term never occurred to her. As to the question of marriage, it did not for a moment enter her head. For her it did not exist.

A sigh drawn from her soul as she stood by his bed had dissipated all that, and discovered to her immense longings, womanly, motherly necessities which she had never realized before and which she imperfectly comprehended now. She perceived him no longer as a comrade, but as the new need of her awakened nature.

She had imagined love as impassioned, headlong, and impetuous, and, in the place of this ideal, she felt only the confident, weak appeal of Barabant to her ministering tenderness. The sensation was acute, poignant, disturbing; the happiness that had possessed her then was too big, too strange; it frightened her. She feared such a transforming, all-consuming love. To give herself utterly thus she felt, in her intuitions, would mean only disaster. So she fled from herself, trying to stifle that immense emotion to which she had no right,—so fraught with peril. So when, through all the rumble of sound and the ceaseless rabble of the boulevards, there returned the silent room under the eaves, and the feverish smile that answered to her soothing touch, she incessantly cried to herself:

"No, no. I would love him too much. The end would crush me."

Little vagrant of the people, she knew well what that end inevitably must be.

VIII

THE MOTHER OF LOUISON

Barabant, baffled and incensed at Nicole's desertion, vowed that he would be through with such a coquette. Where pride begins there is a limit to gratitude, and that limit she had overstepped. He washed his hands of her. So, having decided—irrevocably decided—that Nicole had removed herself from any interest of his, and that it was a matter of indifference to him whether or not he saw her again, he determined to bring her to reason by paying attention to Louison.

Accordingly he contrived to meet her in the passageway the morning after his unceremonious desertion by Nicole.

"Salutations, Citoyen Barabant," Louison cried. "No luck this morning. Nicole has already left."

"Nicole is out of the question," he retorted.

"What!" Louison opened her eyes in astonishment.

"I say, we have nothing to do with Nicole," he replied coolly. "Where are you bound?"

"To the flower-market."

"I understand the route is dangerous at this time of day."

"Exceedingly dangerous."

"Then I had better accompany you."

"I think you had."

With this light introduction, they set out through the stirring city, greeted by the slamming of opening shutters, and escaping the clouds of dust that rose from the brooms of concierges. Louison was the first to speak.

"Well, comrade, and how goes it with you?"

Barabant affected ignorance.

"What, is it not serious with you and Nicole?"

"Serious is a big word," he answered, resolved not to yield an inch.

"I see, a little interest, but not—not the grand passion, violent and sacred!" She added, with a false sigh, "Poor Nicole, it is serious with her."

"Of course."

"I know it."

"You imagine it."

"I know it by one sign: she is jealous. There you are!" She laughed. "She is always jealous of me when it's serious. This time, though, there is no cause. I shall not interfere." She placed a flower to her lips and shot a quick glance up at him. "Though I met you the first."

"Do I count for nothing—or my preference?"

"Nini!" She shook one finger slowly back and forth. "Let us talk of other things. I might unconsciously break my promise."

The air grew fragrant as they entered a square blotted out with tents. Masses of red and pink, of white and yellow, met the eye through sudden lanes in the petticoat crowd.

"Leave me now to my bargaining," she said. Stopping in the perfumed alley at a tent, where the swinging sign-board bore the name la Mère Boboche, she cried tartly: "Good morning, citoyenne. The flowers are very stale this morning."

A thin, bent woman turned her one good eye, and recognizing a daily opponent, rose, drawing in her lips and nodding.

"Eh, they are dear this morning, but you have brought your muscadin. You can pay well to-day after the way you cheated me yesterday."

"He is my brother," Louison said coldly, turning over the flowers.

"Oui dà!" La Mère Boboche dropped an anxious glance at her counter. "Isn't he handsome, though, her muscadin? What arms, what a chest, eh? Solid that!"

Louison, observing that Barabant was uneasy under this chaffing, was about to interpose when a shrill voice rose in taunt from the opposite stall.

"What a monster of immorality! Allons, la mère, it's time you forgot such things."

Instantly the two enemies let loose at each other floods of vituperation.

"Listen to the evil tongue!"

"Hark to the old hen, what a cackle!"

"Corrupter of youth!"

"Cheat!"

"Impostor!"

Louison, profiting by the outcry, selected her flowers and escaped the fray.

"Now for some white ones and I am done. Aïe, what a jam!"

She took his arm, and as they entered the press of the main alley, once or twice was swept up against him with great force.

"Pardon; aïe, aïe, pardon! What a scramble this morning!" She was swung face to face with her protector, her eyes matching his in height. They freed themselves and reached another shop.

"Thanks, citoyen; your arm is strong."

Louison, giving a look of admiration at his limbs, began her bargaining. Barabant, though aware of the artifices, resisted weakly the direct attack. With a new interest he studied the liberty-cap that flamed in the black, sinewy wave of her hair. She was dressed in a yellow bodice, falling to a short skirt of light-blue fustian. The ankles thus revealed were shapely, and attracted the eye with their bright bit of red stocking. He began to ask himself if she were not really beautiful, as he watched the figure, unusually erect, every motion of which was made with grace and ease.

Louison, observing Barabant's study, from time to time turned her head to send him a smile over her shoulder. Occasionally she frowned and, as though to discourage his examination, shook her head.

Barabant forgot the curious impression she first had made upon him. He saw only a face with great capabilities of expression: mobile, flexible, obeying the capricious thought. The eyes more than ever arrested his attention and baffled it. They opened to him a way; but when he looked it was as though penetrating into a vast darkness.

"Why do you look at me so?"

Barabant recovered to find Louison at his elbow, her purchase made, regarding him with amusement.

"You mystify me," he said frankly. "There is something about you I cannot place. What is it?"

She shook her head.

"Don't. Besides—Nicole."

"You have been very solicitous to leave me to Nicole," he said, with a smile. "You choose excellent means to gain your end."

He had expected to catch her confused and blushing. Instead, she discovered a row of white teeth, and nodding her head, said:

"Eh, you are not so slow after all." Before he could reply, she exclaimed, "Hello, there's mama!"

She indicated a wig-maker's, where, on the door-step, a woman of about thirty-five or-six was sitting, carding a wig. Despite the difference of ages, Barabant noticed a similarity in the color of the hair and in the span of the eyebrows.

"Good morning, mother!"

The woman raised her head, but as her glance reached them started back, as though from a feeling of repulsion, and immediately dropped her head.

"Thank you, I am well," Louison cried mockingly. "Good day, mother, we can't stop." She turned in perfect good humor to Barabant. "There's a model mother for you; no trouble at all!"

"And your father?" Barabant inquired, as much struck at her philosophic attitude as at the maternal indifference.

"There's the trouble, voilà." She held her thumb-nail against her teeth and clicked it. "She has never been willing to tell me his name." She shrugged her shoulders. "That's stupid, isn't it? Why not?"

Barabant asked her curiously how long they had been parted.

"Since I was five years old. I only remember some dreadful scene at home,—I don't know what,—and all at once her manner changed to me. The next day she drove me out."

"At five?"

"Nothing extraordinary in that," Louison answered, surprised at his astonishment. "Ah, you do not know our Paris. She married soon after; perhaps it was for that, but I think not." She was silent a moment. "I think she discovered something about my father: that he was an abbé or an aristocrat."

"And you?"

"I begged. I found a corner in the cellar at la Mère Corniche's. You have never been in that pleasant abode?" She made a wry face. "There are rats; you don't get much sleep. Then it smells bad and it is black; though of course at night that makes no difference. I did not stay there long."

"What did you do?"

"Oh, I passed from corner to corner." She stopped in the square and seated herself on a bench. She emptied her flowers and held them out to Barabant. "Hold these while I make my cockades. I passed from family to family. I was well treated. They gave me a crust or a bone, and let me crawl into a corner at night. Of course I worked. It was interesting!" She wove the flowers deftly into cockades, taking them from his lap, their hands brushing each other from time to time. "Does that amuse you? Good. Then I'll continue. At ten I began to sell flowers, and then they treated me better—I shared meals."

"What a life! It must have been rough at times?" Barabant asked the question not without a mixture of curiosity in his pity.

"Yes, at first." She returned thoughtfully over her history. "But I stabbed a fellow who was annoying me. He lived, but the result was just as good. They are all afraid of my temper, and there is no protection like that." She rose, having finished the cockades, and faced him with a smile in which struggled a temptation. "You know I have a temper; oh, but a temper—a temper to make your hair stand on end!"

"I can believe it," Barabant said, studying her.

"Would you like to see?" she asked mischievously.

Without waiting a reply, she halted, caught her breath a little, and drew back. The mouth dropped open, the eyes fixed themselves. Then by the sheer power of her will she banished the blood from her face. The lips closed in a thin, cruel line, the nostrils dilated, while in the eyes glowed such malignant, tigerish hatred that Barabant, with an oath, sprang backward, placing the bench between them.

Immediately a low laugh rang out. The features changed from the hideousness of wrath to a look of amusement, and Louison, again erect, sidled up to him with a smile lurking in the corners of her lips.

"Did I frighten you? I like to do that." Her face had regained its composure, but it was a cold constraint; she was still pale from the force of the emotion. "It is so amusing to frighten people. You see, I am able to protect myself."

"That I can believe," Barabant cried, finding his voice. "It is unpleasant!"

"Don't be frightened; I reserve that for my enemies. I know how to please, also."

She laughed, amused at his horror.

"And now I must get to selling my cockades. You can return with me only as far as the Seine. A companion such as you, you understand, would never do; it would not be professional."

Arranging her cockades in the basket, which she transferred to her arm, she retraced her steps.

"Ah, there's mama again," she exclaimed, as they neared the wig-maker's. "Let's see if she'll greet us more cordially."

Suddenly she stopped and, with a gleam of mischief, caught his arm.

"I have an idea. Follow me. I'll make her speak."

They approached the woman on the step, who, after the first quick glance, abased her head without further recognition.

"Good morning, mother."

The woman continued silently to card the wig.

"Eh, Mother Baudrier! It is I, your daughter—Louison. You won't answer? Good-by, then." Louison turned as though to leave, calling back: "By the way, I've discovered my father."

The woman, with a cry, staggered to her feet, and, choking for utterance, fell back against the house; while in her eyes was the wild light of abject terror. Then perceiving by Louison's mocking laugh that it was a trick, without a word she gained the doorway and tottered into the house.

Louison, amazed and perplexed, remained fastened to the ground.

"Bon Dieu," she said at last, thoughtfully, "extraordinary! Who could he have been?"

Barabant echoed the question, while the memory of the scene sank into his mind, and with it a silent resolve to investigate the mystery further.

IX

THE TURN OF JAVOGUES

Barabant spent the remainder of the morning in rambling through the markets, skirting the shores of the river, seeking everywhere the thoughts of the people, listening to their ambitions, their desires, and their hopes. Toward noon he drifted among a throng of masons who, dispersing languidly over blocks of stone, were crowding into the nearest café.

"Salutations, citoyens!" he cried to them, according to the custom of free greetings that obtained. At the sight of the sling he still wore they hailed him warmly, asking:

"You got that at the Tuileries, citoyen?"

"Why, I know him," one suddenly exclaimed; and pushing to the front, he cried, "You are the Citoyen Barabant who spoke so well in the Place de la Grève." He turned to his comrades: "Aye, he can talk, too."

"Bring him in!"

"Citoyen, eat with us."

"Yes, join us, comrade," echoed a swarthy Picard, throwing his arms about Barabant, who, nothing loath, answered:

"Gladly, citoyens."

They took possession of a corner in the café, calling the other occupants—two coal-carriers and a seller of lemonade.

While the soup was devoured one or another would turn to Barabant with a wink or a laugh, crying:

"It was glorious, eh, the taking of the Tuileries?"

"We fought well—the Sans-Culottes."

"The fat Louis was trembling that day!"

As they fell to eating their long loaves of bread, spread with cheese and washed down with an execrable mixture of wine and water, groups of two or three sauntered in, to smoke and discuss, among whom Barabant recognized the Marseillais who had borne him in the square. Javogues, greeted uproariously, in turn perceived Barabant.

"Why, it is my little orator!" he cried, and was advancing with open arms to infold him in a bear-like hug, when his eyes encountered the sling. "Mordieu," he exclaimed, "you were wounded!"

"Slightly."

Contenting himself with a wring of the hand, Javogues settled his body into a seat opposite, exclaiming: "There is a patriot, citoyens; I'll vouch for him!"

A chorus of grunts and a bobbing of heads showed Barabant the value of such an indorsement. Across the table his companions cried to him:

"He's a terrible fellow, eh, the Citoyen Javogues? No hesitation about him."

"That's the kind of men we want!"

They finished eating, and sprawled back to discuss.

"What I want to know is, where are we going?" Javogues demanded.

"We are going nowhere; we are rooted."

"The Convention does nothing but discuss."

"What's the use of overturning the throne, after all?"

"We must have the Republic!"

"What say you, Citoyen Barabant?"

"I say no step backward!" A lull gave him the attention of the room. "We must advance or perish. If we lack in daring, we deserve to perish. The Revolution, comrades, as I see it, is not against an unworthy king or any king: it is to reconstruct society. Citoyens, there is but one true end: the Nation must be one family. No more classes, no more titles, no more king, no more first estate, no more third estate. We are brothers, brothers all in one family—France!"

"There's the word!" Javogues cried, amid the salvo of glasses and bravos that acclaimed the speaker. "And out with all lying, plotting priests!"

A chorus approved.

"Right!"

"That's it!"

"Now you're talking!"

"Curse the blackcoats!"

"What has kept us down all these centuries? What? Tell me that! The Church! What has been the ally of the aristocrats? The Church! What taught us to be content with our lot, with fetters, with a crust, with the yoke of taxation? The Church!"

"Aye, the Church!"

"Down with it!"

"Down with the lie!"

"Bah, the Church! the Church! I too was fool enough to believe in it." Javogues swept his huge fist over their heads, and crashing it upon the table, shouted, "There is no God!"

A few mumbled approval, more laughed, while one voice cried:

"There he is again, with his God!"

"I tell you, it is with such superstitions that they enslave us!" Javogues drew back, defiant and aroused, and assembling his anger, he thundered again, as though to bear down all opposition, "There is no God!"

The laughter increased, while another scoffer cried:

"Well, if there is, he does us little good."

To this all agreed. Barabant, smiling, added:

"Citoyen, one thing at a time. Let us depose Capet first."

They arose amid laughter, Javogues's protests lost in the confusion. Barabant, impelled to enthusiasm by the ardor of these laborers, opened his arms and exclaimed:

"Comrades, when Frenchmen are united, we fear no foreigner. What nation has ever fraternized as we? We all are brothers, all working for the great end. When we grumble at delays, let us not forget what the Revolution has made us!"

Then the voice of Javogues arose:

"Brothers, before we separate, let us embrace!"

With one impulse, such as countless times animated the populace in these days of exaltation, the group fell into one another's arms. Javogues, extending his hands covered with soot, exclaimed:

"Glorious emblems!"

Barabant echoed the cry, but as they moved off he surreptitiously brushed away the stains, asking, to distract his companion's attention:

"And Dossonville, did you get him?"

"He escaped—for the time."

"Are you sure it was he? Did you see him again?"

"What difference does it make whether I saw him or not?" Javogues answered impatiently. "I know he was there."

"How?" Barabant asked, in astonishment.

"By the look in his eyes the day I met him. That is all I need to tell an aristocrat!"

Barabant, seeing the impossibility of swaying the fanatic by reason, kept silent until they parted.

In the Rue Maugout, la Mère Corniche cried to him from her tenebrous sentry-box:

"One moment, citoyen." The window-hinges spoke and a shadowy head appeared. "There's a tall fellow above in your room."

"In the uniform of the National Guard?"

"That's it."

Barabant, who had left Javogues too recently to derive any pleasure from a visit of Dossonville, was hastening away when again the querulous voice halted him.

"Not so fast, citoyen."

"Well, what? I'm in a hurry."

"You've seen the Citoyen Marat?"

"Marat?"

"What! you've not presented your letter?"

"Oh, my letter!" Barabant cried, and hastily covering his mistake, said: "But that was days ago."

"You didn't forget to speak of me?"

"Come, now, la Mère Corniche, I'm not an ingrate!"

"And what did he say?"

"It brought tears to his eyes."

"Truly?"

"Pardi! The Citoyen Marat has a heart."

Barabant, on the staircase, congratulated himself on his escape from a bad position, little realizing the danger of the present one, and excusing the subterfuge on the light pretext of giving pleasure to the old woman. He hurriedly determined to say nothing to Dossonville of his danger, preferring first to question him.

Dossonville, the greetings over, announced his purpose with the question:

"Well, young pamphleteer, what have you ready?"

Barabant replied by tapping his arm.

"I see,—at the Tuileries?"

"You were there, of course?"

"What Frenchman wasn't?"

Barabant, noticing the equivocation, pressed him.

"With what section, citoyen?"

"I was with no section."

"Within or without the Tuileries?"

Dossonville rose up.

"Again! I thought you were convinced at Santerre's."

"You do not answer my question," Barabant insisted.

"Why do you ask it?"

"Because, Citoyen Dossonville, there are those who claim to have seen you among the defenders."

"What's that? Who says that?" At once Dossonville was all alertness.

Barabant repeated, adding: "If it is so, citoyen, no matter for what reasons you were present, you cannot ignore the danger you run if recognized."

As though to confirm the warning, the stairway suddenly gave out the hurried fall of feet, the door opened, and Nicole appeared, breathless and frightened.

"Citoyen Dossonville," she cried, "I come to warn you! Javogues is below!"

Dossonville threw a glance to the window, his hand going to his pistol. Then correcting himself, he said:

"So this is your trap, is it?"

"I am not a spy," Barabant disclaimed indignantly. "You have an escape by the roof; the gutter is solid; once opposite — "

"Yes, yes," Nicole added; "pass into my room, through the hall, and out!"

"You mistake me," Dossonville interrupted. "I have nothing to fear. Go to the landing. They may stop on the way."

Barabant obeyed. Dossonville, turning his back, snatched a paper from his redingote, rolled it into a ball, and tossed it into the gutter.

He looked a moment at the astonished girl, then shrugging his shoulders, he committed himself to her mercy with a wave of his hand. Already from below came the rush of feet. With a sudden inspiration, Dossonville divested himself of his pistols and sword, laying them conspicuously on the bed. Then retreating as far away as the room permitted, he seated himself and folded his arms, facing the horrified girl with a calm smile, as though to say:

"Dispose of my life!"

Nicole, struggling between her patriotism and her womanly instincts, heard Barabant calling from the landing:

"Who is there?"

"Javogues."

"What do you seek?"

The next moment half a dozen Marseillais stormed into the room, while Javogues, at the head, shouted:

"When he moves to escape, shoot him down!"

But on the instant Dossonville, erect and holding out his hands, cried:

"I am unarmed; my weapons are on the bed. I submit. There is no need of murder. What is the accusation?"

Javogues, baffled at the turn, still greedily covered the prisoner with his pistol, but his face showed indecision and the longing for a pretext.

"Lower your pistol," Dossonville continued calmly. "Citoyen Barabant, I call you to witness that I surrendered willingly and am now under the protection of the Nation. On what charges do you, without warrants, arrest an officer of the National Guard?"

Javogues unwillingly dropped his weapon. But immediately, his anger rising at being so thwarted, he advanced and, as though to crush his enemy, thundered out:

"Dog of an aristocrat! I'll tell you. I arrest you for firing on the Nation from the Tuileries."

"What, Citoyen Javogues!" Barabant cried indignantly. "If you have taken this step on the evidence you gave me, I declare it an outrage!"

One of the band spoke up:

"I saw him, too,—I, with my own eyes,—firing on us with the Swiss."

"Citoyen, you are mistaken," Dossonville replied. Then realizing the danger he ran, he continued rapidly, "At what hour?"

"Nine o'clock."

"At nine you have said!" Dossonville cried triumphantly, extending his arms. "Citoyens, I demand to be taken at once to prison. The moment such an accusation is made I insist upon my right to vindicate myself. At nine o'clock I was in the presence of the Citoyen Marat. Take me to the Abbaye and let the Friend of the People answer for me. Citoyen Barabant, I shall need you too."

The effect of that powerful name was tremendous; even Javogues was stunned at the sudden counter, and sullenly gave the order to descend. Even Nicole, tortured by the crisis, remained still in doubt. She made a step forward as though to reveal what she had seen, but meeting the eye of the prisoner, she halted before its eloquence, and, bowing her head, allowed them to pass. Dossonville signaled Barabant to place himself behind him, and thus they plunged down the pit, where twice Barabant thought he caught the sound of a chuckle. But when they emerged into daylight, the face of Dossonville remained inscrutable.

At the prison of the Abbaye they entered without difficulty. There the gate stood open day and night. At the desk, when the accusation had been read and the alibi announced, Dossonville extended his hand to Barabant and said:

"Thanks, citoyen. You need trouble yourself no more."

"No more!" Barabant exclaimed, in astonishment, for he had expected to testify to the meeting with Santerre.

Dossonville smiled grimly and, with a curious twist of his back, said:

"My back itched a little in such company, especially in that devil's descent of yours, where little slips might occur. You were necessary to my peace of mind! Thanks, citoyen."

Then, as he was about to be led away, he turned to the turnkey and cried rapidly.

"Citoyen, it is useless to disturb the good Friend of the People. He will pardon me if I used his name to insure a hearing before a properly constituted court of justice." Then with his silent, parted grin, he added, "My true defense I shall present at the proper time."

He disappeared in custody, not before he had sent a glance of malicious enjoyment toward his enemy, who, astounded, did not immediately recover. When he did, it was with the rage of the wounded lion suddenly surprised by the trap.

X

A TRIUMPH OF INSTINCT

"Holà above, Barabant."

"Holà below, Goursac."

"Come down."

"What for?"

"Collenot is condemned. We're going to the execution."

"What, at eight o'clock at night?"

"Immediately. I am just back from the trial."

"I'm coming."

The Revolutionary Tribunal, inaugurated two days before, had deliberated ever since upon the fate of Collenot d'Agremont, seeking to fasten on the King and the Court the onus of the battle of the Tuileries. But beyond Barabant's desire to see the execution of this first victim of the anger of the Nation, was his curiosity to witness the second installation of that strange machine which had carried the name of Dr. Guillotin beyond the boundaries of France.

"And your Nicole?" Goursac asked when Barabant had joined them. "Why don't you bring her?"

"She's not in her room."

"You called her?"

"Yes, yes." Barabant, not wishing to discover their estrangement, hastened on: "Did Collenot implicate the Court?"

"He would say nothing. To do him justice, he was very firm."

"And the Tribunal?"

"Impressive. The people were awed. The judge pronounced an eloquent harangue,—they always do." He flung out his arm and repeated sarcastically: "'Victim of the law, could you but read the hearts of your judges you would find them crushed and saddened. Go to your death courageously. The Nation demands from you nothing but a sincere repentance.'"

"That's well put!"

"Repentance—and your head!" Goursac amended sarcastically. "What an absurdity!"

"Not at all," retorted Barabant, disciple of Rousseau and the sentimentalists. "The Nation mourning and forgiving its enemies, even when pronouncing sentence, is a spectacle, I say, that is sublime."

"Bah! What good is sentiment when you lack a head? No, no. These grandiloquent harangues of mercy and advice disgust me. They are nothing but self-advertisement. If I were a judge, I'd say:

"'Collenot, my friend, the Nation has proved you guilty; I pronounce upon you sentence of death; for further details consult Monsieur de Paris. Bon voyage!'"

"And the guillotine, Citoyen Goursac: do you find it insincere to despatch an enemy with the least pain?"

"Ah, the guillotine! There is a tremendous advance in human thought!" Goursac exclaimed, without deigning to open an argument. "There is something to be proud of. I foresee great innovations from this simple invention. To have learned to suppress human life painlessly is a true sentimental advance. We shall go further."

Barabant, seeing that he was started on his theories, said good-humoredly:

"Well, what next?"

"The day will come when society will regard it as a crime to allow children to grow up who are hopelessly destined to suffering—such as weaklings, monsters, hunchbacks, and the other deformed. The State will suppress them."

His companion groaned in horror.

"More than that," Goursac contended, "the day will come when the aged, the infirm, the decrepit, the mortally stricken, will be painlessly released from their suffering. Yes, death, when inevitable, will be made instantaneous, and society will approve."

"And how soon do you expect this magnificent idea to fructify?" Barabant asked scornfully.

"In about two thousand years," Goursac answered, with a hitch of his head. "That is the time necessary for an idea to conquer society."

"My dear friend, you are either joking or mad."

"The condition of prophecy is to be scorned," the theorist said dryly. "You remember Cassandra."

They entered the Place du Carrousel, where the guillotine, whether by conscious or unconscious irony, was established under the frowning shadows of the abode of kings. The dim square was hidden by a loose, shifting network of variegated colors dominated by the bright flecks of countless liberty-caps, which, in measure, as new groups arrived, contracted into mists of red. Above this bobbing field of heads two thin shafts started upward, nearly lost in the descending dusk. Goursac, extending his hand in the direction of these, said:

"There is the guillotine."

"It does not seem very terrible," answered Barabant. "Let us stay here; it is, perhaps, a false report. In ten minutes it will be too dark."

Others with the same idea lingered on the outskirts of the crowd or turned away. The faces of the throng could no longer be distinguished, when suddenly afar there sprang up a circle of torches, and the scaffold emerged from the night.

The two friends hastily made their way through the crowd until, at the end of twenty minutes' patient endeavor, they reached the foremost ranks. A calm spread among the unseen throng, broken by sudden tensions at each new alarm. The people, who had greeted the first appearance of the guillotine with cries of disappointment and demands for the more spectacular gallows, were now impressed by the cloak of mystery the night drew about the scaffold. The machine was no longer mere wood and iron; it had tasted blood: it was human.

Barabant, from his position of vantage, could distinguish the upright shafts, where from time to time, as Goursac explained the mechanism, some reflection from a torch falling on the knife above, there appeared the dull display of steel like the sudden threat of a brutish fang.

Turning from the scaffold, Barabant examined the crowd, where, seeking for Nicole, he perceived Louison worming her way toward them.

Suddenly a whisper ran over the heads and rose to a breeze of exclamations. The masses tightened. Those in front were swept against the guards as those behind surged forward, stretching to tiptoe. Louison, caught in the press, was imprisoned not twenty feet away. This time the alarm was not vain. From all sides burst the growl of the mob.

"Hu! hu! hu!"

A long, tedious moment succeeded, then suddenly the scaffold swarmed with dark figures. The hooting and the screeching gave place to a burst of hand-clapping. Barabant, astonished at the implacable ferocity of the crowd, turned to examine it, but his eye encountering Louison, remained there.

The radiance of a neighboring torch redeemed her figure from the obscurity. Her head was strained slightly forward, while one hand clutched the kerchief at her throat as though to restrain her eagerness. The lips were parted, the eyes glowed with the intensity of fascinated contemplation, but her whole figure, in contrast to the unbridled passions of the crowd, remained, as during the attack on the Tuileries, controlled and insensible.

So unnatural was her attitude that Barabant could not have averted his eyes had not the hand of Goursac recalled him to the drama before him. He sought in the gloom and the shadows, seeing nothing, until suddenly out of the darkness came the shoot and the thud of the knife.

A woman, with a cry, caught his arm, burying her head in his sleeve. Another woman, holding a baby, was shouting wildly:

"Bravo! Bravo!"

A tottering veteran, in the costume of the Invalides, questioned him eagerly:

"Is it over? Tell me, citoyen, is it over?"

The woman on his arm continued to gasp hysterically. Himself recoiling at this death out of the darkness, he returned to the contemplation of Louison.

Her pose had relaxed, while a slight smile of disdain appeared as she watched the frantic crowd acclaim the head which a bourreau held to them. On her face was neither horror nor anger, neither disgust nor passion. As calmly as though before her own mirror, she smoothed out her dress and replaced the cockade, torn by the contact of the crowd, with a fresh one from her basket, scenting first its perfume. She raised her eyes, and her glance met that of Barabant, overcome with disgust. She frowned, and turning her shoulder, was lost in the crowd which now flowed out in widening circles.

"What is there about her!" Barabant exclaimed, turning to Goursac.

"About whom?"

"Louison," he said impatiently. "You did not see her? She made me shiver!"

"She affects me like a snake," Goursac answered. "She is a creature of the night, in her element at such a time. They say she never misses an execution. Well, citoyen, what of the machine?"

"Horrible!"

"You are wrong," Goursac protested. "It does not take life: it suppresses it, and that by a process more charitable than natural death. That is the way a nation should avenge itself." He repeated several times in a transport of enthusiasm, "Magnificent!"

"There, look at it now!"

At Barabant's summons they paused at the gate, looking back at the dim circle of lights around the guillotine unseen but divined, while Barabant continued:

"The first time did not count—it was only a thief. To-night is the true beginning of the guillotine—a sinister and ominous beginning."

"Still, what a spectacle!" Goursac exclaimed. "What could be more dramatic?"

"Too much so," Barabant retorted. "I admit I am impressionable, but to-night the blow seemed to fall from above our own heads."

"You are superstitious. You will be telling me next that you had a premonition about your own neck."

"Hardly; but, my friend, yours is so long and the chances of politics are so many— "

"Don't trouble yourself," replied Goursac, laughing, and with a mock gesture he extended his fist. "As for my neck, Madame Guillotine, I defy you to take it." He turned to Barabant. "You, my friend, are so gallant that I won't answer for yours."

They passed into the Rue Royale, Goursac slightly in advance. Barabant, rubbing shoulders with the departing crowd, felt a pull on his arm and heard the voice of Nicole saying mischievously:

"Barabant, are you very angry with me?"

Too astonished to make answer, he remained dumbly gazing into the teasing countenance; but at that moment Goursac, perceiving them, called out indulgently:

"That's right, children; we don't live long enough for lovers to quarrel. I'll keep discreetly ahead."

Barabant persisting in his silence, Nicole continued pleadingly:

"Then you are still angry?"

"Yes."

"I am sorry."

She said it in such a gentle tone, sighing slightly, that Barabant's anger held no longer; still, as a measure of policy, he kept silent.

Goursac, preparing to wheel into a side street, called back, with a laugh of which only Nicole could guess the cost:

"Good-by, my children; I leave you in peace. Love-making is disconcerting to the older generation. Reconcile yourselves quickly."

Barabant and Nicole, thus left to themselves, continued arm in arm silently homeward, avoiding the thronged thoroughfares, the noise and the lights, plunging by preference down quiet ways where only an occasional window reddened the sides of the night. Barabant struggled to maintain his just anger; Nicole, who had yielded to an impulse in accosting him, searched for some means to regain the ground which she felt she had surrendered.

"You don't answer," she said at last, withdrawing her arm half-way. "You want me to go?"

He freed himself brusquely and faced her with the angry cry:

"Coquette!"

"No, that I am not!" she cried, and seizing his arm, she said rapidly: "Barabant, it is not true. You have no right to say that!"

"You have a right to be what you wish."

Nicole, checking herself, said sadly:

"You still believe I am playing with you?"

"I do."

She withdrew a step and shook her head.

"No, it is not you I am playing with."

Barabant, who did not fathom the allusion, started to ask her what she meant; but Nicole, immediately perceiving the danger, retreated from her serious mood, and slipping her arm through his, said imperiously as they started on:

"Barabant, have you ever been in love—seriously in love?"

"Oh!"

"But seriously?"

"No."

"I was sure of it."

"And why?" Barabant demanded, nettled at her assumption.

"Because you understand nothing of a woman." She continued rapidly: "Listen to reason, my friend. You assume rights over me and my actions, and yet what right have you? You have never once told me that you love me. Yet you are angry because I insist upon being wooed, foolish, ignorant fellow!"

Her reproof, which she designed to be heavy, weakened despite herself, until at the end she pronounced it almost caressingly.

"Is that just, Nicole?" Barabant cried, seizing the opening. "Why am I angry? Because you will not give me the opportunity." He drew her closer to him. "Nicole, listen to me but once."

"No, no," she checked him imperiously, "I do not wish to. You are too headlong. Barabant, I tell you, you do not know yourself."

"I—I don't know what I feel?"

She checked him again.

"If you do, then respect my wishes." She added almost pleadingly: "Not too fast, Barabant. Be reasonable and I will not avoid you again." Then peremptorily changing the subject: "Did you see Louison? She is always at an execution."

He accepted the turn reluctantly.

"I saw her."

"How did she affect you?"

"Like a snake," he answered, using Goursac's expression. "There is something about her that repels me."

"I was afraid she might attract you," she confessed, with a laugh, in which showed a little relief.

At No. 38 they groped into the entrance, feeling the walls with their hands. The crow set up a raucous crying, while la Mère Corniche appeared at the door, shading her candle to discover their approach. They passed on through the first court to the bottom of the staircase, where a single torch flickered in its bracket. Nicole held out her hand, averting her face.

"Good night, Barabant, and until to-morrow."

The hour, the place, the torch that allowed her body to melt into the shadow and illuminated only the eyes, the lips, and the smile that tempted him with the mystery of what it hid, overcame his resolutions. He caught her by the wrists and drew her toward him. Nicole gave a little cry, resisting feebly.

"I cannot understand you," he cried fiercely. "What are you? What do you feel? Do you love me or do you not?"

She answered faintly, struggling against his arms:

"Let me go."

"Nicole, dear Nicole, I love you, I adore you."

"No, no, no!"

He released her, and throwing himself at her feet, he stretched up his hands to her, crying:

"Look, look!"

Nicole, with her hand to her cheek half turned from him, could not but believe. In his eyes she saw the tears appear, and moved, despite herself, by his emotion, she took his forehead between her palms, saying softly:

"Calm thyself, Barabant."

"You love me; you do, you do!" he cried. He caught her hand in his and repeated, as only the lover knows how: "I love you! I love you! I love you!"

She pressed her hands to her eyes to steady herself.

"And how long will it last?" she said solemnly, her voice reverberating in the hollow of the silent hall. "Three months, Barabant? And then — "

"For life—forever!"

Nicole shook her head incredulously, but her breast rose in long, tumultuous breaths, trembling with the memory of the word.

He mounted the stairs, turned and held out his hand to her. She dared not look at him, for victory was in his eyes.

"Nicole, Nicole!"

Then she looked at him, her hands to her throat, fallen back against the wall. He smiled to her, waiting confidently. Up the dark ascent was love, mystery, anguish, jealousy, doubt,—but always love.

She moved a step toward him, fascinated and drawn on, until their fingers touched. Then suddenly she shrank away, and with a cry, spreading out her hands to screen him from her sight, she fled. Only the instinct had survived, but the instinct had conquered.

XI

THE MAN WITH THE LANTERN

Then between Nicole and Barabant began one of those subtle conflicts of the sexes in which the one who loves the more unselfishly is foredoomed to defeat. Until the night of the execution Nicole had combated the very thought of love. Her flight at the staircase was the last spark of resistance. She had drunk of the cup, the poison was in her veins. The next morning she resigned herself to the bitter, determined, cost what it might, to have her hour of happiness.

She gave up the struggle against herself, but began another to safeguard her happiness. Her intuitions told her to resist—that the longer he was compelled to woo, the more he would prize her. In her uneasy doubts she had recourse to coquetry, but that coquetry which is unselfish and pathetic, and is nothing but the instinct of self-preservation.

To Barabant, who neither knew the depth of her longings, nor could have understood them had he known, the hesitation and delays of Nicole were incomprehensible. Resolved to meet her with like tactics, he assumed toward her the attitude of a comrade, avoiding all expression of sentiment.

Nicole readily fathomed the artifice. She countered by an equal show of indifference, leaving him always after a moment's conversation. Barabant retaliated by devoting himself anew to Louison.

The manœuver brought Nicole back. It was the one move she had not foreseen. It threw her into a panic of jealousy. Not that she did not understand his motive, but she feared, from his being thrown with Louison, results of which he had no thought. She admitted her mistake and relinquished the struggle. She returned uneasily to him, showing him from time to time, by a word or gesture, that he had only to ask. Barabant, blind to the extent of the change, though instinctively perceiving its import, redoubled his attentions to Louison; treating Nicole always as a comrade, hailing her joyfully, gay and charming in her company, but saying never a word of what she now impatiently sought.

Meanwhile events had been hurrying on the inevitable conflict between the Commune and the Convention. On the 25th of August the news of the treacherous surrender of Longwy to the Prussian army ran through the arteries of Paris as an inflaming poison. The Nation rose from the fall in the fury of its anger and wounded pride. From the windows of the Hôtel de Ville an immense banner rolled its folds over the city, bearing the inspiring inscription:

"The Fatherland is in danger!"

From all sides recruits rushed in to swell the legions of defense. The city, as though the enemy were already at its gates, converted itself into a camp, established posts and sentries, while at all hours the streets shook under the footfall of passing patrols. Searching parties ran from house to house, filling the prisons with suspected aristocrats.

The Convention, urged to abolish the monarchy and establish the Republic, hesitated. Only the Commune was resolute, vociferous, and implacable, shouting for the massacre of the traitors at home before marching against those abroad.

Lafayette deserting, Verdun rumored betrayed, traitors everywhere,—in the army of Brunswick, in the Assembly, in Paris,—nothing but a great example could strike terror in the hearts of aristocrats at home and abroad. What that example was, so clamorously demanded, few doubted who beheld the frenzied crowds that infested the gates of the prisons, gloating over the list of prisoners there exposed.

In the midst of these alarms, to the dismay of Goursac, Javogues took up his residence in the landing below them. Shortly after, Nicole reported another disquieting fact: la Mère Corniche had closed her cellar, refusing admission to all. Occasionally Barabant saw Javogues running the streets at the head of searching parties, in a whirlwind of disheveled forms and rushing torches, while the room of the Marseillais was filled with uncouth figures in secret gathering, of whose character Barabant, knowing the temperament of Javogues, had no doubt.

On the night of the 1st of September Barabant, who had enrolled for the defense of the city, began his patrol at the junction of the Rue St. Antoine and the great, gloomy square where had stood the fortress of the Bastille. The mass of citizens, foreseeing the massacre on the morrow, had retired early, barring the doors, leaving the streets to be swept by restless bands of the lawless: vultures stirred up by the prospect of carrion.

The hours lagged, and the tramp of his step seemed endless to Barabant. His reflections were bitter; for him, the Girondin, it was not simply the massacre of aristocrats, but the fall of his party, that he apprehended.

At twelve Nicole was to join him for the remaining hour. There was still three quarters of an hour before she would come. The increasing sound of voices restored him to the consciousness of his trust.

Soon a party of five emerged, preceded by a small muffled figure gliding with feverish steps ahead, as a flame devours its path. Barabant, following them on his beat, strove to recall the familiar stride of the leader. The patrol approaching him from the opposite direction cried:

"Is it you, Citoyen Sentry?"

The figure advancing assumed human shape.

"Hé, you are alone to-night?"

"Until twelve."

"You are lucky." He shifted his musket and laughed. "Mine leaves me alone to-night. We had a bit of a quarrel. I had to break a bottle over her head. And now, the devil take it! I have to stand guard alone." He added angrily: "That's the way with women."

"One moment, citoyen. You saw the party pass just now?"

"Aye. Did you not recognize him?"

"Who?"

"Some one who'll be busy to-night,—the Citoyen Marat." He raised his voice cheerily and sang:

"Ah, ça ira, ça ira, ça ira; Les aristocrates à la lanterne! Ah, ça ira, ça ira, ça ira; Les aristocrates on les pendra.

"By to-morrow night there'll be no need of sentries!" he broke off. "It's long, eh, when there's no one to keep you company? The devil take the woman!" He shouldered his musket. "Citoyen, Salut et Fraternité."

He turned on his heel and joined the darkness, while back came the unmusical voice:

"Dansons la carmagnole, Vive le son, vive le son! Dansons la carmagnole, Vive le son— "

The rest lost itself faintly among distant roofs.

Barabant, recommencing his tedious pacing, returned to the Rue St. Antoine, where the sound of light footsteps warned him of the approach of a woman or a child.

"Can it be Nicole?" he thought hopefully, but his spirits fell as the woman came on doubtfully in a wavering line.

"Good evening, citoyenne," he said gallantly. "There are not many of your sex abroad to-night, and alone."

The woman gave the countersign, "The 10th of August."

Barabant, seeing that she was not inclined to enter into a conversation, cried:

"Take pity on the patriot, citoyenne. The hours are dull."

But the woman, with only a slight shake of her head, passed quickly on. Barabant, thus repulsed, grumbled to himself:

"She is neither young nor pretty or she would have stopped." But remembering the sentry he had left, he continued: "Perhaps it is the fair one with the broken head. If it is, she doesn't seem any too eager. No, she's turned away."

Suddenly he drew himself up with an exclamation. He saw the woman halt as with the twinkle of a lantern the figure of a man joined her, while to his astonishment she drew back in evident shrinking from her new companion.

Barabant, who had followed this scene with such intentness as to have become unaware of his surroundings, suddenly bounded back at the touch of a hand on his shoulder.

"What vigilance, Citoyen Barabant! What a model sentry!"

It was Louison who had stolen on him silently, and now stood mocking him. To Barabant the apparition was so in keeping with the strange impression which the girl had made on him that he was too startled to answer immediately.

"Why are you always afraid of me?" Louison said impatiently. "It isn't pleasant to inspire terror."

Barabant excused himself, recounting the scene he had just witnessed; but Louison, not to be put off, returned to her question. "So I inspire you with fear?"

"The expression is exaggerated," Barabant returned evasively.

"Come, frankly, there is something about me that has repelled you?" She continued seeking the answer herself. "Was it the day we went to the flower-market and I pretended anger? That was but play." Her eyes sought his face, as though she could find its expression despite the darkness. All at once she said, "It was at the guillotine?"

"That's true."

"I knew it; but why? I don't understand," she said almost angrily. "What is there about me that gives such an impression? I am not conscious of it."

"First, answer me this," Barabant said, "and frankly. At an execution you have no feeling of pity or horror, have you?"

"No," she answered thoughtfully. "Why?"

"Because it is too evident."

"How do I seem?" she said quickly.

"You seem utterly indifferent to any human suffering."

"That is true," she said slowly.

"It is not only that," Barabant continued, "but—how shall I say it? There seemed to be almost a fascination to you in the spectacle that ordinarily sickens the human heart."

"What!" the girl exclaimed, astonished, "are you not curious to see how a man can die?"

"Curious, yes; but the spectacle is disagreeable to me."

"Why? What is more ordinary and commonplace than death?"

Barabant, in despair of making her understand, remained silent.

"How curious! And when I am at an execution I look different from this?"

"Yes."

"I seem—?"

"Unhuman."

She tossed her head in displeasure and said sharply:

"I do not like that."

"I am frank."

Louison remained thoughtfully silent, perturbed and frowning. Then lifting her head, she said gaily, in quite a different manner:

"Very well, then; I shall take care how you see me in future."

She turned in the direction of the Bastille, and fastening her glance upon the ring of light, said:

"It seems to be going away. Perhaps we shall see the woman now."

"She comes faster this time," Barabant said as the sound of footsteps warned them of her approach.

The next moment a bundle of draperies passed them as a ship scudding before a storm. Louison, watching the woman, closed her hand over Barabant's wrist, allowing an exclamation to escape her. Then, springing forward, she cried:

"Eh, mother! Wait a moment!"

The fleeting figure turned as though stung, then dashed wildly into the darkness. Louison, with a bound, sprang after her, but suddenly clapping her hand to her forehead, turned and broke past Barabant, who heard only, as she shot on toward the Bastille, the words:

"The man with the lantern!"

XII

THE MASSACRE OF THE PRISONS

The next morning Nicole and Geneviève, having breakfasted at noon near the Temple, where the throng collected daily to insult the ears of the royal family, returned slowly toward the Tuileries through the hushed and apprehensive city.

Toward three o'clock the long-awaited tocsin sounded from the other side of the river, then the chance burst of a musket and the assembling roll of drums. But this time, in contrast to the night of the 9th of August, there came no spontaneous outpouring into the streets. As the tocsin continued to disturb the air with its violent voice, timid faces appeared at the windows, searching with anxious glances the streets, the opposite walls, in doubt of their neighbors; even the air, as though to discover the reason of the uproar.

The streets were emptied; small groups wavered in the entrances, waiting for the first rumors to guide them. As the two girls hesitated, a woman appeared, running toward them, dragging a child at either side. From window and doorway a clamor of questions arose, while many, running into the street, surrounded her and sought to stop her progress. But the woman, resisting all entreaties, cleft the crowd and disappeared, repeating frantically:

"They are massacring the prisoners!"

The street grew noisy with exclamation and conjecture, while those above, in the windows, screamed down for the rumors that flew from lip to lip. A little later another messenger arrived,—a waif of the slums, to whom the marks of poverty and vice had given the semblance of an incongruous manhood. The boy came romping down the street, bare-legged, disheveled, brandishing a knife. At times he flung up his hands and screamed in childish treble:

"To the Abbaye, citoyens, to the Abbaye! The tyrants are being exterminated. The justice of the people is beginning! To the Abbaye! To the Abbaye!"

Behind the frenzied boy there fell a silence, and the crowd, in a sudden, senseless panic, retreated indoors.

"The Abbaye!" Nicole cried in consternation. "And Dossonville! We must hurry there."

A baker's wife, seeing them hastening on, cried:

"Are you going to the Abbaye, citoyennes? Is there any danger?"

"Not for us."

"Wait, I'll join you."

A cobbler made a fourth, then two apprentices from a cloth-merchant attached themselves, then a fishwife and a tow-headed newsboy. As they crossed the Seine the crowd increased, while horrid figures of depravity and suffering, vermin of Paris, broke past them. Cutlasses and pikes appeared, and from the panting throng shouts burst out:

"Death to the traitors!"

"Death to the betrayers of Longwy!"

"Death to all aristocrats!"

"Death to priests!"

At the Abbaye they found the sanguinary remnants of the prisoners who, transferred from the Conciergerie, had been swept from the carts into the maw of the mob at the very gates that opened to shelter them. On the prison itself there had been as yet no attack. The mob, seeking vengeance on the priests, had swept on to the convent of Les Carmes.

At the sight of the strewn corpses and the blood-bespattered pavements the baker's wife halted, crying:

"I've seen enough; I'm going back."

The cobbler hesitated, listening across the houses to the faint cries of the mob in the Rue Vaugirard. The apprentices sprang forward, while the newsboy exclaimed impudently:

"Come on, comrades, we must see what's doing!"

Nicole, who had come solely to assure herself of Dossonville's safety, likewise recoiling before the spectacle of butchery, was yet so impelled by the subtle, morbid fascination which such scenes exercise over the human mind, that without a thought she hastened on. The fishwife and the cobbler joined them; even the woman who had already started to retreat acceded to the common curiosity and returned, protesting:

"It's too horrible! Turn back."

"After all," the cobbler answered, "that's what the aristocrats would like to do to us!"

"Aye, citoyen, you've hit it right!"

"And the women?"

"They'll leave them alone."

"We'll see."

About the convent a loose throng was churning, bristling with pikes and crudely fashioned spears.

"Keep together," the cobbler cried, "and bear toward the wall!"

By this manœuver they penetrated to the front, where, their band disintegrating, Geneviève and Nicole succeeded in reaching a position at a grill in the wall.

In the garden, not thirty feet away, a black mass dotted with the white of human faces was huddled together, shrinking from the gates and apertures that swarmed with axes, scythes, swords, and barbarous faces more pitiless than the steel.

At Nicole's side a mason extended his cutlass toward the priests, bellowing:

"Eh, you fat fellow over there! Wait till they let us in! I'll carve you!"

Another shouted:

"I choose to shave the tall one; I'll make a true monk of him!"

The priests encouraged one another; some knelt, others lifted their arms, their voices, and their eyes serenely above. A few blanched before the approach of martyrdom, while others in whom youth's natural impulse to life was strong calculated the surroundings and weighed the desperate chances of escape.

All at once there was an upheaval in the herd of the besieged, a swaying toward the walls, and a sudden parting that opened a path to the chapel beyond, where a swarm of the populace, who had broken through, was spreading over the steps. From the crowd without a wild shout went up; those at the locked gates, stretching their arms through, strove to prod the victims with their pikes.

On the steps, face to face with their prey, the new assailants hesitated, seeking some pretext before striking. But one, more impatient than the rest, burst from the back and fired point-blank into the herd. The impulse once given, the assassins fell upon their victims, who on their knees welcomed the end.

Forty or fifty of the younger members, revolting at such surrender to death, bounded away to scale the farther walls. A very few passed over and escaped to outer courts before the bandits flung themselves on the fleeing. Then everywhere could be seen bodies clutching at the brim of the wall, tumbling and pitching backward in the horror of the overtaking fate. Arms that grasped liberty suddenly contracted in the convulsions of despair; faces that already looked on life appeared a moment above the wall and fell back with the sharp summons to death.

"Shall we go?" cried Nicole, suffocated.

"Yes."

But they could not move. The scene enchained them.

The hunt consummated, the hunters flung themselves on the unresisting, and as though to stifle the smallest spark of pity, redoubled their fury and their cries.

In front of the two girls a Marseillais felled a priest with two strokes across the scalp, and drove his pike into the stomach with such ferocity that the point refused to move. The assassin, in rage jumping on the lifeless body, stamped and tugged, cursing the resistance of the corpse which sought to retain the weapon that had struck it down. Everywhere the butchers, not content with the death-dealing blow, flung themselves on the lifeless bodies, piercing them with infuriated stabs, as though the last insult was this mutilation of the dead.

Finally, despairing of satisfying their vengeance on this inert mass, the leaders forced those who remained into the church, some who still breathed being borne on the arms of those who but deferred their murder. Two by two they were led out and butchered.

From this moment the massacre, in its clock-like procession, abated its fury. The executioners themselves, exhausted and listless, struck mechanically.

The crowd, grumbling at the monotony, moved away. Nicole and Geneviève found themselves in the street, packed in the press, beside their late companions. The crowd, animated by the lust of curiosity, became that most fearful of the manifestations of humanity—a mob.

Geneviève and Nicole, no longer individuals, but atoms, became cold, pitiless, maddened with sensations, hungry for new; invaded by a fury which they did not understand, an anger and a hatred of which they knew not the cause.

Some one cried:

"On to St. Firmin. There are eighty priests there!" A hundred voices took up the cry, and the mass, set in motion, rolled toward the prison.

The fishwife, with streaming hair, bellowed:

"Cut the throats of every one. No priest must escape!"

Farther on in the press of bodies, Nicole saw the two apprentices, transformed with the frenzy.

The cobbler had armed himself with some weapon; even the tow-headed newsboy near them screamed hysterically:

"À la mort! À la mort!"

"I can go no farther!" Nicole protested.

"Yes, yes," Geneviève cried, seizing her arms and impelling her, but half resisting, into the rush of the multitude. "We must see it! We must see everything!"

She was a child no longer, but a savage akin in fury to the beast enraged by the red flash of blood.

At St. Firmin's the vanguard broke into the prison. The night was filled with shrieks of terror and of furious exultation. Body after body, dead or dying, was hurled from the window, to be pounced upon below and torn to pieces. More than eighty lay quivering in mounds.

Then at last the mob, by that strange organization by which it moves without commands, turned face and, sparkling with torches, inundated the narrow street that led down to the Boulevard St. Germain, and returned to the prison of the Abbaye. It was now deep into the night, and for hours a semblance of a trial had been going on within the court. The mob, thus balked by the routine of justice, softened and dissipated into a throng of spectators, bewildered and recovering slowly from their delirium.

Nicole, fearing for Dossonville, pressed forward for a nearer view. About the gates were a score of executioners, so saturated with blood that at first glance the butchers seemed more like the butchered. Eight or ten waited in two rows the arrival of the new victim. As many more leaned wearily against the wall with nodding heads. One stooped to light fresh torches.

Suddenly the gates disclosed to Nicole the flaring courtyard and the wild figure of a prisoner propelled to destruction by two guards. At first he marched to his death with firm tread; but all at once, with a horrid heave of his breast, he stretched out his hands before his face to hide the hideous doom. Shoved forward, his arms raised in the instinct of self-preservation, he suffered untold tortures: his arms, hacked to spouting stumps, received a dozen gashes, while the revolting body sought to strike back against the sting, until the last blow silenced the shriek on shriek that called on merciful death.

Two men dragged aside the half-naked corpse and flung it on the mound of bodies. At the shock of the new arrival there was a sudden settling and shifting in this inert mass, a quivering adjustment that gave the ghastly semblance of life, as though a hideous welcome of the dead to the dead. Geneviève, with throbbing pulses and dilated nostrils, shuddered and turned to Nicole. She was so rigid, so ghastly with the horror, that Geneviève seized her arm.

"Ah! ah! ah!"

At her clutch Nicole screamed in mortal dread, then burst into hysterical weeping. Geneviève put her arm around her and drew her away, through the morbid crowd, seeing dimly the baker's wife pressing feverishly forward to seize their place. Then Nicole, covering her eyes, began to scream:

"Take me away, away, away!"

But at every tenth step she stopped and struggled to go back, her glance seeking the caldron. The third time, to her horror, the gates opened once more, and, heavily borne between two guards, she saw the figure of Dossonville.

XIII

DOSSONVILLE IN PERIL

"The Citoyen Dossonville to the bar! The Citoyen Dos-son-ville!"

The call, resounding along the stone corridors, reached the prisoners huddled in the main hall of the Abbaye.

"The Citoyen Dos-son-ville!"

A turnkey under a snarling torch penetrated the group, drawing one after another to him with rough hand.

"The Citoyen Dossonville! I summon all on peril of their lives to discover to me the Citoyen Dossonville!"

Out of the mass extended a hand with long, accusing forefinger, and a voice exclaimed:

"Over there."

The hand was snatched back, while a fomenting in the crowd showed where the informer was burying himself from recognition.

The turnkey stopped before a figure stretched in sleep, and incredulously thrust his torch into the face. But the sleeper continued to inhale long breaths methodically, until, convinced of the genuineness of the sleep, the turnkey proceeded to wake him with a vigorous thrust of his foot.

Dossonville started to a sitting position, opening his eyes on the suspicious visage above him and the background of fellow-prisoners who, afraid to show too much interest, held themselves at a distance and followed from the corners of their eyes.

"What do you want with me?"

"Are you the Citoyen Dossonville?"

"I am."

"The Nation summons you to appear before the bar of the popular justice!"

"At eleven o'clock at night? The justice of the people never sleeps, then?"

"Be quick!"

Dossonville lifted himself to an upright position, restoring his pillow to its rightful function of cloak.

"I will not bother about my other possessions now," he cried sarcastically. "Citoyennes and citoyens, to the pleasure of seeing you again, or not, as you prefer. Now for the justice of the people!"

Under the lightness of his manner, his mind worked with the desperation of an animal at bay. Of what he was approaching he knew nothing. Yet as he advanced along the reverberant corridors, his mind assembled a dozen stratagems to meet either a whirlwind of assassins or the travesty of a trial. His eye, meanwhile alert for every detail, enveloped each portion of the journey at a glance, running the walls as a wild animal tracks his cage.

Gradually his waiting ear distinguished a muffled hum, a buzz of voices, increasing in volume until out of it escaped the piercing shriek of a woman.

The next moment there burst upon his hearing a hundred cries,—shrieks of terror, shouts of vengeance, cries of pity, commands and groans, drunken and maddened notes,—sharp to the ear, rushing over his mind in a storm of confusion. The gate opened and the volume smote him with the fury of a blast.

He stood in the courtyard, blinking at strange forms and the crossing and recrossing of torches, striving to collect his wits. Two guards had seized him, presenting the points of their reddened swords to his breast.

His eye went to the center of the courtyard, to a table flanked by torches, littered with papers, bottles, and the glint of steel; behind which, installed as judge, Dossonville recognized the huissier Maillard. A score of Marseillais, stained with blood, reeling from sleep or drunkenness, churned about this improvised tribunal, interrupting with their revilings the testimony of the accused, or swaggered back and forth through the gate that led to the mob. Some clustered in corners to drink from the bottles that a wine-merchant constantly renewed; others nonchalantly lighted pipes, stretched their arms and yawned. In the lull between executions Dossonville heard a snore. Amid this carnage one man, stretched on a bench, was unconcernedly asleep.

"There's a man who's not disturbed by trifles," he muttered.

At the slight shift he made, one of his guards pricked him with his sword, crying angrily:

"Move again, and I'll cut you to ribbons!"

"I am become a statue," Dossonville answered coolly. "Only, do not bear too hard. I am ticklish."

Ahead of him, a priest without hope told his beads; while before the tribunal was a man so bowed with years that he had to be supported on either side.

All at once, seeking in the crowd, Dossonville perceived Javogues.

"Aïe! aïe!" he mumbled uneasily at the sight of that gloating face. "What ferocity! He is bound to make sure of me. The animal!"

He turned stoically from the Marseillais to the judges, where, to his amazement, he perceived a movement of clemency toward the accused. Suddenly the voice of Maillard appealed to the crowd:

"Citoyens, whatever the condition or the crimes of this feeble plaything of time, I declare to you that it is unworthy of the Republic to pursue here its vengeance! When nature, for eighty years, has spared one from peril of sickness, shock of accident, and the din of battles, man cannot show himself more pitiless than nature. Citoyens, I demand the handful of years for this venerable man."

An approving murmur saluted this oratorical appeal, broken by the strident voice of Javogues:

"Traitors have no age. If he is an aristocrat, let him die!"

Maillard, encouraged by the cries of dissent, extended his arm over the broken figure and said impressively:

"Whatever this man has been, exists no more. The Republic can take no vengeance here, for it can deprive this man of nothing. Citoyens, let him be acquitted."

"Well said."

"He speaks well."

"Free him!"

"Bravo. Free him!"

The acquitted man, aware of what had happened, was led away by the guards. The priest was put in his place, Dossonville moving nearer.

But now the executioners without the gates, growing impatient, smote the air with their cries:

"More victims!"

"Hurry up!"

"No ceremony with the aristocrat!"

"Hurry up! More! More!"

"Give us more! We want more!"

"Maillard, we are thirsty!"

The judge, addressing the quiet victim, proceeded methodically:

"Jean Marie Latour?"

"I am he."

"Called Brother Francis?"

"Yes."

"Priest?"

"Yes."

"You refused the oath of allegiance to the Nation?"

"I did."

At this a howl more of triumph than of anger burst from the listeners, and the judge, recognizing the hopelessness of the case, said shortly:

"To La Force."

Three men seized him and bore him, unresisting, to the shambles, while two more propelled Dossonville roughly forward.

Hardly was he in position when three piercing shrieks announced the death of the priest. Dossonville, shuddering despite his will, heard a voice cry boisterously:

"Eh, what a squeal the animal gave!"

The guards fell back, guarding his retreat, while Dossonville, disdaining to notice, felt rather than saw the Marseillais take his position at his side.

"Armand Roger Dossonville?"

"The same."

"Lieutenant in the National Guard?"

"Yes."

"You are accused of being in the Tuileries on the tenth day of August and of firing upon the Nation."

"Who accuses me?"

"I accuse you."

"And I."

Dossonville turned, met the angry eyes of Javogues, and seeking the second speaker, recognized one of those who had arrested him. He turned to the tribunal.

"The witnesses are mistaken. I was not at the Tuileries."

His accusers burst into a roar of denunciation, but Maillard, quelling them, said quietly:

"That should not be difficult to prove. With whom were you on the tenth day of August?"

Dossonville nodded his head in assent. Then, seeing the trap into which he was being led, he asked:

"First, does not that register relate that on my arrest I claimed an alibi with the Citoyen Marat and later renounced it at this prison, giving as a reason that I used it as a protection to insure my reaching prison and a trial?"

Javogues broke in furiously:

"Do not listen to him! He prepares some new lie!" Then grasping Dossonville by the collar, he shook his fist in his face. "I swear that if he is acquitted, I myself will cut his throat."

"The Citoyen Javogues," Dossonville continued, without changing the level of his voice, "unfortunately for me, from the day we met has hated me with an obstinate hatred. I adopted the subterfuge only because I believed that otherwise I never could have reached the prison alive. The proof is, I denounced it immediately and explained my reasons. You will find it there. I will now tell you with whom I passed the day."

He waited a moment for quiet, Javogues thundering:

"He lies! He lies! He lies!"

"The man whose testimony I invoke is known to you, Citoyen Maillard. Of his patriotism there can be no question. Unfortunately, he left immediately after for the Army of the Rhone. From ten o'clock of the night of August 9th until ten o'clock of the morning of August 10th I was in the house of the Citoyen Héron."

There was a movement of stupefaction in the assemblage, even Javogues recoiling. But the first words of Maillard fell upon the ears of Dossonville as the sudden fall of a sword.

"The Citoyen Héron did not leave for the frontier. Let the Citoyen Héron be roused and corroborate the accused!"

Two or three threw themselves upon the sleeper to bring him forward. The mind of Dossonville, thus faced with certain defeat, did not give a second to despair, but, with the last instinctive grasping for life, gathered for a supreme effort.

"It is unnecessary," he cried hurriedly. "That night I performed secret services to the Nation that cannot be made public. But my life is at stake; I demand Santerre. Santerre will vouch for me."

But what he said was lost in the chorus:

"Spy!"

"Liar!"

"Traitor!"

"Liar! Liar!"

"Santerre now!"

"Robespierre next!"

"He was nursing Danton, perhaps!"

Dossonville stretched out his hand appealingly, but recognizing, himself, the impossibility of his position, he changed the gesture into one of command, and looking Maillard calmly in the face, said:

"Well, hurry it up then!"

"To La Force!"

Dossonville, wheeling to meet his escorts, found himself face to face with Javogues.

"Ah, traitor," the Marseillais cried, planting himself in his path with folded arms, "have I caught you at last?"

With a sneer, he turned contemptuously on his heel, while Dossonville, seized by his two guards, began the fatal journey. Already from the gates savage faces peered in expectation, while from the courtyard cries of warning arose:

"Another! Another!"

"Make ready, comrades!"

"A tall one this time!"

"Make ready!"

Half-way to the gate, Dossonville stumbled and went down, sprawling. Instantly he was up, but catching at the arms of his guards, who, trying to shake him off, cried:

"Let go, there, or I'll stab you."

"Citoyen," answered Dossonville with an exclamation of pain—"Citoyen, I have turned my ankle. Support me!"

"Come, come, no nonsense!"

"Citoyen, it is because I do not wish to appear to shrink. Remember that I am a Frenchman; I desire only to die bravely. Give me your support."

"Give it to him!" growled the other.

"Citoyen, I thank you; unfortunately, we shall not meet again."

The one who had spoken continued gruffly:

"When you pass through the gate keep your hands behind your back; you'll suffer less."

"Thanks again."

The next moment the door of the human furnace flung open upon his eyes the horrid spectacle of dead and living: of the living more horrible than the dead.

"One step more!"

The butchers, but five deep, seeing a man borne to them by their comrades, relaxed their tension; those farthest away even lowering their dripping blades.

"There, citoyens, steady me one moment."

With a sudden powerful lunge Dossonville threw the two guards back and leaped headlong into the gauntlet, pierced it, bounded across the open, and dove headlong into the friendly crowd, disappearing like an enormous fish, with only an eddy in the crowd to show his passage.

XIV

GOURSAC AS ACCUSER

For two days, while the massacre ran its course, Paris, in terror of a few hundred assassins, was silent and empty. Bands of marauders scoured the streets, robbing and pillaging under pretext of the right of search. No shops were opened, all industry was suspended, while the law-abiding occupied themselves with fortifying their doors against immediate assault.

Nicole, broken with the horror of her experience, remained in her room, in utter collapse. Barabant, who likewise was ignorant of the escape of Dossonville, sick at heart, passed the day in the room of Goursac, mourning the fall of the Revolution of Ideas. Louison, alone of all the court, ventured out, bringing back such tales of the ferocity of Javogues that Goursac in his anger vowed that he would strike him down. The day was pervaded with the stillness of night. Across the roof arrived the faint traveling cries of victims; beyond that, the air was empty.

After three days of butchery, came the reaction. The assassins, after slaughtering indiscriminately women, children, old men, priests, forgers, and other criminals, blinded with lust of blood, hurled themselves on La Correction, where the children of the people were confined, maltreated and covered with vermin. Thirty-three were led out and put to death.

Then at last Paris revolted. The Commune, itself horrified, rose up and ended the slaughter. On all sides the nursed wrath of the people exploded in cries of vengeance, as they thronged to the section-halls with angry denunciations and demands for prosecution.

After two days of fever and stupor, haunted by visions of the mocking face of Louison and of Barabant, Nicole made an effort, and rising from her bed, set out for the section-hall in the company of Geneviève. When they had entered the hot, choked hall and had taken seats, they found Goursac at the tribune stirring the assembly with pictures of the massacre of women and children. The audience, relieved of its personal fear, vented its anger in wild cries for vengeance. Goursac, having demanded the arrest and condemnation of the Terrorists, descended.

Across the boisterous hall Nicole beheld, with a sudden thrill, Barabant springing impetuously to take his place. But as he reached the tribune and turned to address the crowd, her eyes, which had followed his every movement, were distracted by a violent interruption at the entrance. A cry of indignant anger exploded from the crowd, a cry of despair from Geneviève, whose fingers buried themselves in Nicole's arm; and Nicole, seeking through the overheated, clamorous atmosphere, beheld, flanked by two companions, the wild figure of Javogues.

The crowd, taken unawares, remained vacillating; while the Marseillais, confident of his reception, advanced, and lifting his hideous arms, shouted:

"Citoyens, behold the blood of traitors and rejoice!"

No answering shout was returned.

"Citoyens, France has been purged of its tyrants!"

Nicole, shrinking from the horror of the Marseillais, was yet fascinated by his scornful courage.

For a moment the individual dominated the mass, as yet divided, awaiting the moment that should produce its leader. From somewhere in the back came the answer:

"And La Correction? Is the blood of children also on your arms?"

At this solemn denunciation, Javogues, for the first time realizing his danger, drew back a step, seeking the speaker in the craning of the crowd.

"Butcher! look this way! It is I—the Citoyen Goursac—who challenge you."

With a sweep of his arms, Goursac freed himself and began a zigzag descent down the benches toward his enemy, pausing at every step to cry:

"Butcher! Assassin! Cutthroat!"

Javogues, watching his approach, was at first too astounded to gather his senses; but when Goursac, piercing the last rows, emerged with accusing finger, Javogues advanced a step and closed a hand over his knife.

The mass, watching every motion of these two men, with one movement of its hundred arms loosened its weapons. The action unified it. It became an organism, hostile, menacing, and alert for the first outburst.

Goursac, gathering anger as he advanced, cried:

"Assassin of children! butcher of women! murderer! cutthroat! do you dare to show yourself in this assembly?"

Javogues's answer was lost in the clamor. From all quarters arrived the accusing question:

"La Correction? La Correction?"

"I was not at La Correction!" Javogues thundered above the tumult. "There is no blood of children on these arms."

"And of women?" Goursac caught up. "If you say those arms have not been stained with the blood of women, I tell you, you lie!"

Javogues snatched up his cutlass, but, changing his tactics, appealed to the assembly:

"Hear me!"

From all sides they cried angrily:

"No! no!"

"I demand the right of speech."

"No! no!"

"Hear him!" Barabant cried from the tribune. "Condemn no man without hearing him."

Nicole, with a swift premonition of an overhanging vengeance, started to cry:

"No, Barabant, no!"

But Geneviève, entwining her arms about her, besought her, crying:

"Mercy, Nicole, mercy! I love him!"

At points in the crowd others caught up Barabant's cry, until, after five minutes of fury and storm, the noise dwindled and went out.

Javogues, facing his accusers, returned his weapon to his belt, spread his legs as though to withstand the impending shock, folded his arms, and ran his eye over the banks of his enemies.

"Citoyens, I have answered that I was not at La Correction. You ask me if on these arms there is the blood of women. This is my answer: I do not know!"

"He mocks us!"

"Insolent!"

"Liar!"

"Impostor!"

"This is the blood of traitors," Javogues cried when the outburst had subsided, "and that is all I know. Traitors have no sex. When I see a traitor, I do not stop to ask if it be man, woman, or child, old or young! A traitor is a traitor! Were the mother who brought me forth or the child of my flesh to conspire against the Nation, I would strangle them with these my own hands!"

Again the clamor rose to drown his words, but this time Goursac, rushing from side to side, shouted:

"Let him continue! Let him continue!"

"Of what I have done I am ready to give an accounting," Javogues continued disdainfully. "At the prison of Les Carmes, my hatchet sent down to Hell the soul of that arch-conspirator Dulan." He lifted his arms. "That is the blood these arms bear, and I glory in it. At the Abbaye, I myself purified the Nation of five traitors. At La Force— "

But from the angry crowd rose the cry:

"Enough! Enough!"

One voice, deep and rumbling with an accent of doom, made itself heard:

"We give the right of speech to a citoyen to defend himself, not to a criminal to recite his crimes!"

Goursac, mounting to the tribune, secured a lull.

"You have recited these executions," he cried, addressing Javogues. "By what authority did you constitute yourself a judge?"

Javogues, opening his arms, said:

"By the authority of popular justice."

"Where is your warrant?"

The Marseillais did not answer. The section, seeing where he was being led, kept an intense silence as Goursac's voice, rising in denunciation, continued:

"You admit these deaths. You claim popular authority. Show us your warrant from any popular body, from any section, and you march from here unmolested."

Javogues, turning to his companions, said in a low tone: "Save yourselves. I remain." The two moved—but forward to his side.

The eyes of the assembly were on Goursac, who, white with the intensity of his passion, slowly stretched forth his finger:

"Well?" He waited a moment, his figure rigid in denunciation. "No answer? Then I pronounce, before this assembly, that you have lied! I here declare that what you have done is not the work of a judge, but of a murderer! That when you declared you acted by popular authority, you slandered the Nation, and tried to fasten on it the stain of your guilt and the odium of massacre!" Then assembling all his powers, he shouted at the top of his lungs, "Slanderer of the Nation!"

He turned to the section.

"Citoyens, these are the vipers that assail every life. No one of us is safe. They threaten the Assembly. They do not conceal their desire for its massacre. But to-night we hold one, this monster, this scum of the earth. We hold him, self-confessed and convicted. Citoyens, I declare to you we shall be guilty of cowardice if we now allow this monster to live another day!"

"Aye, to prison with them!"

"À la mort! À la mort!"

"À la guillotine!"

Above the confusion one shrill voice rose victorious, bearing the final decree of the mass.

"No, citoyens! À la lanterne! À la lanterne!"

The next moment all other cries were swallowed up in the wild outburst:

"À la lanterne!"

A hundred hands were stretched out to grasp the Marseillais, when Barabant, to the despair of Nicole, flung himself in front of Javogues, and with appealing arm sought to be heard. But the torrent he faced was relentless. He saw nothing but open mouths, clenched fists, black brows; pistol, knife, and hatchet tossing above the surge of arms. His friends thundered in his ear:

"À la lanterne!"

Those in the back, climbing on the benches, bellowed down:

"À la lanterne!"

From the tribune, frenzied and terrible in his anger, Goursac whipped on the tempest:

"À la lanterne!"

Barabant, with all effort of his lungs, could not utter a sound against the storm. Those that were near shouted to him:

"Barabant, do not balk us!"

"Barabant, look out for your own neck!"

All at once, through the crowd, the terrified figure of Nicole struggled toward him. She flung herself to his side, catching him violently by the shoulders, panting and hysterical.

"Barabant—for my sake—Barabant—for your own safety—Barabant—if you believe in a woman's premonitions, do not save that viper!"

He shook his head and firmly but gently put her from him. The girl, covering her face with her hands, yielded to her despair and fell back into the crowd; while Barabant, never flinching, fought the uproar until he forced the frantic audience to listen.

"This man," he cried at last, above the persisting clamor—"this man is guilty; he should die!" The uproar broke out afresh. "He has put human beings to death without authority from the people. He must die!"

"À la lanterne!"

"Listen!"

"Shut the doors! Lock the doors!"

"But, citoyens," Barabant burst out, "neither have we the right of death. Denounce him, arrest him, but obey the law. Respect the law; respect justice. Citoyens, I demand the arrestation."

The shouts rose in conflict.

"No! no!"

"Yes! yes! yes!"

"Death to him!"

"Arrest him!"

"Hang him!"

"The law! The law!"

The mob was divided, threatening to clash and annihilate itself. The result was a dozen times in doubt, but after half an hour of lull and tumult the verdict was for the course of the law. Barabant again mounted the tribune and put the resolution of arrest.

Javogues and the two Marseillais were led away; the storm rolled out; the hall emptied; a few loiterers straggled down the benches, staring at Nicole, who, exhausted, sobbed on the shoulder of Goursac:

"What a mistake! What a mistake!"

Barabant, leaving the tribune, approached his friends. Now that the passions of the moment were cold, he began to doubt the wisdom of his act.

"I could not help it, Nicole," he said, moved by her utter grief. "It was right, Goursac, was it not?"

Twice he repeated the question without success; nor did the other answer until they reached the Rue Maugout. Then, at length, his bitterness broke through.

"Barabant," he cried, "I will say but one thing: my life is on your head."

"That is absurd," protested Barabant. "Javogues is in prison. He will be condemned."

"He will not remain there one hour!" Goursac replied curtly; but conquering his dejection, he extended his hand. "Barabant, I know you meant well—but you made a mistake. Remember what I say!"

"Meaning I have betrayed you?"

Goursac made no answer.

Barabant, turning brusquely, repeated the question:

"Citoyen, did I do wrong?"

"Barabant, my young friend," Goursac answered, avoiding the question, "when I meet a snake, I do not stop to ask if it is another's property!"

"Then I was wrong?"

"If Javogues loses his neck and we keep ours, no. If Javogues keeps his—"

He rubbed his own solicitously, it being unnecessary to complete the sentence.

By six o'clock the prophecy of Goursac was confirmed, and the inhabitants of the Rue Maugout learned, without astonishment, that Javogues had been liberated and was in hiding.

XV

LOVE, LIFE, AND DEATH

From above there came the shrill, rebellious cry of a woman. Below, in the court, the tenants were gathered, seeking refuge from the heat of the night. A few lights upon the sheer walls and the faint glow of the descended moon illuminated the dim groups: the men against the wall, the women clustered in the center. The cry was repeated, rising shriller. From the wall the exclamations arose:

"It isn't gay!"

"Sangdieu, two in a week! There's no peace left!"

"Eh, citoyen, if we're to fight all Europe, we must have soldiers!"

A peddler, a transient from la Mère Corniche's cellar, added in high tones:

"Thank God, just the same, we're men!"

The crones listened critically, without emotion, resuming their old wives' tales when the cry had ceased. Once a child, more keenly responsive to suffering, burst into a frightened whimper; but the mother, with an exclamation of impatience, sprang up and with a slap silenced the child, crying:

"Little brat, who told you to do that!"

Under the torch that lighted the entrance to the stairs the ghoulish figure of la Mère Corniche hobbled forth, returning from her inspection.

"Well, what news?" a voice cried.

"Eh, it'll be all night now," she answered peevishly. "I'm going to get some sleep."

The women, hearing this, broke up and departed to their rooms; the men began to grumble:

"What the devil's to be done?"

"I'm for the cabaret."

"You can't stay here."

"There's no sleep to-night. Come on to the cabaret."

"You'll join us, Citoyen Goursac?"

"No; I'm remaining here."

"And you, Citoyen Barabant?"

"I also."

"Morbleu, you've strange tastes!"

They shuffled away, leaving Barabant and Goursac, with their backs to the maple-tree, in possession of the empty darkness.

Presently lights began to splotch the walls, and at the windows appeared the silhouettes of feminine forms, while a running comment resounded:

"Where are the men?"

"Gone to the cabaret, probably."

"They are, if my man's among them."

"They're all weak-kneed."

"The cowards!"

The cry of the woman returned.

"Aïe, what lungs!"

"I yelled so, the police came up."

"You were right."

"Pardi!"

"Let's hope she'll give us some rest."

"Amen!"

The lights, one by one, flattened into the darkness. A single window, under the eaves, continued bright, from which ever descended the cry of battle.

"Does that affect you?" Goursac asked, following the momentary shadows across the panes.

"I don't like to hear it."

"You get accustomed to it, as to all things. Tiens! I was forgetting. I heard to-day that Dossonville had escaped."

"Absurd."

"They said he had been seen with Louison."

"But Nicole says she saw him cut to pieces."

"Then doubtless it was a mistake."

"No news of Javogues?" Barabant took up.

"None."

"That makes three days. You see, he's left the city."

"I doubt it." Goursac added after a moment: "I'll tell you something curious. You know Geneviève?"

"That child who lives with Nicole?"

"She's in love with him."

"What! that little ogre?"

"Eh, the ogre has the spark of the woman in her!" He jerked his head toward the lighted window. "Who's with her?"

"Nicole and Geneviève."

"Much good it'll do them."

"Hanh?"

"Good night. I'm going to philosophize! Are you staying?"

"Yes."

Scarcely had Goursac departed before the form of a young girl emerged from the stairs, and Nicole's voice said softly:

"Barabant, are you there?"

"Here I am."

He sprang eagerly to meet her, but Nicole, retreating before the decisive word, hastened to say:

"Poor girl, it is not going well. Geneviève is staying with her. Have you been waiting long?"

"I? No. I was talking with Goursac. He has just left." Barabant, determined to bring matters to an issue, added relentlessly, "I was just leaving for the cabaret."

"What! you were not waiting for me?"

"I could not count on your coming."

Nicole's eyes filled with tears, and, unable any longer to bear the unequal contest, she cried bitterly:

"Barabant, you are cruel!"

"I?" he answered, with a last effort. "I who have offered you everything? I whom you will not believe when I tell you I love you?"

"I do! I do!"

Barabant, no longer resisting her weakness, cried:

"But I adore thee, Nicole. I am out of my mind with love for thee!"

He seized her in his arms and kissed her on the cheeks, on the forehead, on the wet eyelids, with all the overpowering, reason-consuming flame of love.

She withdrew from his grasp, and looking him anxiously in the face, said:

"You thought me heartless and capricious, didn't you?"

"I have forgotten."

"But you did."

"Perhaps."

"Ah, Barabant, it was because I loved thee that I avoided thee."

"Why?"

His face expressed so much bewilderment that Nicole passed her hand gently over his eyes.

"No, that thou wilt never understand. If I could only tell thee how I love thee!" She wanted him to know the deep maternal longings that he had stirred within her, but all she found to say was, "I feared to love thee too much, and so I fought against myself." Then, with the first awakening of coquetry, she nestled on his shoulder and said confidently, "Forgive me."

"But why? Why?"

"It absorbed all that was in me, and I was afraid."

"Of what?"

She did not want to tell him of her doubts, so she said:

"Women have foolish ideas, Barabant; you must not try to understand them."

She joined her arms around his neck and laid her head upon his shoulder. Suddenly the silence was rent by the inexorable cry. In the heart of Nicole something penetrated like a knife. She began to tremble.

"Why do you shake so?" he asked.

"It is from joy."

"You love me so, then?"

When the silence returned, she said:

"Barabant, promise me but one thing."

"I promise it."

"When the day comes that you are leaving me for another woman, tell me first." She added low, as though she did not want him to hear: "I can kill myself without seeing her in his arms!"

Barabant, recoiling before such a picture of the future, cried from the bottom of a heart of pity:

"Never! Never!"

"No—I could not leave thee, even so," she said, weeping herself at the thought she had conjured. "Let me always be thy servant. I am only an ignorant girl, not fit to be thy companion. Let me take care of thee, though, whatever happens!"

"No, never that! Never! Nicole, it is for life, forever!" he cried with the sincerity of the moment, which is the sincerity of the lover. He was young, generous, quick to pity, and he adored her. "You do believe me?"

"Almost."

He redoubled his protestations, while Nicole, laughing through her tears, cried gaily:

"Go on, Barabant. It is good to hear. Don't stop—more, more!" At last she herself arrested his protestations: "Yes, Barabant, I believe thee. Oh, anything you can say to me I'll believe at this moment!"

"That I want thee while I live?"

"Yes."

"Forever?"

"For—ever." She drew herself up to his lips. "I have been so miserable waiting for thee."

Their lips met and they stood in the darkness as one body, while above, unheeded, from the darkness broke out the cry of life and death.

"Thou wilt not leave me, Nicole, again, neither now nor ever?"

"Do I not love thee?" she said simply.

They passed from the shadow and moved, tightly enlaced, through the dim region of the dwindling torch, slowly up the steep, hard steps into the enveloping darkness beyond. Again was lifted up the cry of anguish and rebellion, the cry of Prometheus, heritage of woman, and again came silence.

PART II

I

FAMINE

On the first day of September, 1793, Nicole left the Rue Maugout with the intention of visiting the Convention. Her step, that a year ago would have been confounded with the hum of life, now echoed down the quiet streets without interruption. Her eye, that once flashed so alertly through the curious crowd, passed with the indifference of habit down the deserted vista, and returned into the fixity of mental abstraction. The passers-by were rare; those who hung on the windows screened themselves. At a few doorways groups of emaciated children watched her progress, eyeing her basket with wolfish eyes. A year had brought but slight change in her. She still retained the bloom of youth, but her glance was more pensive. She was no longer gipsy or girl. A certain thoughtfulness had succeeded, elusive and arch, that told of the awakened imagination.

Twice on her way a band of police enveloping a prisoner passed, as passes a whirlwind over the stretches of the desert. Nicole gave them but a casual glance; such of the inhabitants as the familiar fall of feet brought to the windows retired indifferently, the prisoners themselves stoically adding their resignation to the monotony of the scene.

On the thoroughfares knots of Tapedures, the ruffians of the Terror, became frequent, stalking the town, beating the streets for their human game. Occasionally she met a bill-poster affixing the latest decree of the Republic—violent notes, in blue, violet, yellow, or red, that splashed the walls on every side. About the bakeries and butcher-shops knots of beggars were assembled, often reclining on the ground, watching with dreary, troubled glances those havens of food, ready to battle for a scrap of refuse.

A mother from a distant quarter, drifting from shop to shop, halted before such a group with a timid inquiry. From the loiterers, watching with confident indifference, a hag, extending her shriveled arm, shouted sarcastically:

"Welcome, citoyenne. You want something to eat? Take it; take it. We are so tired of eating meat in this section—nothing but beef and mutton and venison and pheasants here, morning and night. We get tired of that sort of thing in the end, you know. You were right to come here; see how well fed we are, how sleek! Don't believe him, his cellars are full of meat. It's rotting away. No one to eat it!"

From the fasting hags a rumble, rather than a laugh, went up. The woman who had covered perhaps half of Paris melted into a storm of sobs, beseeching a crust or a bone for the sake of her children. Then the hag, her raillery changing to anger, burst out:

"And we, have we no children? Are we not mothers, too? Hark to the woman: she thinks she's the only one to be pitied! Be off! Leave us in peace with your eternal wailings!"

At other times, women from the quarter itself, returning from a scouring of the markets, would awaken a sudden flame of interest.

"What luck?"

"What did you get?"

"Bread?"

"Meat?"

The scouts always denied success. Then a chorus arose:

"She's hiding it!"

"Show us your basket!"

"Eh, and under your dress!"

Once, in the Rue St. Honoré, a slip of a girl had almost freed herself of the questioning crowd, when a lean dog with a sharp nose bounded, sniffing, to her side. There was a quick turning in the crowd, and the nearest woman, leaping to her feet, shouted hysterically:

"I smell dried fish!"

The next moment, up the street a scuttling speck fled before a frenzied cloud from which shot out white arms and grasping hands.

Through such mad scenes of famine, Nicole arrived at the Hall of the Convention; where, being early, she entered the Tuileries to await the arrival of Barabant.

The gardens that once resounded with the hum of life, that once were gay with the swish of many colors, were now brown with the uninterrupted stretch of earth, rustling with the pervading sigh of leaves. Already in the trees, in the air, and in the tired soil was the melancholy of the parting season. Each breath that disturbed the branches, however slightly, set free a caravansary of fluttering leaves, and the leaves were sear.

She seated herself on a bench and abandoning the basket and clasping her knee, watched the whirling leaves heap themselves about her feet. One or two poised on her shoulder, in her hair, without her heeding them. Presently Goursac, also on his way to the Convention, joined her.

"This is the work of the cursed Montagne!" he said grimly, viewing the desolate gardens. "And yet Javogues is not satisfied. He would turn it into a cemetery!"

"Listen, my friend," she said earnestly. "If the Girondins fall, you will not stay to sacrifice your life to Javogues?"

"Do you think that I, a Girondin, would fly from that rascal!" he cried indignantly. "He works in the dark; he is incapable of striking in the open."

"And if the Girondins fall?" she persisted. But he refused to entertain the suggestion.

"This reminds me," he said, with a sweep of his arm, "of the time we were here a year ago. Do you remember?"

She nodded.

"Well," he said brusquely, "are you happy?"

"Yes."

"As happy as you thought?"

"No," she said slowly, "but it is my fault. The fault of my position, if you wish. I am jealous!"

"Of Louison?"

"No! Of what may happen."

"Why shouldn't he marry you?" he said angrily.

"Because I have not asked him," she answered wearily. "And because I would not have it."

"Why?"

"Because I love him, my friend," she said in rebuke. "And because a waif of the streets does not marry a man of education and position unless she wishes to drag him down."

Goursac, to her surprise, leaned over and patted her hand; then, as though ashamed to have shown such tenderness, he added gruffly:

"That is the only thing that can make you happy."

She did not deny it.

"I know what you have passed through."

She shook her head incredulously.

"It is but the history of womankind," he said laconically.

She took a leaf that had fallen on her hair and tore it slowly to shreds.

"Yes," he continued, warming to the subject, "you but resume in a year what woman has struggled for throughout the centuries. What is marriage but the instinct of self-preservation? Who imagined the bond? The weaker being, woman; and all the advances up the social scale have resulted from her silent striving toward equality with man. Without marriage you are a slave at the mercy of an angry word or a hostile mood; a slave who, in her search for security, must learn, without tears or show of fatigue, to render herself indispensable to the man."

Nicole rose abruptly, frowning, and with nervous fingers; but immediately she reseated herself with a forced laugh.

Presently, seeing that he had said more than he should have, he withdrew, leaving her immersed in the reverie his words had awakened.

Goursac had guessed truly. What womankind has endured, she had begun from the bottom. The instinct of self-preservation within her had awakened the immense intuitions that in the silent, enduring conflict of the sexes alike direct the wife, the mistress, and the outcast. She had studied Barabant, seeking the needs of his temperament, discovering his faults, and leading him to gradual dependence on her. Her imagination awoke. She saw the peril of mere domestic companionship. Where at first she had belittled the force of passionate love, she had come to realize its necessity and the need of constantly provoking his curiosity. She hid her thoughts from him, making of herself a mystery, employing that coquetry which, to the seeing eye, has at the bottom nothing but pathos. She had loved as a child. She had become an actress.

But in her heart of jealousy and doubt she knew well all her artifices could avail no longer than her youth. In marriage alone was peace and security. The daring of the thought frightened her. She knew it to be beyond her lot, nor in her devotion to Barabant would she have it so, but each day the dream returned, as from a pit one sees a star, or from a wreck the beacon on the forbidden shore.

Barabant found her lost in reverie, the leaves again unnoticed on her shoulders.

"The effect is pretty," he said, smiling down at her.

"On whom the leaves fall and rest, the earth will fall before the year is out," Nicole said. "That's the superstition."

"Nicole, I forbid you to say such things," he cried sharply. "They hurt me, and you know it!"

Satisfied with this evidence of his affection, she sprang up, brushing away the leaves, and saying with a smile:

"There, they have no power now."

"You are early."

"Yes; I was a little melancholy; I wanted to reflect. The gardens are delightful for that."

"I do not find them so."

"The mood is gone, now that you are here." She took his arm, smiling up into his face. They strolled through the alleys of chestnut and maple, Nicole drawing her skirt across her, placing her feet daintily, shaking her head in pretended anger as from time to time a leaf fluttered against her cheek.

"And the Girondins, mon ami? You have told me nothing of them."

"It grows worse and worse for them. The Jacobins are relentless."

"Don't identify yourself too much with them, then."

"But that is cowardice."

"No. If the Girondins fall, all the more will the Nation need the Moderates," Nicole answered anxiously, for her one dread was of his impulsive nature. "Why play into the hands of our enemies?"

Leaving the gardens, they entered the Place de la Revolution. The vast square that had swarmed with the multitude on the day of the execution of the king was devoid of movement, except where a few curious, wandering toward the emplacement of the absent guillotine, streaked like insects across the placid expanse.

Nearing the plaster statue of Liberty, Nicole was attracted by the lank figure of a man.

"Look over there," she said, drawing Barabant's attention. "Wouldn't you say that it was Dossonville?"

"There's a little resemblance."

"Much."

Barabant, who continued to study the figure, exclaimed:

"Really, the resemblance is striking!"

At this moment the man, turning, disclosed indeed the familiar features, while the well-known voice cried:

"Mordieu! It is Nicole and my little orator Barabant! Well, what's the matter? Touch hands!"

For Nicole, with a movement of superstition, had crossed herself, while Barabant, stock-still, remained staring stupidly at the apparition, until he was able to blurt out:

"What, it is you! Then you're not dead."

"Not even once!" he cried, slapping his hand emphatically across his chest. "I give you my word, it is not true! Come, feel of me. Is this the arm or the chest of a specter?"

"Still, I saw you," exclaimed Nicole, unable to reconcile the fact to her memory—"I saw you at the gate of the Abbaye—"

"My dear girl," Dossonville responded, with much good humor, "believe me, I am not dead; and, what's more, I never have been dead that I remember."

"But—"

"Mordieu, Nicole! are you determined to exterminate me?" Dossonville cried. "Let us reason. You saw me at the gate, but you didn't see me cut down, did you?"

"No."

"Then I reject your theory."

The three burst out laughing, until Dossonville suddenly exclaimed:

"But come, Louison must have told you."

"Louison!" echoed Barabant and Nicole, more and more amazed.

"Extraordinary woman! She can even keep a secret then!" Dossonville cried. "Why, it was Louison who found me in the crowd and piloted me to safety."

He recounted shortly the events of his escape, adding, as he extended his arm in a sweeping embrace of the horizon:

"And here I have lain concealed. I don't say where; the secret is too good. For ten months I lay like a rat. For the last two I have gone out only after midnight. To-day is the first trip into the blessed sun."

"Do you dare to risk it even now?" Barabant cried.

"Yes, now. Everything is arranged," he answered carelessly. "It was a little long coming, but it came."

But suddenly Nicole, remembering, exclaimed: "Barabant, you must warn him that Javogues is back."

"Back!" Dossonville repeated. "When did he leave?"

Barabant, in his turn, recounted the arrest and disappearance of the Marseillais, concluding:

"He reappeared with the rise of the Terrorists."

"Aïe, aïe!" Dossonville cried, having followed the recital with interest; "I cannot say that the situation is pleasant for the Citoyen Goursac."

A shadow passed over the brow of the young man, and he answered bitterly:

"I was a fool. We should have crushed the monster when we had him."

"There's good in him."

"What! You say it?"

"He wanted to cut my throat," Dossonville replied; "but that's nothing. He is sincere. It is true, from his point of view, there are not three men who should be alive in France to-day; but that is only a prejudice. I am keeping you; where are you bound?"

"To the Convention."

"Always a Girondin?"

"Well," Barabant answered doubtfully, "the Girondins had their chance, and they could not control the Convention."

"I say it's their own fault if they fall," Nicole interjected hastily.

"Nicole, you are right," Dossonville replied. "Moreover, they are about to lose their heads." He drew his finger across his neck. "In a political party, that's a grave failing."

"What, guillotine the Girondins!" Barabant exclaimed. "Guillotine Vergniaud, Brissot,—they would never dare!"

"Bah! you look upon it too seriously," Dossonville retorted. "What is the guillotine? Simply a vote of censure. But Louison—where can I find her?"

"At the Prêtre Pendu," Nicole answered. "You'll find her there about noon. That is, if there is no execution this afternoon."

"The Prêtre Pendu? Don't know it."

"It opened lately in the Rue Maugout, opposite No. 38."

"You call it— "

"The Prêtre Pendu."

"Charming!"

"I warn you, Javogues will be there."

"You are positive?"

"Absolutely."

"Good. Then I'll set out at once."

II

DOSSONVILLE EARNS A KISS

Dossonville, taking the river bank, proceeded with many inquiring halts, inhaling the air and sunshine in full breaths. He strolled into the halles, where the stalls, in state of siege, extended in long, deserted barracks; no buying, no selling, no provisions, only in the shadows the same clusters of limp basking beggars, slumbering with one ear alert.

As he languidly pursued his way, a door at his side was flung violently open and a man bearing on his back an enormous side of beef scurried across the place toward a butcher-shop, the door of which swung open to receive him. Instantly, with a hue and cry from every corner, there was a swift leaping of famished men, women, and children. Before Dossonville could leap aside he was caught in the rush, elbowed, buffeted, and thrown off his feet. When again he rose, the butcher was buried under a mound of ravenous humanity, thirty feet from his destination, while the square was obscured with the multitude that battled over the shreds of meat which came up from the bottom of the heap.

Hardly had he extricated himself from the tangle when, in the Place de la Bastille, a group of savage boys, pursuing a dog with a bone, swept by him, snatching at the fleeing animal, unmindful of its anger. One hand at last, more fortunate than the others, closed over the brute, and the human children tore the bone from the beast. Pursuing now a haggard boy, they returned in a cloud, panting, with famine-inflamed eyes, while the lean, infuriated brute at their heels struck with angry jaws into the pack.

Beset on every side by troops of children too weak to extend their hands, Dossonville arrived at the Rue Maugout, readily recognizing the Cabaret of the Prêtre Pendu by its figure of a priest, which, swinging from a miniature gibbet, advertised the republican principles of the host.

Seeing no one before the entrance of No. 38, he penetrated into the inner room of the cabaret, where, the two or three groups occupied with cards being unknown to him, he exchanged salutations with the hostess, asking genially:

"Your husband, citoyenne, I hope, is frying me a bit of steak?"

"My man's with the army."

"A patriot, then."

"And there's no meat."

"An omelet will do."

"No eggs, no fish, no vegetables."

"Diable! that leaves nothing but bread and cheese."

"No bread, no cheese!"

"Mordieu, what am I going to lunch on?"

"Soup."

"Ah!" Dossonville nodded, with understanding. "True! As long as the material world exists, soup is possible. Well, soup be it, citoyenne, soon and hot."

He passed curiously to the card-players, for his ear had caught such strange expressions as these:

"I play the Liberty of Marriage."

"I the Genius of Peace."

"The Equality of Rank."

"Liberty of the Press."

"Taken by the Genius of Arts."

Dossonville, much perplexed, moved to a survey of the pack. He found the Monarchs indeed dethroned; the Kings succeeded by the Geniuses of War, Commerce, Peace, and the Arts; the Queens replaced by the Liberties of Faith, Professions, Marriage, and the Press. The Knaves themselves, as though suspected of royalistic tendencies, had yielded to the Equalities of Duties, Color, Rights, and Rank.

"The sentiment is perfect," he murmured to himself, "perfect, but perplexing."

The hostess appearing with a capacious bowl, he returned to his corner, where he contemplated the soup with that respect and curiosity which a Parisian gives to a dish of which he has not had the making. He stirred it doubtfully, and at the first taste drew a long face.

"Tonnerre de Dieu! They've put the aristocrats in the soup," he grumbled. "However, being good patriots, we must eat it."

He was bending over the bowl, when a shadow darkened the open doorway, and with the fragrant scent of flowers came the voice of Louison, chanting:

"Cockades, patriots; cockades, my Sans-Culottes. The last ones I have been able to save for you."

She passed among them, calling to them by name, tapping them on the shoulders, but receiving nothing but banter.

"Are they good to eat—your cockades?"

"As a salad, nothing is better." Taking up the idea, she repeated laughingly: "Buy my salads, citoyens; buy my patriotic salads!"

Wishing to enjoy her surprise, Dossonville kept silent, leaning forward, his chin in his palm, smiling expectantly. Thus Louison discovered him. The very slightest look of astonishment passed over her face, a fugitive amazement that she immediately controlled.

"Louison, you are discretion itself," Dossonville said approvingly, his smile extending to a grin as he stretched forth his hand. "If ever the Revolution places women in power (and what is impossible to-day?), I'll recommend you for Minister of Foreign Affairs."

"Citoyen, citoyen, you are mad to enter this place," Louison cried. "Do you not know that this is the headquarters of Javogues?"

"I know it; but see you, Louison, that animal is so stupid."

Divining that despite his careless manner he was fortified against the encounter, she relaxed and said more calmly:

"Really, I didn't expect that you'd escape."

"My dear Louison, it is not so difficult."

"In these days it is."

"A man has as many lives as a cat," he said ironically. "It is the imagination that is lacking."

As though to put this theory to the test, a voice jarred upon the stillness, crying:

"Where is the spy?"

The next instant the cabaret was thrown into turmoil as Javogues, at the head of three or four companions, rushed in.

"Good day, citoyen," Dossonville's cool voice was heard saying above the uproar, "and how goes it with you since we parted last?"

Guided by his voice, Javogues precipitated himself toward his enemy, but as his hand shot forth it stopped in mid-air, and he fell back in astonishment.

Dossonville, never losing his poise, with an imperceptible movement of his hand had rolled back the lapel of his redingote, disclosing on his breast the shield of an agent de sûreté.

"Impossible!" Javogues exclaimed, recoiling. "You an agent de sûreté! It's a counterfeit!"

Dossonville checked the second rush as coolly as the first. His hand went into his breast pocket and withdrew a document, which he tendered to Javogues on the tips of his fingers, saying:

"Read, and grow wise."

The Marseillais passed it to a companion, who shook his head and passed it to a third, who read in a piping voice:

OFFICE OF THE COMMITTEE OF SAFETY

The Citoyen Santerre having appeared before us and established the alibi of the Citoyen Dossonville on the day of the Tenth of August, we declare the Citoyen Dossonville innocent of all suspicion. Furthermore, as it appears he refused to disclose the nature of the secret mission, in the interests of the Nation, on which he was engaged, even at the risk of his life, we declare the Citoyen Dossonville a patriot who deserves the gratitude of his country.

We further appoint the said Citoyen Dossonville agent de sûreté, with the following powers—

"The rest is quite technical," Dossonville interrupted. He turned to Javogues, who, thus robbed of his dearest vengeance, remained transfixed with stupor. "You see, Citoyen Javogues, you cannot always tell a traitor by the look in his eyes."

Stung by the taunt, Javogues advanced furiously:

"It's a lie," he cried. "It's another of his tricks. The paper is a forgery." Then turning to his companions, he shouted: "Don't let him out of your sight until I return!"

Dossonville, erect and solemn, checked him sternly:

"Enough! Enough, citoyen, do you hear? What you have done I forgive—but go no further! An act such as you contemplate is a defiance of the Nation. I represent the Nation. Citoyen Javogues, I warn you, at the next attack you make against me I'll have you on the scaffold within twenty-four hours."

Javogues, impressed despite himself, found no encouragement in the faces of his comrades. He turned on his heel and went dejectedly toward the door. There he wheeled, and shaking his fist, cried:

"Dossonville, if I am not to hate you, arrest me, guillotine me at once. For, as long as I live, it is war between you and me! If you want me, you'll find me here, at five."

Dossonville remained a moment pensive and erect.

"Mordieu!" he exclaimed at last, "the fellow is genuine. Devil take me if I can help liking him." Then turning to Louison, who had followed him with fascinated eyes, he said: "As for you, ma belle, I owe you everything. To begin with, I swear an eternal love."

And, taking her in his arms, he kissed her on the cheek, and then sat down.

In a moment the room was swept of its terrified guests, while the proprietress, disappearing through a back door, left the memory of a red stocking.

Louison, at the familiarity, recoiled, while anger like a blast from an oven inflamed her face. Her hand stole to her bosom, and with a sudden movement she hid a knife behind her.Dossonville, feigning ignorance, appeared engrossed in the selection of a cockade from the abandoned basket. But as the girl in her passion leaped at him, he sprang aside, whipped out his sword, and flung himself behind a table.

Then, those without, flattening their noses against the window or peering through the doorway, beheld a furious combat between them; the man, always cool and alert, checking the rushes of the girl with the point of his sword, turning, retreating, or advancing as his assailant, with the rapidity of a bird, flew from point to point, darting, feinting, or striking for an opening. Meanwhile above the scuffle and the patter of feet the voice of Dossonville rose imperturbably in running comment:

"Hoop-là, parried! A little more to the left and you had me. Mordieu, who'd have thought a pretty woman would resent a kiss? Such a fraternal kiss, too, so full of gratitude! Perhaps that's the trouble; you never can tell with a woman. What now?"

Bounding on the table, the girl without a pause leaped full at him.

"Bravo! That's a jump for you. What a woman! Louison, you are splendid. Dame, what fury! À toi!"

Hard pressed with the recklessness of her attacks, he threatened her throat so closely that, with the slightest stiffening of his arm, he would have run her through.

"A life for a life! there's gratitude for you!"

From outside they cried to him offers of help.

"Never; any man that interferes, I'll shoot down. This little affair is between us,—eh, Louison? What now?"

He sprang away, barely avoiding a chair hurled to break down his guard.

"That was well imagined. Mille diables, what a woman—and not a sound! Louison, I adore you already. Louison, my dear, do you believe in another life? If you would only guarantee me another, I'd give you this out of courtesy,—only then I couldn't adore you. What energy! If you are getting tired, Louison, rest a while."

But her answer was to fling herself again at him, seeking to come inside his guard by stooping suddenly to one side, grasping at his blade with her free hand. Dossonville, forced to meet the fury of the onslaught, a second time presented the point of his blade to her throat; but this time, so impetuous was her rush that only the instant withdrawal of the weapon saved her.

"A second time, Louison, I spare you. My gratitude, you see, is eternal. Louison, you fight too recklessly, you expose yourself. You rely too much on my sense of gratitude. Hoop-là! Again I had you! If it's only a matter of a kiss that stands between us, you might give it back to me. Ha, ha! Well struck, Louison! Where will it end? My gratitude restrains me, and you must realize what a good fellow you are trying to end— "

Suddenly, to the astonishment of all, Dossonville included, Louison halted, panting and heaving, restored the knife to her bosom, and burst out laughing.

"Dossonville," she cried, flinging out her hand in acclamation, "you're a man!"

He dropped on both knees, exclaiming: "That word disarms me. Do me the favor of cutting my neck."

With a movement as swift as her attack, the girl passed to his side, and, bending suddenly, kissed him on the forehead.

"That one, Dossonville," she cried, "you have deserved."

And with a laugh, she flitted into the street, where the spectators, respecting her sudden whims, prudently left her an open passage.

III

WAITING FOR BREAD

In this season of famine, when the supply of bread barely sufficed to feed one half of the population, by six o'clock in the evening long lines began to form in front of the bakeries, to await through the long night the morning distribution of loaves. Javogues, who took the occasion of this assembling to study the crowd for signs of traitors or faint-hearted republicans, returned each evening, toward five o'clock, to the Prêtre Pendu in a gale of patriotic ferocity.

But this afternoon, to the astonishment of those who were accustomed to quail before his glance, his lagging step, his knotted club trailing at his heels, and his head relaxed on his shoulders gave every appearance of dejection. At the Prêtre Pendu he sank gratefully into a chair, covered the table with his arms, and plunged moodily into his thoughts.

Presently, arm in arm, bristling with weapons, in villainous shoes wound about with strips of rags, appeared three Tapedures,—Cramoisin the mountebank, Boudgoust the waiter, and Jambony the crier,—thrown together by the strange tides of the Terror. In the middle, Boudgoust strode with hang-dog head, as though his height had overshot his strength. The shriveled, furtive mountebank clung to one arm, while at the other waddled the bloated, leering cub of the gutters. So tightly huddled were they that they seemed one unclean body with three heads—an incongruous union of malignant age, stultified manhood, and vicious, insolent youth.

Perceiving Javogues silent and absorbed, they slackened their pace, and Boudgoust said cautiously:

"Cramoisin, he's still in bad humor."

"It's that cursed Dossonville, my little Boudgoust. If it worries him, why doesn't he get rid of him?"

"Javogues's the devil when aroused," Boudgoust continued apprehensively. He turned to the boy: "Jambony, throttle that voice of a carriage-crier and speak softly. It might be best to slip away."

But Javogues, lifting his head, beckoned them.

"Well, watch-dogs, what luck?"

Cramoisin and Jambony looked to Boudgoust, who turned his pockets inside out, showed the flat of his palms, and answered:

"Nothing."

"An unfortunate day—for all of us," Javogues said gloomily, and relapsed into bitter reflections on his encounter with Dossonville.

"What luck!" exclaimed Cramoisin. "We escaped easily. Suppose we eat something."

Jambony opened his mouth, and the voice, trained to rise above the jargon of the street, resounded from one end of the street to the other.

"Food!"

The invariable bowl of soup and a bottle of thin wine were placed in front of each. Boudgoust, whose appetite was in proportion to his length, accomplished his portion in one swallow, and being thus reduced to philosophizing, exclaimed:

"All citoyens should be made to eat together."

"Nothing new there," Cramoisin interjected querulously. "We have the Fraternal dinners, haven't we?"

"That amounts to nothing," Boudgoust retorted. He leaned his elbows on the table, scratching the back of his hands as he talked: "But every day, every meal. That's democracy! Or, better, no citoyen to eat more than another! If I saw any one eating meat to-night I'd arrest him. All citoyens should share alike."

Jambony, having now emptied his bowl, declared in his stentor's voice:

"And I am for equality of dress. No distinction between citoyens on account of dress! A national costume—one for the men and one for the women!"

Presently, while he launched into the details of his scheme, a raven, with a croak and a flap of its wings, hopped from the gloom of the opposite entrance, followed by the diminutive figure of la Mère Corniche, who, giving a nod of understanding to the four, installed herself on a stool and began to knit.

"There's one who's no Girondin," Boudgoust grunted.

"She's a tiger since the death of Marat," Jambony remarked in a thundering whisper. "She was very devoted. They say—"

And he proceeded to detail one of those fantastic tales which the Parisian playfully attributed to any woman, were she eighty or eighteen.

Cramoisin, having caressed the last drop in his bowl, now exclaimed:

"Jambony, you are tiresome, you and your national costume. You go half-way. What we must restore is the primeval innocence!" As he spoke he pressed a flat thumb on the table, while from under his eyebrows shot the shrewd dagger glances of the madman. "The primeval innocence—there only is the truth! Nothing but that can restore republican simplicity. No clothes at all! A return to the simplicity of Adam and Eve—the true, the real republicans! There's something that would be sublime!"

"Allons, Cramoisin, you have too much vanity!" Boudgoust replied.

"Yes, he wants to display his beauty," put in Jambony, who retained the spirit of raillery gathered at the doors of the theater. "We know that trick, old fellow."

Cramoisin was beginning a furious answer when Javogues, turning impatiently, demanded the hour.

"Close to seven."

"They come later every night," Javogues grumbled. He rang the table with his fist. "Perhaps they think they can hide their guilty faces in the dusk!"

Presently, from the entrances, people with baskets began to appear, directing their way toward the Bakery Gobin, a rod below, to take up the vigil that consumed the night.

Those who passed the Prêtre Pendu waited anxiously their welcome from the mouth of Javogues, whose salutations varied according to his estimate of their patriotism.

"Greetings, patriots."

"Greetings, citoyens."

"Greetings."

To some he simply nodded in return. Occasionally he stiffened and, without recognition, fastened his scrutiny on the eyes of a new arrival, as though to tear away the mask and wrench forth the secret.

Marching purposely toward them, looking Javogues disdainfully in countenance, came Goursac. So implacable were the glances the two enemies exchanged that they seemed to clash midway in the air. Arrived within ten feet of the group, Goursac turned curtly on his heel and departed toward the bakery without having recognized them by word or nod. The Tapedures cursed; Javogues, following him with his glance, muttered:

"Sacré! Girondin, wait a little longer!"

Several women passed, among them Nicole, who received a friendly greeting from Javogues, Boudgoust commenting:

"Fine woman that, Cramoisin, for all you say!"

Cramoisin scowled for an answer, following the girl with a glance of implacable hatred.

"Eh, yes," Jambony added, sinking his voice. "As for me, if it weren't for Javogues I'd not keep her long chained up to that cursed Barabant."

"Barabant," growled Boudgoust, "is an indulgent. He is forever talking of mercy."

"He who speaks of mercy in these days," cried Cramoisin, purposely raising his voice, "is in league with aristocrats. He should be denounced."

Javogues turned angrily:

"Enough! Barabant is a patriot. I know it!"

Boudgoust, who disliked quarrels, interrupted:

"Hello, who's this brat?"

A girl of six or seven was approaching, carrying in her arms a stool.

Javogues, at once suspicious, stopped her.

"Who sent you out, my little one?"

"Papa."

"And who is your father?"

"The wig-maker there," she said, showing the shop with her small finger. "He's coming to take my place later."

"Ah, your papa is a good Royalist."

The child, frightened by his looks, remained twisting from side to side, while Javogues, softening his voice, repeated the question.

The child shook her head.

"What does he say of us?" It was Boudgoust who put the question.

"Don't know."

"But he suffers much with this famine, doesn't he?" suggested Cramoisin, slyly.

"Oh, yes," she answered, the innocent face brightening. "Papa says we suffer more now than before."

Cramoisin, triumphant and smiling, drew back; the child toddled on.

"Ah, Citoyen Flaquet," Javogues cried in triumph, "who doesn't dare pass us in the daylight and who regrets the royalty, we hold you at last!"

Among the next to leave No. 38 was a girl of sixteen, who, in greeting Javogues, faltered a little in her walk. It was Geneviève, suddenly blossomed into a woman. Her eyes, that formerly were too black and large on her sallow face, were now in fair relief to her cheeks, that had flushed with the glow of womanhood. She moved lightly, and even the carelessness of her dress could not conceal the full figure, erect and flexible.

The four men watched her pass on and take her place in the lengthening line.

"The best of the lot!" Cramoisin said.

"She was ugly enough last year," Boudgoust replied.

"She was not a woman then," retorted the other, who seized the opportunity to broach his favorite theory. "Women, they're good enough in their places. They're put here to give men to the world. I believe in the community of women. No marriage. Women discriminate according to a man's being old or ugly or poor. All discrimination is unrepublican. There should be no distinctions."

"Yes, my old fellow, but halt there," Jambony said impudently. "No community of men."

"Why not?"

"You'd fall to the lot of la Mère Corniche."

Cramoisin angrily resented the interruption. He passed to the sociological aspect of the reform, and declared that with the Nation battling against all Europe such a measure was needed to fill in the gaps of war. Other bottles were brought and torches.

Below at the bakery, two torches disclosed the undulations of the monstrous queue, but the faces and the outlines of the figures were confounded in the night. Sometimes a brief song would mount up, a few whispered communications could be heard, and the steady snoring of a sleeper.

From there, in the narrow circle of light under the figure of the priest, which swung in grotesque outlines, the four Tapedures could be seen, drinking and discussing. At times their voices, impassioned and drunken, reached the line, the high pitch of Cramoisin crying: "Primeval innocence! community of women!" or the bellow of Javogues, "There is no God!" as the four, without listening to one another, debated furiously their sublime ideas.

From time to time others arrived through the darkness, relieving those in line. Toward midnight Barabant replaced Nicole. Several of the new arrivals were fresh from cabarets; many of those whom no one relieved began in drunken boisterousness to scream upon the night ribald songs and jests, foul anathemas of the party in disfavor.

The noise of kisses and tipsy laughter became frequent. The women and children, accustomed to the scene, retired under shawls and sought to efface themselves against the chilly walls. Some women, more vicious than their mates, joined in the drunken carnival, which toward three o'clock, when the torches dropped back into the night, knew no bounds. And all the while, amid this licentiousness, muffled or in brazen outcry, the line asleep or cringing, whispering or ribald, waited stolidly for the dawn.

Shortly after three, Javogues and his body-guard quitted the cabaret to make the rounds. A single torch held aloft by Boudgoust lit up the huddled queue. They passed down the line, Jambony and Cramoisin embracing the women, Javogues compelling all to cry "Vive la Nation!" and "A bas les Indulgents!" As luck would have it, Cramoisin perceived the face of Geneviève, which, in her curiosity, she momentarily displayed.

The drunkard flung himself forward and seized her in his arms. She defended herself furiously, averting her face, resisting all his efforts to drag her into the street; until Cramoisin, getting his arm around her waist, wrenched her forth screaming in her terror:

"Citoyen Javogues, Citoyen Javogues, protect me! Don't let him take me, Citoyen Javogues!"

Javogues, recognizing the voice, ran up.

"Who've you got there?"

"Don't you see I've got a woman?" Cramoisin said surlily. He added an obscenity that caused the girl, in despair, to exclaim:

"Oh, Citoyen Javogues, save me, save me!"

"None of that," Javogues cried angrily. "Let her go."

As the drunken Cramoisin started to protest, with a blow of his fist he knocked him down. Geneviève, carried down in the fall, flung herself at the feet of Javogues, grasping his knees.

"Thanks, thanks," she cried hysterically. "Citoyen, you are good, you are kind!"

Then fearing to become too prominent, she hurried to her place, enveloping her head with a shawl and crouching back into the friendly obscurity.

Cramoisin, whimpering, disappeared; Javogues, Boudgoust, and Jambony reeled away. Fatigue stilled even the noisiest. The night was achieved in sleep.

Toward six the line roused itself, as two inspectors of the municipality arrived to preside over the distribution of the bread. The doors were opened and the frantic rush began, those in the rear crowding forward with frenzied inquiries, which changed into the familiar shrieks of despair when the doors were closed with a third of the line unserved.

Geneviève, who had received her maximum of bread among the last, avoided the outstretched hands of the unsuccessful and escaped up the street, to where la Mère Corniche, at her post, exacted a tithe from each lodger. Dropping her tribute in the basket, she was hastening on when the concierge retained her with the cry:

"The Citoyen Javogues wants you."

Thinking that it was to fetch water from the Seine, the girl sought her bucket and hastened to the room of the Marseillais. At the sight of the bucket, Javogues frowned and asked:

"What are you doing with that?"

"Don't you want me to fetch water?"

"No."

"Ah."

"Leave the bucket in the corner."

Geneviève obeyed. Javogues shut the door, returned, and frowned again as he saw that she was trembling.

"What is the matter?" he said roughly. "Why do you tremble?"

She shook her head.

"Are you afraid of me?" he said, advancing.

"Oh, no."

"Then what is it?"

"I'm glad—that's all."

"True?"

All at once the girl, flinging herself at his feet, caught his hands and cried:

"I love you, I love you, I love you!"

"What, me!" Javogues cried, amazed, retreating a step. "You love me!"

"I adore you. I think of nothing but you. You are my god!"

"There is no God!"

"Yes, when one loves."

"Then you love me—it's true?" he said, raising her to her feet. "Why do you love me?"

"Why?" She drew a long breath. "You are so big, so heroic!"

Javogues fell back into a chair, repeating:

"Extraordinary! I don't understand."

She threw herself into his arms with the movement of a child, and, without seeking to conceal her thoughts, repeated a hundred caresses while he continued to mumble stupidly:

"Extraordinary! Extraordinary!"

Finally her emotion penetrated him. He took her in his hands and held her from him, she coloring with pleasure at this show of force, which came to her as a caress.

Suddenly a tremor ran through his immense body, an upheaval out of which came something gentle and softened. He continued to hold her before him, without shifting the glance that plunged into her eyes, while the girl, turning in his grasp, repeated, "Let me go!" for, child that she was, she divined what was passing in him.

"But why," he repeated stupidly—"why do you love me? I don't understand. No other woman ever has."

"Because you are so heroic. All the others understand nothing of poverty and sorrow. You—you understand. You give hope to such as I. When I hear you speak those sublime thoughts, my heart swells. You too have suffered; you know the abyss." She added, not without elation: "I loved you from the first day. I never thought you'd notice me."

"It's true—really true, then—what you say to me?"

For all answer she looked at him and smiled.

"It's curious. I don't understand it," he said at last. "But I believe I'm beginning to love you."

Then, without quite knowing why, she lowered her eyes.

IV

SIMON LAJOIE

The inhabitants of the Rue Maugout, astounded by the sight of Geneviève arm in arm with the overshadowing Javogues, had not recovered from the shock of this evidence of human feeling in their tyrant when the next day brought them a further surprise.

Toward five in the afternoon Dossonville, with the evident purpose of impressing his enemies by a new accession of strength, made his appearance, with a body-guard of two. The onlookers, enjoying the amazement of the Marseillais, were yet themselves astonished and perplexed at the incongruity of the new reinforcement.

One, short and contracted, gave the impression that by some mysterious settling his head had shrunk on his shoulders, his shoulders had moved toward his waist, and by this gradual process his whole body had been telescoped into his legs. A huge, flattened nose, or rather beak, imposed itself upon the yellowish, parched face and empty cheeks, while from two slits under the overhanging brows, the half-hidden eyes, without deviating from their forward direction, absorbed the outer world.

His companion, in contrast to the dragging gait of his fellow, moved in short steps, picking up his feet. The sharp nose, set as close as is possible to the perpendicular, pointed the way to the head, which, set forward on the craning neck, seemed in turn to be running ahead of the frail body.

Dossonville, with his loose amble and important tilt of head, gave the cabaret a "Salut!" and continued twirling in his hand for his only weapon an ivory baton a scant two feet in length. Behind him the watch-dogs paused, one grim, taciturn, and furtive, the other loquacious, florid of gesture, and loud, while, as a cur at the approach of a strange dog draws himself up snarling and apprehensive, Javogues and the three half started from their chairs.

Satisfied with the discomfiture of the Terrorists, Dossonville led his followers to the Place de la Revolution, where he found the execution over and the crowd, with a scattering hand-clap, dispersing.

On the terraces of the Tuileries a few spectators still lingered curiously, looking down on the scaffold that violently interrupted the peaceful vista of the woods beyond. Threading his way through the widening network of women, soldiers, spies, muscadins, and laborers, Dossonville perceived Louison, who, having at last quitted the environment of the scaffold, was returning toward the Cabaret de la Guillotine to dispose of her cockades.

"Well, Louison," he cried, "you have a bored air! It was stupid this afternoon, then? The show did not interest?"

"Nothing but a priest to-day—all priests die in the same way," she answered. "However, yesterday it was better. They guillotined twin brothers. That was something out of the ordinary." She added thoughtfully: "It's curious how alike men are on the scaffold."

All at once she perceived the two who had halted obediently at a distance of twenty paces. Dossonville, when her glance had traveled from them to him, and back and forth, in amazement and inquiry, opened his wide mouth and said with pride, indicating them with a flourish:

"Aren't they darlings, though? My assistants, my lambs, my watch-dogs!"

Louison, seized with a sudden, mad laughter, found a moment to say:

"Where, please, did you find such a pair of cutthroats?"

"From the galleys."

"And you trust them?"

"Do you think I'd trust an honest man?" Dossonville exclaimed, with a laugh that left the girl in doubt as to his seriousness. "What is an honest man? A man who has not been sufficiently tempted. Give me the rogue every time. Depend on no man until he is a rogue—a rogue you hold, by his past. With an honest man you are at the mercy of his future." He again designated his assistants. "A word from me would send them to the guillotine. That is the only way to insure tranquillity."

"That's a new theory," Louison exclaimed, much amused. "And there is sense in it. What do you call them, your trusty rogues?"

"You see the short one with the borrowed legs?" Dossonville answered proudly. "I call him Le Corbeau, from his beak and blinking eyes. I picked him up in the Cour des Miracles, ex-beggar, ex-cripple, ex-thief, hidden in a cellar. I offered him protection from arrest in return for services. He accepted; I supplied a coat and a hat, and there he is.

"The other who stands there shaking in the wind is Sans-Chagrin, ex-priest, recanted and reformed. On the subject of our bargain I say nothing, only that I dispose of his neck as easily as mine." Dismissing them by a signal, he took Louison's arm. "Now for us. What do you say to a drop of something in the Rue de Bourgogne?"

"I say, on to the Rue de Bourgogne!"

At the scaffold they made a detour to escape the contact of blood, which made the place abhorrent and carried on the shoes of those who passed in front of the scaffold the red trail for blocks about.

Louison, as they went, was crying her cockades, when suddenly they were aware of a shrinking and a widening in the crowd, and looking up, perceived Sanson, the executioner, and his sons advancing, impassive to all demonstrations. Seized with a mad desire, the girl stepped toward them, crying:

"A cockade, Citoyen Sanson, a red cockade!"

The next moment Dossonville had jerked her away.

"Mordieu, Louison!" he cried angrily. "Why did you do that?"

"Why not?" she said, laughing. "The Revolution has abolished prejudices!"

"It cannot change human nature," he retorted. "You can call him Executor of Public Judgments, Avenger of the Nation, he is always the executioner." He added frankly, "Louison, ma belle, there are really moments when you are not human. At an execution you are like granite!"

"Very well, do not notice me."

"That's easy to say," he grumbled. "Besides, I'm curious."

"Indeed."

"Barabant has been telling me about that extraordinary mother of yours."

"Barabant?" Louison said uneasily. "He doesn't like me."

"I like nothing so well as a mystery," Dossonville continued enthusiastically. "I have three plans already to make her speak."

"Five would do no good."

"Why not?"

"She has left for the provinces."

"Diable!"

"Besides, I do not care to be mysterious," she said impatiently, "and I do not like to be thought strange."

"Speak no more of it," said Dossonville, though inwardly relinquishing nothing of his purpose. "In future I'll consider you only as a commonplace woman."

Louison regarded him maliciously.

"Determine that for yourself."

"Satané de femme!" he exclaimed. "I'll be very careful what I determine. Louison, you are not a woman who can be loved comfortably. I tell it to you frankly. The place seems good; let us sit down."

Several nights later, Dossonville, resting on his rounds, was seated at a table in front of the Café de Valmy, in the Quartier des Bonnes Nouvelles. The bells had announced the midnight; from the intersections of the square the streets yawned to him out of the impenetrable darkness.For once Dossonville abandoned himself to reverie—a mood evoked by the memory of Louison. Since his encounter, the mystery of her birth had continually teased his imagination. The terror of la Mère Baudrier when Louison had announced the discovery of her father, and again the mother's strange rendezvous in the Square de la Bastille, suggested such an unusual solution, without offering a clue, that his mind returned again and again to the problem.

In another corner, Sans-Chagrin, late in his cups, disputed with the host upon the value of religion, while Le Corbeau, who by his silence gained the majority of the decanter, pretended indifference to the discussion.

"I know what I say," Sans-Chagrin was declaiming. "Religion is a farce and the Assembly will do well to abolish it!"

"That is not so certain," objected the listener.

"It will come."

"Perhaps— "

"Religion will be abolished! I know what I'm saying. I was a priest myself."

"Come, now!"

"True. They expelled me. And why? Why? Tell me that."

"Out with it."

"For instituting reforms. Religion is a farce!"

A woman, scenting a story, issued from the door, and leaning on the shoulder of her husband, said:

"Come, Citoyen Sans-Chagrin, tell us of that."

"I reformed the confessional," Sans-Chagrin began querulously. "Aye, and it needed it, too. Every day and every hour I had to be disturbed for a confession. I said to myself, if there's so much wickedness, it's because the confessional isn't rigid enough. That's logical, isn't it?"

"And what did you do?"

"Only this. I announced that, in future, to avert confusion and to better impress the penitent with his crime, I would hear confessions thus:

"On Monday, all the liars.

"On Tuesday, all the misers.

"On Wednesday, all the slanderers.

"On Thursday, all the thieves.

"On Friday, all the libertines.

"On Saturday, all women who lead bad lives."

His listeners burst out laughing, while the woman said, "And no one came?"

"No one came!" Sans-Chagrin repeated indignantly. "No one came! And the Church, instead of adopting the reform, expelled me. They said I wanted to be rid of confessions. What a farce, my friends, what a mockery!" He spread out his arms in appeal to their judgment, slapped his chest three times, and fell back loosely in his chair, exclaiming, "Oh, oh, oh!"

Dossonville, who had lent a moment's amused attention to this farcical recital, rose and returned to the march, a manœuver which caused Sans-Chagrin and Le Corbeau to choke in their haste to empty the decanter.

They had gone but a short distance when Dossonville's ear caught the slight rasp of a window opening overhead. Flattening himself against the wall, he covered his lantern with his cloak, with a whispered caution to his followers as the window continued to give forth its low complaint. There was a minute's silence, and then it was drawn shut, and the slight click of a bolt was heard.

Hearing nothing further, Dossonville finally resumed his walk, but at the next corner some one muffled in a cloak fell into his arms.

The man, with a dozen pardons, sought to make a detour, but Dossonville's long arm, shooting out, grasped his shoulder.

"Not so fast, citoyen. There's a little formality we must not forget. Name and errand?"

The stranger, perceiving him neither to be surrounded with pistols and knives nor to have a very threatening air, answered:

"Citoyen Clappier, Section des Bonnes Nouvelles. I am hurrying to seek a doctor."

"Show your card of citizenship, and pass."

"The devil!" the man exclaimed, after a show of searching in his pockets. "I forgot to take it out of the coat I wore this morning."

"Really, citoyen, you are in bad luck," Dossonville replied. "I shall be forced to accompany you." He summoned Sans-Chagrin and Le Corbeau out of the shadow, and gave him into their charge, with a "Lead the way!" Then he dropped behind, murmuring, "Provided one does not enter that doctor's by the window."

They journeyed silently for several minutes, until suddenly the three ahead halted, and Sans-Chagrin, returning, said:

"The citoyen wishes to speak with you."

Dossonville, who had expected this dénouement, had the prisoner brought to him.

"Well, citoyen, what is it?"

"Citoyen, I ask a moment's private conversation."

"With me?"

"With you alone."

"It is important, then?"

"Very."

"Good!"

Perceiving that their walk had brought them near to their starting-point, Dossonville led the way to the Café de Valmy, passing through which, he entered a small room, giving orders to his body-guard to remain without. Then shutting the door, he straddled a chair, rested his arms on the back, and with a smile awaited the opening.

"Citoyen Dossonville—" the man began.

"What! You know me?"

"For a long time."

"Indeed!" Dossonville exclaimed, astounded and nonplussed by this knowledge.

"Citoyen Dossonville," the man continued, "I ask of you one promise. If I convince you of my patriotism and my citizenship, will you guard my secret? I ask you as a man of honor."

Dossonville inclined his head.

"Agreed. I promise to keep the secret, on condition that you convince me of your patriotism—that is, by showing me your true card of citizenship."

"That will not be necessary."

Throwing back his cloak, he removed a wig and mustaches, discovering to Dossonville the features of Sanson, the executioner.

"Do you recognize me?"

At this sinister figure, Dossonville recoiled with a movement beyond his control, but recovering, he exclaimed:

"Pardon."

"It is nothing," Sanson answered flatly. "I am used to it."

"Pardon. What surprises me is this," said Dossonville, hiding his own emotion. "That you who have been imprisoned for suspected Royalist interests should expose yourself to suspicion for any cause."

"Have you not guessed my errand?" Sanson said, with a frown.

"Until you disclosed your identity, yes," Dossonville retorted sharply. "But such adventures do not necessitate a disguise at one o'clock in the night. Citoyen Sanson, had I met you otherwise, I should have nothing to say; but disguised and under a false name is different. I shall have to report it."

Sanson reseated himself.

"For thirty years I have assumed disguises and another name. Do you need to be told the reason? You yourself gave it but a moment ago,"—he paused,—"when you recoiled."

"I do not understand," Dossonville said coldly, resolved to push him to the end. "Explain fully. If I am to risk myself thus, I must know all."

"What you cannot understand—you cannot understand!" Sanson broke out irritably, while his eyes sought the face of his captor, doubting the sincerity of the objection. The movement of anger passed; recognizing the peril of his position, he extended his hand and began in a flat, monotonous voice:

"Citoyen Dossonville, it is disagreeable, but I cannot make conditions. Citoyen, I need not tell you that we have always lived apart from society. As far back as we know, every male of our family, from father to son, has been of the same profession. All others are barred to us. Three have tried to bury themselves in the outer world. They were driven back. Every woman has married an executioner, every man a daughter of one. The office I hold was given Charles Sanson in the year 1688. My grandfather, my father, and myself have inherited it. It will descend from son to son, whether King or Republic succeeds. Nothing will ever change that!"

He paused a moment in distaste before continuing:

"When we appear in public, a space is opened to us. We pass in any crowd without touching a shoulder. The poor, to whom we give alms, recoil before our touch. The woman who would speak to us would be cast out, as a pariah. But no woman, recognizing us, would wish to speak to us. We had hoped the Revolution would free us from the universal prejudice—vain hope!" Then, as though he had said enough, he broke off acridly: "And yet you cannot understand why I disguise myself?"

Dossonville, lost in the strange vista which the recital had opened to his imagination, did not at once reply.

"And you keep the secret from every one?" he asked at last.

Sanson, perceiving the question was one of personal curiosity, replied curtly:

"I have said that no woman knowing us has ever spoken to us. I should have said, except one." He smiled, if the curling of his lips could be called a smile. "A bouquetière who was with you one day on the Place de la Revolution."

"The story is on your word alone," Dossonville said, irritated by this allusion. "It lacks evidence."

"Then you do not remember me?" Sanson said.

Dossonville, startled at the turn, for a moment lost his self-possession as he strove to penetrate the allusion.

"Citoyen Dossonville, can you recall the Café Procopé about twenty years ago, and a certain Simon Lajoie who sometimes played a game of checkers with you in the evening, and who inspired you with a great deal of curiosity?"

"Perfectly," Dossonville replied, staring at him in perplexity.

"Do you remember that his visits ceased the day your interest prompted you to follow him from the café?"

"What!" Dossonville cried, rising, and extending his hand in question. "It was—?"

"It was I."

"Tonnerre de Dieu!"

And falling back, he stared in empty, stupid amazement.

"Are you convinced?"

"I am."

"I hold your promise?"

"Yes."

Sanson readjusted his disguise, while Dossonville sought some pretext to retain him and make him talk.

"Citoyen, one question."

"Well, what?"

"I should like to know," Dossonville said, "does the popular hatred affect you?"

Sanson frowned, hesitated, and then answered in two words eloquent with meaning:

"Not now."

Then, without offering his hand, he turned, saying peremptorily:

"Adieu!"

Sans-Chagrin and Le Corbeau, who would not have allowed the devil himself to pass without an order, brought him back. Then Dossonville, springing to his feet, cried:

"Set the Citoyen Clappier free! The Citoyen Clappier is an industrious patriot!"

V

CRAMOISIN PLOTS AGAINST NICOLE

Cramoisin, since the day of his humiliation before Geneviève, had vented his spite on Barabant, seeking thus his vengeance on Nicole. Several times, in measure as the trial of the Girondins neared its end and it became evident that their condemnation was inevitable, he had sounded Javogues on the score of Barabant, only to be repulsed with decided negatives. But each defeat, by feeding fuel to his hatred, only increased his determination. Convinced, at length, that nothing could be accomplished for the present through Javogues, he had recourse to la Mère Corniche, hoping to find in her an ally.

The shrewd little woman was not long in perceiving his intention. So having sufficiently enjoyed his timid skirmishes, she summoned him to her early one morning, after the distribution of bread, and said point-blank:

"Out with it. What do you want to say to me?"

The face of Cramoisin artfully showed surprise.

"Come, old fellow, let us understand each other. You hate Barabant, eh?"

"Barabant is a Girondin," Cramoisin ventured, and then, deceived by her mood, he plunged on: "He is a Moderate, a contre-Révolutionnaire. He is against Robespierre and the Jacobins."

"Not a bit," la Mère Corniche interrupted, having now entrapped him. "He is a follower of the great Marat!"

"Who are you telling that to!" Cramoisin cried contemptuously.

"Hark, old fellow, no airs with me," the concierge retorted sharply. "The Citoyen Barabant came here with a letter to Marat. I saw it. As for you, I know what you're after, my fine patriot,—your eyes are on the girl!"

Cramoisin, now thoroughly alarmed, sought only to retreat.

"Never in the world," he cried indignantly. "Come, mother, you mustn't wrong a fellow-patriot. I bear no hatred to Barabant. I thought him a

Girondin; he is always with that cursed Goursac. But if you say he's not, I'm glad to hear it."

"Oui dà, of course you are! You look it," she retorted scornfully. "Come, get out of my way; leave me in peace, old hypocrite. You don't fool me an instant. Be off!"

Cramoisin escaped to the cabaret; la Mère Corniche, mumbling to herself, settled back in her chair; as the distribution of bread ended, the lodgers issued forth with buckets, to get water from the Seine. Resolved to put Barabant on his guard, she had stopped him, when, to her delight, she perceived Cramoisin disappearing into the cabaret in such pitiful fright that she made a pretext and allowed Barabant to depart, resolved to prolong for a few days the agony of the terrified bully.

She began the round of inspection which, at the expense of her strength, she never failed to accomplish each morning. She passed through the empty rooms, scenting and prying, fumbling among papers and garments, viewing one room with a glance, ransacking another for the taint of aristocracy or the earmarks of a traitor.

Arrived on Barabant's landing, she made a satisfied, careless survey of the room, entering to rest from her labors. On a chair, in a state of mending, was the blue redingote the young fellow had worn on his arrival. More from habit than from suspicion, she ran her fingers through the pockets, and drew out the paper they encountered. It was the envelop addressed to Jean Paul Marat.

She regarded it stupidly, contracting her brows, seeking an explanation, before, with a cry, she tore it open. A sheet, empty and white, slipped to the floor. La Mère Corniche, overcome by the evidence of the duplicity, fell back against the wall.

It was five minutes before she could realize how she had been duped. Then from the miser, and the devotee of Marat, a long howl of rage broke forth, and clutching the letter, she fell from the landing, rather than descended the stairs, gained her room, and abandoned herself to the transports of her rage.

A half-hour later she hobbled forth, white but controlled, to the entrance, where, perceiving Cramoisin, she cried with a furious gesture:

"Come here."

At this angry summons the Terrorist would have slunk away had not la Mère Corniche cut off his escape, crying:

"Cramoisin, idiot, imbecile, come here!"

She seized him, trembling at her tone, and impelled him into the entrance, exclaiming:

"You hate Barabant? Answer me, you hate him!"

"I swear—" he began, when she cut him short: "Fool, I despise him! Do you hear me? I despise him!"

While Cramoisin remained, with gaping mouth, incapable of words, the old woman poured out her reviling. At last he asked, in amazement:

"What do you want of me?"

"I want your help to destroy him."

"Then why didn't you say so at first?"

Fearing to be forced into explanations, she abated her fury and more calmly demanded:

"You have a plan; what is it?"

"It's true?" Cramoisin said, still unconvinced. "You'll join me?"

"I swear it."

"We can't convince Javogues," Cramoisin began, "unless we can make Nicole betray him."

"But how?"

"Jealousy."

"Jealousy? Is there cause? Do you know anything?"

"What is necessary we can invent."

"She won't believe it."

"She'll believe it when she hears it from three persons," Cramoisin said, ruffling up his nose and sneering. "A woman'll believe anything three persons tell her. With Boudgoust and Jambony, we are four."

"Is that your plan?" she cried, in disappointment. "It's stupid, impossible!"

Cramoisin continued to argue with her its merits; she accorded it a grunt, then a shake of the head, and finally said:

"Well, yes; it may do. We can try."

"It's agreed, then. We must excite her suspicions,—but nothing definite."

"What, are you going to give me instructions!" la Mère Corniche cried irately. "As though I couldn't handle a woman!"

"Touch hands, then; it's agreed?"

"Yes."

"You must speak the first word," he said hurriedly. "It will be better." Shutting off a reply, he departed, leaving the concierge scowling and angry.

"Oui dà, I'll speak the first word, old schemer. He doesn't want the woman to lay it to him, the toad!"

The next morning, as Nicole was leaving for the flower-market, la Mère Corniche called to her."Eh, Nicole, stop a moment." The girl, who feared her, approached reluctantly.

"You're going to the market?"

"Yes."

"To-morrow is Sunday. I want to put some flowers on the tomb of Marat. See what is going cheap this morning and tell me."

"Is that all?"

"You must stop from time to time to give me news," continued la Mère Corniche, taking her hand.

"You know as much as I do."

"You sell flowers every day?"

"Yes."

"Your man doesn't earn enough, then?"

"With the price of food where it is one can't earn too much."

"You are happy?" the old woman asked brusquely.

"Why do you ask that?" Nicole replied, resenting the question.

"There, don't get angry. You may have friends you don't know of." She released her hand, adding: "If you suspect nothing, I'll say no more."

Penetrating readily the stratagem, Nicole laughed over the encounter, and, perceiving the bald attempt to rouse her jealousy, she dismissed the conversation contemptuously from her mind.

Toward midday, however, the insinuation returned, and forgetting her first attitude, she suffered a little at the very shadow of what her imagination could conjure up. She ended by again laughing at her simplicity, nor did her mind recur again to the thought during the day.

That evening, as she passed in front of the Prêtre Pendu, she encountered Cramoisin, who watched her from the corners of his eyes, rubbing his splayed thumb over his lip in such an ironical fashion that she stopped and demanded impatiently:

"Well, what is it? I seem to amuse you."

"Eh, perhaps you do."

"Come, what do you mean by such looks!"

Then rising, he looked her a moment in countenance, and replied:

"Nicole, they told me you were clever."

"Well, what does that mean?"

"It means that you are either very stupid," he said curtly, "or very blind."

Nicole mounted the steps in perplexity, arresting her journey at every landing to ask herself anxiously what he could have meant. In her room she remained blankly at the window, forgetting the meal she had to prepare. Several times she passed her hand across her forehead, as though to rout the unquiet thoughts, but always returned to the same reverie. The church bell ringing five aroused her, and, ashamed to have yielded to such doubts, she said angrily:

"Come, I'm an idiot! I'll tell the whole affair to Barabant when he returns and we will laugh at it together."

Yet when he entered, her resolution forgotten, she rose quickly, and taking him by the arms, looked anxiously in his face.

"What is the matter with you?" he asked. "Why do you look at me so curiously?"

"I was afraid you would do something rash," she said evasively. "What—what of the Girondins?"

"It is hopeless. To-morrow they may be condemned." But only half satisfied, he returned to the question. "Was that all you wanted to know? You looked at me very queerly."

"I don't doubt it," she said quickly. "Ah, Barabant, I am so afraid that you will compromise yourself with them."

"I must decide—and you would not have me a coward, Nicole?"

She defended her position, she repeated the old arguments, she tried to win him from the thought of sacrifice; but of what had happened during the day she said not a word.

"It is getting late," she exclaimed finally. "I must get into line."

"Let me take the whole night," he pleaded; "you are tired."

"No, no. Not at all."

She hurried below, furious at herself for having betrayed to him her unrest, but when she remembered how instantly he had noticed the strangeness of her look, she could not help thinking that a little suspicious.

The next morning she prepared to meet the concierge with a new defiance, but la Mère Corniche did not even raise her head. Cramoisin, to her relief, was absent; only Boudgoust and Jambony were lounging in front of the cabaret. She cast a furtive glance in their direction; they were laughing boisterously.

"They are laughing at me," she thought, all her doubts returning.

She passed a miserable morning, tortured by the fears that now seemed always to have been with her. Unable to bear the tumult within her breast, she determined to recount all to Barabant. If anything existed, she must know it definitely.

Unfortunately, the arrival of Dossonville, who joined them at lunch on the boulevards, prevented the confidence, and during the meal another suggestion added to her suffering. Barabant, in speaking of Dossonville's interest in Louison, expressed his astonishment at the attraction, ending peremptorily:

"As for me,—she repels me."

He had put considerable warmth into his criticism; that and the simple declaration of antagonism made havoc in the imagination of Nicole. She thought the opinion obviously unnecessary. She asked herself if he really were interested in Louison, whom she had always feared, would he not have said exactly what he had. But from logical inquiry she soon flew to conjecture and supposition, to weighing each word and action and seeking a hidden meaning. She thought no longer of confiding in Barabant, but held herself on her guard.

She was not convinced—she but half believed; yet she returned sadly. Her dream was over. Whatever might come, the first breath of jealousy had entered her heart, and, rightly or wrongly, she knew that her tranquillity had departed forever.

VI

BARABANT HESITATES

The Place de la Revolution was choked with the multitude come to witness the end of the Girondins. The populace, indifferent to the sight of two or three executions a day, gathered with common impulse to witness these men, long lifted above their heads, go down to their death in humiliation and disgrace. Many who hungered, cursed them in the need of some object to their hatred; others who feared them, in the savage joy of deliverance; but the mass hooted simply from the delight of seeing them fallen.

Toward one o'clock the procession of five carts, announced by all the tumults of the human voice, cut through the frenzied hordes, who from time to time fell back into silence, astonished at the demeanor of these men; who to insults addressed the crowds with cries of "Vive la République!" or joined in the chorus of the "Marseillaise."

The rumor had circulated that the body of Valazé, who had committed suicide the night before, was to be guillotined with the rest. In the last cart, indeed, the people discovered the corpse stretched among the living.

Arrived at the scaffold, the twenty descended; the one remained. A jailer, to win a laugh, propped up the corpse, crying:

"Hurry up—Valazé's waiting for you."

The crowd applauded with jeers and taunts. The Girondins meanwhile ranged themselves at the foot of the scaffold. When their number was complete, with one movement they embraced.

Several, turning toward the public, lifted up their arms and repeated the cry:

"Vive la République!"

Then, drawn up one against the other, giving front to the torrent of their enemies, forgetting even their individualities in the supreme moment, the condemned began the hymn of the Republic:

"Allons, enfants de la Patrie, Le jour de gloire est arrivé."

Every two minutes one of the fraternity left the ranks and ascended the ladder; but the chorus continued, uninterrupted either by the wild acclaim that greeted the appearance of each victim on the scaffold, or by the thundering shout that told of the severed head.

The chorus thinned to three, to two, to one. The last, without ceasing the chant, mounted to the platform; only the knife interrupted the song.

Then, as far as the eye could travel, over the immense square, over the packed bridges and distant, darkened streets, like an immense flight of released birds there appeared above the crowd the red flutter of agitated liberty-caps. The populace, who believed that from out this hecatomb would come relief from famine, bread and meat to save them, shouted frantically. They also shouted who feared to be silent. The uproar continued for ten minutes before the mass disintegrated.

As Goursac, with heavy heart yielding to the impulse of the crowd, sought his friends, from whom he had separated for the sake of prudence, a touch on his arm checked his progress. To his surprise, he encountered the solemn face of Le Corbeau.

"What do you wish?"

"To talk with you," the lips answered, but the eyes said, "You are under arrest."

"I was expecting it," he replied calmly, "but not from this quarter." He sought his friends, but the movement of the crowd had divided them. "After all, it is better so," he said to himself; "farewell would be equivalent to a warrant." He turned to his captor: "Where are you taking me?"

Le Corbeau, without change of feature, ignored the question and kept the silence. Resigning himself to the situation, Goursac allowed himself to be conducted with the crowd; but all at once, as they entered the Rue Antoine, he felt an impress on his other arm and another voice saying:

"This way."

This time he perceived Sans-Chagrin, who, without other recognition, drew him off the thoroughfare. They penetrated abruptly into a nest of narrow streets, winding and twisting in a manner that left him completely in doubt as to their direction. But as their general progress seemed to be leading them toward the Cour des Miracles, that cesspool of beggars, thieves, and cutthroats, he began to fear that this capture had some other design in view than his imprisonment.

He quitted his attitude of indifference and summoned all his faculties to find a reason for this strange course. Observing that at each corner they turned his captors were forcing him into a wider circle, the conviction grew in him that they took this subterfuge to see if they were followed. At the next corner he himself turned—without success. But at the third attempt he distinguished, lurking behind, the three incongruous figures of Cramoisin, Boudgoust, and Jambony!

Then no longer doubting that he was being led to his death, he resolved that no weakness of his should add to the satisfaction of his enemies.

But at this moment, as for the twentieth time they turned a corner, he was seized under the arms and rushed at a run down an alley. Through an entrance in the end he was propelled through courts, hallways, and passages innumerable, and suddenly emerged into a distant street.

Goursac, now utterly at a loss, made no resistance to this sudden doubling. Only when, after a few anxious blocks, he perceived that they were no longer followed, he again sought to enter into conversation with Sans-Chagrin, to be met by the same obstinate silence.

Their attitude increased his perplexity, which was now augmented by their totally ignoring the direction of the prisons and striking out for the barriers of the city. Not until the Barrière du Trône Renversé itself was in sight did his captors stop. Entering an inn, they gave a sign of recognition to the host, passed down a hallway, and pushed their prisoner into a large room, where he found himself in the presence of Dossonville. At the sight of the agent de sûreté, Goursac drew himself up haughtily.

"So, Citoyen Dossonville, you turn with the wind," he said. "I did not suspect your versatility."

"Heavens, my dear Goursac, yes!" cried Dossonville. "But if I go with the wind, I hope to be of some use to those who oppose it." He pointed to the table. "That package will interest you."

"There is some mistake," Goursac said, as he scanned the document. "This is a passport for the Citoyen Jacques Monestier."

"Well, what of that—Citoyen Monestier?"

Goursac looked at the passport, and from it to the laughing countenance of Dossonville.

"Then it was to save me," he said slowly, "that you had me arrested?"

"Parbleu! You are waking up!"

With one bound, Goursac caught Dossonville in his arms.

"Pardon, pardon! What a fool I am!" he cried. "My noble, my generous friend! Head of an ass that I have on my shoulders! You risk your life for mine! Thanks, thanks; a thousand times, thanks!"

"Good!" Dossonville broke in. "We understand each other now. We have but little time; listen to me." He stopped the other in the torrent of his protestations. "Only remember this, that if a weather-vane turns to every breeze, it relinquishes its base not a jot, not even to the hurricane. I find therein a great moral." He dismissed the thought with a gesture. "Now for you. You must pass the gates immediately. When Javogues discovers your escape, he may give orders to watch all the gates. See here, my friend—you must listen to me."

Goursac was paying not the slightest attention. Seated on a chair, his face aglow, he regarded Dossonville with almost adoration, while from time to time his emotion exploded in words.

"Dossonville, you are heroic! You are sublime! Oh, if I only could acquaint the world with such an action! Magnificent! Heroic! Heroic, I tell you!"

Dossonville, perceiving his joy, thought to himself, "Yes, heroism before death is all very well, but how the hope of life transforms a man!" Aloud he continued, "Take the passport and hurry."

Then Goursac, retreating a step, said but one word:

"No!"

But in the word, with the flash of his eye, with the toss of his head, with the resolution of his lips, there was the eloquence of an oration.

This time it was Dossonville who was overcome with astonishment.

"You are mad!" he exclaimed, seizing him by the lapel. "If you return, it is to the guillotine."

"So be it!"

"Reflect."

"I have. Had I wished to save myself, I should have done so long ago."

"Then you seek death?"

"I will not fly from the scum," Goursac said proudly. "I am a Girondin and a Frenchman. When I can no longer live as a Girondin, I am ready to die as a Frenchman. Liberty? What do you offer me? Exile and a daily cringing from discovery, a miserable, hunted existence in the mud and rain? No!" He took a step forward and grasped his hand. "For what you have risked for me accept my benediction; may it bring good luck."

"At least, take the passport," said Dossonville, desperately, holding it out to him, "so that if you change your mind — "

"So that I may not change my mind — there."

With a rapid motion Goursac tore the passport in two, embraced Dossonville, and went out. Before the Prêtre Pendu, Cramoisin, Boudgoust, and Jambony, more dead than alive, hung their heads in terror while Javogues, like a wounded bull, strode backward and forward before them, filling the air with his imprecations.

"Come, you lie, one and all. You lie, Cramoisin; you lie, Boudgoust; you lie, Jambony. He has bought you with gold! You have sold yourselves!"

"I swear they escaped us through some passage!" Boudgoust cried.

"We searched an hour," Cramoisin put in.

"Shut up!"

Javogues seized him furiously by the shoulders, and approaching his gleaming eyes as though to force the truth from his face, he shouted:

"You lie! You lie! I see you lie!"

Abandoning him, he seized Jambony, shaking him like a whip; but as he opened his mouth to roar forth fresh denunciations, he stopped short and dropped the cub in amazement. At the same moment a murmur ran throughout the crowd, which, parting, disclosed the approaching figure of Goursac.

The Girondin perceived his enemies by the same motion of the crowd; but without faltering, he continued nodding to the acquaintances who now shrank before him.

He had passed the cabaret and was almost at the entrance of No. 38 before Javogues could recover. Then, with a roar, he cried:

"Stop!"

Goursac wheeled, returned, and halted.

"What do you wish of me?"

Javogues, brought thus to the long-desired moment, folded his arms and said brutally:

"You do not rejoice, citoyen, at the death of traitors."

"I always rejoice at the death of traitors."

"You rejoice to-day, then?"

"I grieve."

He pronounced the words sadly.

"You are against the Revolution. Say it."

"I believe the Revolution is so great that its ideas can survive even the massacre that you assassins have begun." Then interrupting the catechism disdainfully, he said: "Enough. I should never have survived this day. Arrest me."

Javogues, too overcome with rage for utterance, consigned him with a furious gesture to his body-guard. From all sides went up a shout of hatred and anger. Children and women crowded about, vying with one another to insult the prisoner; men shook their fists in his face and hooted. Amid curses and raillery, the Girondin walked with collected steps, looking into the ranks of his foes with steady eyes.

They had gone but a block when they encountered Nicole and Barabant. At the sight of Goursac in custody, surrounded by the snarling pack, the two, obeying only their generous impulses, sprang forward with outstretched hands:

"What, you, my friend!" Nicole cried, in astonishment and sorrow. "They have arrested you!"

"No, they are liberating me," he answered, with a smile. He pressed their hands. "Adieu, Nicole; adieu, Barabant; and thanks."

But suddenly the voice of la Mère Corniche rose shrilly:

"He is the friend of the Girondin. He is contre-révolutionnaire. Arrest the man Barabant!"

Cramoisin took up the cry.

"He who pities an enemy of the Nation is a traitor. Arrest him!"

Boudgoust and Jambony, joining in, shouted:

"Arrest him! Arrest him!"

In the abject crowd, terrified by these four men, a murmur, a muttering, a rumble, circulated, which it waited to convert into either protest or approval as Javogues should pronounce.

As the Marseillais unwillingly approached, Nicole, dragging Barabant back, whispered in his ear that eternal cry of woman:

"Save thyself. Thy life belongs to me."

"Citoyen Barabant," Javogues said sternly, "did you greet this man as a Girondin?"

"I greeted him," Barabant said slowly, "as a man who has done me kindnesses in the past."

Before this allusion to his own indebtedness Javogues hesitated, but the cries of the crowd urged him on.

"He evades the question!"

"He's a Girondin!"

"Ask him if he's a Girondin!"

The last cry, from la Mère Corniche, imposed itself above the rest.

"Citoyen Barabant," Javogues asked, "are you a Girondin?"

As Barabant hesitated, Nicole sought the glance of Goursac, invoking his aid. The Girondin, who saw no one but her, perceiving her motive, thought bitterly: "I die, and she cannot spare me a look of pity!"

The crowd was clamoring.

"He hesitates!"

"He refuses!"

"Arrest him!"

At their cries, Barabant decided.

"I am not a Girondin," he said.

A chorus of approval greeted the renunciation, but la Mère Corniche, not to be balked, cried:

"He is deceiving us!"

Those who wished to save him called to him: "Cry, Vive les Jacobins!"

Barabant, all escape denied him, shouted:

"Vive la Nation! Vive les Jacobins!"

Then, while la Mère Corniche and the three were silent in helpless rage, the crowd, which adored Barabant, surrounded him, slapping him on the shoulders, shaking his hand, congratulating him. With one accord the shout went up: "Vive Barabant!"

When the shouting died, Nicole heard the rasping voice of Goursac saying to his captors with triumphant sarcasm:

"I see no further need of delay; proceed."

VII

THE MADNESS OF JEALOUSY

The victory was to the woman, but it was a victory fraught with menace. Nicole understood her danger, but in her anxiety she adopted the wrong defense. On the stairway she infolded Barabant with her arm, seeking to communicate to his depressed body the gaiety and relief in hers, while with all the artifices of the woman who feels herself menaced she sought to belittle the importance of the scene, little realizing the deep wound to the pride of Barabant.

"It was for me you did it," she whispered. "You would not leave me. I alone understood."

He did not answer, and once in their room, fell into a chair, burying his head in his hands. Alarmed at his obstinate silence, Nicole, groping for the right attitude, began to reason, walking the floor in her earnestness.

"After all, mon ami, that is what the Terrorists want—to guillotine the Moderates. Goursac was foolish; he played into the hands of his enemies. You are wise. The duty of the Moderates is to keep silent, to preserve themselves for the good of the Nation. How can you serve the Nation without your head? The times will change, mon ami, and you'll be here to help set things aright."

"Oh, that voice," cried Barabant, "I hear it always."

"Mon ami, you are suffering!" she exclaimed. "I know. I understand."

She threw herself at his feet, trying to separate his hands, seeking to take his head upon her shoulder; but Barabant resisted, saying:

"No, Nicole, no; leave me to myself."

"Don't put me away," she begged. "You are suffering; let me share it."

He took her hands from his neck and compelled her to rise. She went to the window, twice turning to look at the dejected figure that remained unaware of her glances.

"I have made a blunder. Yes, I have made a blunder," she said to herself, pressing her hand against her lips to quell the rising sob. "He blames me."

The next morning she received another shock when he informed her that he wished to be alone all day.

"Then we don't lunch together?" she cried, frightened.

"Not to-day."

Not daring to contradict him, she let him go without a word.

"He blames me. He blames me," she told herself, until all at once, like a thunderclap, came the thought: "Or is it only a pretext?"

Her judgment tumbled before the suggestion, and on the moment she was surrounded by the old doubts. She hurried out, morbidly sensitive to the glances of the concierge, of the loiterers before the cabaret, of the bouquetières her comrades; seeing everywhere mocking glances or looks of sympathy. Despite Barabant's wish and her better judgment, she scoured his haunts with the one desire to know what he was doing.

After a day of agony spent in fruitless travel, she returned to their room, without a glimpse of Barabant. Having prepared the meal, she sat down before the fire to wait impatiently the hour of seven, when he would return. Beside her chair she placed a redingote of his and sewing-material. In the disorder of her mind all her naturalness had departed, and seeking everything with artifices, she wished him to come upon her as she watched their supper and busied herself with his wardrobe.

"That will soften his resentment, perhaps," she thought. "And that everything may be cheerful, I must be singing."

So, when later the stairs gave out the sounds of footsteps, she hurriedly possessed the mending, humming as she sewed; but the steps ceased two flights below. The redingote slipped from her hands, the song stopped, and, overcome with disappointment, she cried:

"Oh, mon Dieu, it is not he!"

When seven arrived and she began to be anxious, she consoled herself with the thought that the effect would be better if he found her waiting without complaint. A burning smell warned her that the dinner was spoiling. She removed the pots from the fire, placing them for warmth in the ashes, and, abandoning all thought of the picture she had imagined, went to the window, where she remained, pressing her hands against her temples, staring into the misty night.

At nine o'clock she returned into the middle of the room, and looking about at the scene of her happiness, she said with conviction:

"It is ended!"

Traveling ceaselessly back and forth like a panther, she cried: "Yes, yes, it is ended!" Still, as long as she repeated it, she continued to hope, and at each fancied creak she ran to the landing, leaning over to catch his first footfall. But when she returned, she still said:

"No, no; I knew it. It is ended—ended!"

At ten she ceased to repeat it,—she was convinced. She collapsed on the bed, brain and body incapable of effort, while the cruel minutes, in their inexorable procession, inflicted each a separate torture.

When midnight announced itself, the last thread of hope snapped within her. She bounded up, lit a candle, descended the flight, and entered the room, calling, "Goursac!"

She had forgotten the arrest. The fact appeared to her as an evil omen, presaging calamity.

In fear of the sepulchral stillness, she fled back, rushing in a panic to her room, where she gazed about helplessly, asking herself what she was to do. All at once, at the window, staring at her old room, she cried:

"If it is Louison!" And emitting an "Ah!" that had in it the note of murder, she passed out of the window.

The night was filled with fog, out of which descended the sharp sting of rain. She moved slowly, her body pressed to the roof, seeing with her fingers until the dormer-window struck against her foot. Once into Louison's room, she crept to the bed, stretching out her hand. It was empty.

"Oh! oh! oh!"

The cry was of something collapsing in her soul. Without returning to her room, she sped down the stairs, through the two courts, and into the street. In her unheeding rush, she turned to the right, missing Barabant, who was at the moment returning from the opposite direction.

When she could run no longer, she dropped into a walk until, recovering her breath, she broke again into a run. At the street corners the bracketed lanterns suffused the fog with a floating radiance that guided her over the glistening, slippery stones. The mist that threatened the world with a destiny of gloom, the rain that gathered on her eyelashes and weighted her hair, she welcomed as the fitting touch to her misery; but the chill abated not a jot of the fever in her veins. Out of the blurred night occasionally long lines of watchers emerged, crouching under shawls, hugging the walls to escape the rain. A dozen brutish arms snatched at her, but eluding all, she arrived, panting and trembling, at her destination, crying to the servant who answered her knock:

"Citoyenne, is this the Committee of Safety?"

"Yes."

"I must see them."

"Do you come to denounce some one?"

"I do."

"Enter."

Nicole found herself in a hall.

"Name, citoyenne?"

"The Citoyenne Nicole, bouquetière. The Citoyen Couthon will know me."

The servant passed to a door at the back and knocked timidly. At the second repetition a voice cried:

"Come in."

The door opened on a group of men about a table littered with papers.

"What is it?"

"A citoyenne who wishes to make a denunciation."

"Name?"

"The Citoyenne Nicole, bouquetière."

"Tiens! I know her," exclaimed a voice. The spokesman, on this evidence, gave a sign of permission to the servant, who ushered in Nicole.

A voice said approvingly:

"Look—she is pretty."

"Haven't the time."

Several, attracted by the exclamation, gave her a casual glance; the rest, without raising their heads, continued the low hum of their conference. From the farther side a man wrapped in blankets, deformed, infirm, seized with sudden chills, greeted her.

"Well, Nicole, you've come to denounce some one? That's right."

"Citoyen Couthon," Nicole blurted, "I—"

At the aspect of these machine-like men industriously busy with the lists that fed the guillotine, all her anger dissolved—she could not pronounce there the name she had loved.

"Well, well," Couthon said encouragingly, "you want to denounce whom? Come, let us get at it. Not the Citoyen Eugène Barabant, at least," he said, with a good-natured leer.

The sound of that name in this spot, without pity, terrified Nicole; she now sought only an excuse to retreat.

"What name's that?" cried a little man from the table. "Eugène Barabant? Wait a moment; wait a moment. Let me search."

Couthon lounged to the side of the speaker, who, turning to his neighbor, demanded the list of suspects to be arrested, while Nicole, flattened against the wall, dazed by a sudden fear, remained trembling at the snatches of conversation that reached her.

"A man offered me one thousand livres to-day if I'd slip in the name of his wife."

"That was cheap!"

"Héron is becoming insupportable. He's sent in the name of every one in his building. To-day it's the woman above him."

"She makes too much noise, no doubt."

"What's the difference? The Nation needs the funds. We must coin money on the Place de la Revolution; the guillotine is the mint of the Nation."

"You're a financier."

"I'm proud of it. Guillotine the rich—there's my finance."

Couthon raised his head.

"That's strange; I too thought I'd seen the name."

The others, attracted by his exclamation, asked:

"What name?"

"Barabant. Eugène Barabant."

A small man spoke up.

"Denounced last night by the Citoyen Javogues and an old hag the size of a child. Do you remember?"

A chorus of assent greeted him.

"Barabant denounced!" Nicole cried. "Barabant denounced!" She extended her hand. "La Mère Corniche?"

"That's the name."

"Come, Nicole, a lover is easily replaced. I've sacrificed two already to the Nation," Couthon cried. "Don't lose your time; denounce your suspect. We are short to-night."

"A pretty patriot like that has right to a dozen suspects," cried another, amid laughter.

Overwhelmed, dizzy, and horror-stricken, she shook her head, felt with her hands until she found the door, and, backing from the room, fled from the house—fled back through the ghostly city.

Goursac's door was opened; Geneviève herself, with solemn face flushed with the light of her candle, was waiting for her.

"Tell me quick!" she cried, apprehending what had happened.

"You know, then?"

"Know what?"

"Barabant has been arrested."

She recoiled to the wall shrieking:

"Arrested!"

"An hour ago."

"Where?"

"Here."

"Here? Then he came back?"

"Yes."

Without waiting to hear more, she fled to their room. The lantern he had lighted shone over the stone floor, the cheerless walls, and the kinks in the roof. It was all empty—terribly empty. On the bed she perceived the belt and the coat he had left. Forgetting her jealousy, her anger, her mission, remembering only that he had returned, knowing only that her dream was ended, she stretched out her helpless arms and cried:

"Barabant! Barabant!"

Then, overcome with hunger, weariness, and the ravages of her emotion, she slipped to the floor in a heap.

VIII

LA FÊTE DE LA RAISON

On the 20th of Brumaire, day of the Feast of Reason, maddest day the world has ever known, the Revolution, having overturned the social order, abolished the clergy, introduced the monetary system, instituted fraternal banquets, established popular education, and renamed the calendar, now, as though unwilling that aught should exist save in its image, decreed the abolition of religion and set up the cult of Reason. The neighborhood of the Prêtre Pendu, accustomed as it was to the vagaries of its tyrants, was yet astounded at the pitch of frenzy to which exultation stirred the Marseillais and his companions.

The ecstasy of Javogues terrified all with its frantic joy; for him the consummation of the human race had arrived. He spent the morning before the cabaret, astride a vat, dispensing wine and hand-shakes, his arms in the air haranguing the crowd that trembled to be present and dared not stay away.

"Religion is dead!" he bellowed to all comers. "The farce is ended! The impudent bubble is pricked!"

Boudgoust and Jambony, on either side, imitated his fury and his gestures, while Cramoisin, twisting in the crowd, made all he met shout to the cry of:

"Vive la Raison!"

The listeners for the most part simulated enthusiasm, with an eye to escape. A few echoed:

"Down with superstition!"

La Mère Corniche, hobbling into the midst of them, extended her hand to Javogues in rough familiarity, crying:

"Well, my big fellow, are you happy? What a day, hanh? No more superstitions for us! Touch hands."

"Touch there, mother!" Their hands met with a clap. "Didn't I tell you, from the first, there is no God?"

"Aye, you did. He never feared, that man!"

"I say it now," Javogues cried, and thrice he shouted: "There is no God!"

Suddenly, flinging from the vat, he cleared a space about him with his arm, and, seizing Geneviève by the shoulder to steady himself, cried:

"If there is a God, let him strike me down. Let the moment decide between us. I defy him!"

He raised his fist to the sky and remained waiting, while more than one closed their eyes in terror. Then as the skies disgorged no thunderbolt, his arm relaxed, descending to his side, and the scornful lips with a sneer pronounced:

"Bah!"

"Vive Javogues!"

It was the voice of Cramoisin that acclaimed the victor.

Abandoning Geneviève, Javogues caught from the crowd a bakeress and a fille de joie and forced them into each other's arms, crying:

"Embrace; the Revolution declares you sisters!"

Leaving the frightened women cowering, he again seized Geneviève as a prop, and clearing the throng, rolled up the street, invoking each window with the exulting shout:

"Vive la Raison!"

While Cramoisin and Boudgoust combated for the relinquished vat, Jambony, serving the spigot, impudent and mocking, bellowed:

"Citoyens, it is not enough to wipe out cults: we must level the steeples. Steeples are aristocratic. What's the use of making Temples of Reason of the ci-devant churches if steeples are to lord it over us. Steeples are the princes of the city!"

"Citoyen, the Section des Bonnes Nouvelles has already done so!" a woman cried.

"Then Vive la Section des Bonnes Nouvelles!"

With the departure of Javogues the crowd grew noisy, disputing and haranguing. From the top of the vat, which he had gained, Cramoisin bellowed in vain to them to listen to his ideas on the primeval innocence and the community of women. The throng had turned to another who, applauding the laws of burial, declared, beyond interring each citoyen under the simple tricolor flag, perfect equality could be obtained only by identical tombstones.

All at once la Mère Corniche, who had remained on the fringe of the crowd, shrank into it with an exclamation of fear. At the entrance of No. 38 appeared Nicole. On her face was the brooding and the color of death. For a moment she leaned against the wall, searching uneasily among the crowd. Then, still seeking, she approached, swaying from side to side, and her eye fell on la Mère Corniche—and passed.

"It is not I," the old woman muttered, still trembling from the suspense. "It's Cramoisin."

Then as Nicole, shaking her head, turned wearily and went down the street, rubbing from time to time against the wall, la Mère Corniche said to herself, "Ah, it is Javogues!"

She sought the eye of Cramoisin. He was still on the vat, struck dumb in the midst of a furious harangue, following the girl as she disappeared from sight.

The concierge, in her fear, had guessed rightly: Nicole sought the Marseillais. Her doubts of Barabant, dispelled on the instant of his arrest, had given place to bitter reproaches, to self-accusation, and to an immense, confused hatred of the man who had betrayed him. The separation was irrevocable; she could see nothing ahead. In the desolation of her hopes her anger turned against the Revolution. Barabant guilty! Barabant, the generous, impulsive advocate of great ideas, a traitor! At such a thought her whole being rose in revolt against the Revolution that would destroy him. Without distinguishing its abuses from its truths, reasoning from men to ideas, revolting at the doctrine of the community of women that menaced her pure ambitions, she saw the Revolution only in the furious figure of Javogues, brutal, despotic, and mad. Shrinking from her comrades, without faith, without hope, adrift, with the figure of Charlotte Corday ever before her, tormented with the thought of martyrdom, she followed Javogues, restlessly keeping him under her eye, seeking him with an instinctive impulse that gradually and fearfully shaped itself in her resolution.The streets where she wandered were filled with barbaric processions from the sack of the churches. Unshaven heads crowned with gorgeous miters, ragged bodies clothed in purple robes, smudgy arms brandishing golden chalices, crucifixes, and relics swept by with exultant, mocking chorus. In the churchyards troops of beggars demolished monuments and leveled the tombs, while still others beheaded the stone images in the niches of the doors.

Toward night the lowest elements of the social order were unchained. The drunkards, the thieves, the idiots, the pariahs, the beggars, the destitute, the morbidly curious, the shrews, the hags, the harlots; all who hated the good and many who had been taught to regard religion as the shackles that fastened them to servitude, erupted into the night, to mock the Church and dishonor it.

Listless, troubled, and uneasy, through the demented city Nicole continued her search, stopping neither for lunch nor for supper, sorting, without success, each successive throng, while every scene of license and sacrilege that inflamed her anger steadied her resolve.

In the church of St. Gervais she stopped, appalled at the riot. Within, shrieks of laughter mingled with hoarse shouts of men and the surging rhythm of music. Horror and rage possessed her, and she plunged in, seeking Javogues, while her hand went nervously to her breast.

The church was dim with the smoky glimmer of lamps, which veiled the interior in a mantle of fog. The fishwives from the Marché St. Jean offered salted herrings to all comers, poisoning the air and disgusting the nostrils, while on their track followed limonadiers with overtopping tanks, rattling their cups and hawking their beverage.

In the Chapel of the Virgin a hundred couples were dancing, bumping into one another, hilarious with wine and hoarse with shouting; while above the carnival, enthroned on the altar, a blue and white Goddess of Reason, a girl of fifteen, watched the rout, arranging her scarlet liberty-cap or extending her hand with conscious smiles to those who acclaimed her.

Among these women whirling with closed eyes and tumbled hair, among the reeling men, Nicole glided until satisfied that the Marseillais was absent; then she left the unholy halls and ran, panting, to St. Eustache.

There, inside the entrance, the uproar halted her, and she remained, in bewilderment, gazing down the enormous length, asking herself if her senses had departed.

The great vista was transformed into a country-side; at her elbow were rustic huts and clumps of trees, while in the distance, hidden under the foliage of thickets, rose mounds that echoed to the creaking of planks under the rush of feet. Suddenly a hand caught her arm and Dossonville's voice cried:

"Nicole, are you mad!"

Angry at this interruption to her plans, she turned with a gesture of impatience; but Dossonville, without relinquishing his grasp, continued sternly:

"You cannot stay, you cannot!"

"I am going to."

The next moment some one seized her by the waist; she turned with a scream. It was Cramoisin who, unaware of her identity, had caught her.

At the sight of Nicole he relaxed his hold, in such utter terror that he stumbled and fell on his back, when a band of women seized him by the arms and legs and bore him raging into the crowd.

"Diable!" Dossonville muttered to himself. "If the beast recognized me, I am done for." Then taking the girl's arm, he repeated: "Nicole, you cannot remain; it is impossible."

"I can protect myself," she said savagely.

"Nicole—"

"I must stay!"

In a moment Dossonville guessed something of her design, and withdrawing a step, said sternly:

"Whom are you seeking?"

"No one."

"You are meditating something desperate."

"No."

"You will not come?"

She shook her head impatiently.

"Then my life is in your hands; I will not leave you."

Satisfied with this solution, that offered her a certain protection, Nicole inclined her head, and caring little how far she betrayed herself to him, hastened feverishly into the throng. The loathing and hatred which communicated itself to her body banished all other senses; her breast rose tumultuously, her forehead grew ugly with anger, while her restless eyes beheld the saturnalia without comprehension.

Silently she dragged him about the great space. On the altars of the chapels were spilled bouquets and bottles of wine pell-mell with sausages, pâtés, vegetables, and meats. A score of hands clutched the food, scattering it over the steps, splashing the altars with the red stains of wine. The people gorged, drank, embraced, and fell sprawling; while at times, with a drunken cheer, some one in the tangle would hurl a sausage or a ball of dripping bread at the statues and portraits above, crying:

"There's for you, ci-devant Virgin!"

"Eat a little and become a good republican!"

Out of the scramble, boys and girls were thrust forward to plunge their tiny hands into the food in sign of liberty, while bottles of wine, snatched from the famished lips of beggars, were held out to them, until in their intoxication they furnished amusement to the ribald crowd.

"Pass on, pass on," cried Nicole.

A rush of women brushed them against the wall. In the procession were tossing a dozen statues capped with liberty-bonnets. In front of them, a woman, leaping forward, embraced a statue in her arms and bore it crashing to the floor.

At the next chapel, Dossonville felt a sudden tension on his arm. Within, a band of madmen and crazy women were performing a mockery of a mass. Before a half-naked girl in stupor on the altar Boudgoust was kneeling, while Jambony, insolent and sneering, swung a chain of sausages to and fro as censers.

Below the figure of the Goddess of Reason had been placed a hastily constructed guillotine, which Boudgoust elevated and replaced, pouring over it a libation of red wine, announcing:

"The blood of aristocrats we offer thee!"

Then turning, he led the uproarious congregation, crouching below, in a litany:

"St. Guillotine, protector of patriots, pray for us. St. Guillotine, terror of aristocrats, protect us. Lovely machine, have pity on us. Admirable machine, have pity on us. St. Guillotine, deliver us of our enemies!"

"Pass on, pass on," Nicole cried, after the unavailing search.

"If it is not they, it is Javogues," thought Dossonville, who had been wondering whom she was seeking.

They left the chapels and emerged into the aisle, where no sound predominated and everything was heard; where it seemed that Hell, having overturned Heaven, was struggling toannihilate itself in the need of venting its wickedness.

For a moment Nicole forgot herself, aghast at the frenzy of her kind. She raised her eyes in terror to the deep vaults stretching upward undisturbed, serene and awful, as though from the dim regions, which in her childhood she had peopled with visions, the avenging thunderbolt was about to smite the scoffers.

On every side the shouts grew wilder. Vile women, dropping the mask of their sex, pursued men in long, haggard, furious lines over the artificial mounds that groaned under the chase. The half-naked figure of Cramoisin appeared, surrounded by bacchantes, exhorting the crowd to return to the primitive innocence. Forms meaningless and confused flitted, whirled, reeled before them in an unending danse Macabre, while mingled with the tempest came the ever-exultant shout:

"Vive la Raison! Vive la Raison!"

Suddenly, by the catch of her breath and by the involuntary "Ah!" Dossonville knew that Nicole had found Javogues.

Without awaiting her leap, he hurled himself on her and bore her back into a thicket, struggling and pleading and burying her teeth in the hand that muffled her screams. Then when the mad struggles had snapped the bonds of consciousness, he picked her up in his arms and bore her quickly out through the unbridled mob, who broke into applause, believing her overcome with drunkenness.

IX

AS DID CHARLOTTE CORDAY

Behind Dossonville the riot and the tumult fell to a whisper; the titanic upheaval ended with the walls. Above, the night was solemn and gentle, and the Seine, toward which he bore Nicole, unconscious of the revolt, flowed with the serenity of ages. Depositing the girl on a bench, he busied himself with recalling her to the quiet world.

When consciousness returned, it was by flashes where the incoherent words, jumbled and wild, showed she was still in the saturnalia, preparing to spring at the hated figure of the Marseillais. Fearing that her cries would attract a crowd, Dossonville shook her. She opened her eyes, saw him, and sat up, seeking to assemble her thoughts. Then a groan escaped her as memory returned.

"Ah, my friend," she said pitifully, "why did you stop me? It was the moment."

She put down her feet, smoothed her dress, and stood up, while Dossonville, rising, said peremptorily:

"Where are you going now?"

"Home. Give me your arm. You were too strong; I am tired."

"Nicole," Dossonville began, in the hope of diverting her mood, "let us reason a little. That is not the Revolution: that is the scum. Judge it not by that."

"You say that," she answered wearily—"you?"

"Aye, the Revolution has proved too immense, and the leaders too weak. It has rolled over them; but the world is its path, and time will right it."

But Nicole, despite all his artifices, refused to say another word until in the Rue Maugout he cried sternly:

"Nicole, what do you intend to do?"

"Is that so difficult to guess?"

"Nicole! You are not going to take your life!"

"My life?" she answered, shaking her head. "That is all that is left to me to use."

"Javogues's?"

She took his hands, smiling, and said:

"To-night I was mad and you could stop me; now I am calm and you can do nothing. Good night. Forgive me if I have endangered your life. Good night, my friend, good night."

From the profound sleep of exhaustion Nicole, the next morning, struggled to open her eyes with the echo of Goursac's name sounding in her ears."Nicole! Hé, Citoyenne Nicole!"

She rushed to the window, and, leaning far out, beheld below in the misty court the abhorrent figures of the three Tapedures. At her appearance they sent up the exultant shout: "Goursac dies to-day!"

"To-day," she repeated dully, watching their departure without emotion.

It was still early, and the weak sun, filtering through the fogs of the November morning, cast yellow shadows where shadows showed at all. Silent and calm, the girl withdrew and began to dress. Within her soul the torment of the last days had given place to quiet. What she had recoiled from doing as an individual now appeared easy to her as the instrument of a high vengeance. In her now were the revolt of womanhood, the anger of the Christian, and the resolution of a Charlotte Corday, which is the resolution of a people.

Slowly and with great care she dressed, examining herself often, selecting her best attire, and as she dressed she began to sing, wondering the while that she could feel so light-hearted. From the bureau she took her dagger and a ring that Barabant had left, slipping it on her finger, saying wistfully:

"Poor Barabant. I might have betrayed you. Ah, I shall make reparation."

In the elevation of her soul he seemed very distant, and the room of her happiness, as she paused meditatively, unreal and no more a part of her life. She went to the bed and knelt, closing her eyes and stretching up her clasped hands. Suddenly she took the dagger from her breast and placed it as a cross before her, fastening her eyes upon it as her lips repeated her prayers.

She rose, passed out of the room, and without a tremor descended the stairs. But at Goursac's landing the sound of voices below compelled her to halt and withdraw into the room. In the turning her skirt caught on a splinter and was torn.

"Ah, what a misfortune!" she said to herself, unconscious of the incongruity of her words. "My best skirt, too."

Her mind, before the immense decision, took refuge in trifles. She sought a pin and occupied herself with hiding the rent, while from time to time she exclaimed impatiently:

"They are taking a long time!"

Unable to remain still, she passed out to the landing, whence, fancying that she had detected the name of Barabant, she stole down the steps as far as the turn would permit, shrinking against the dark walls. Almost immediately the door opened and the voice of Javogues said:

"He shall not escape, I promise it! Within three days Barabant shall look through the little window of Mother Guillotine!"

"But how'll you find him?" replied the querulous voice of la Mère Corniche. "Some one has transferred him from the Luxembourg."

"Never fear. I'll search the prisons and drag him out, in spite of all the Dossonvilles in Paris."

"But when?"

"This morning. There, will that satisfy you, old patriot?"

A grunt came for all reply, and the next moment the ascending flight creaked with the weight of the concierge.

Nicole, thus threatened with immediate discovery, seized her dagger in a desperate resolve, but the advance stopped and the voice of la Mère Corniche whispered:

"Nicole has gone out, hasn't she?"

"No, she is above."

"Then it is better to wait."

To the inexpressible relief of the trembling girl, the old woman turned and descended. Left in security, Nicole resumed her composure. Without fear of failure, without once debating the means she should employ, confident that all that was essential was to be in the presence of the tyrant, she descended, entering the room so softly that Javogues turned with a startled:

"Who's that?"

"Nicole."

"What are you stealing in like a cat for?"

"I have come to speak with you."

"Speak."

"Why do you persecute Barabant?"

"He is a traitor!"

"But he said he was not a Girondin."

"He lied."

"But what is his offense?"

"He would show mercy to the aristocrats."

"Mercy!" she cried. "Have you forgotten to whom you owe your life? You did not scorn his mercy!"

Instead of the expected explosion, Javogues, without resentment, replied:

"Because I remembered that I did not listen when they told me Barabant was contre-révolutionnaire. I have done a great wrong: I considered myself instead of the Nation." He rose with the glance of the fanatic. "Yes, I am guilty—I, Javogues! But I will denounce myself. If the Nation decides that I must be punished, let my head warn others against moderation!"

"Javogues," cried Nicole, recoiling, "have you not a drop of human blood in you? Have you pity for nothing? Does not the sight of all the blood spilled on the guillotine satisfy you?"

"Satisfy me?" he laughed. He elevated his arms, repeating it with a clap of laughter. "That little pool of blood satisfy me? Only an inundation can purify France. Twenty executions a day would not satisfy me. The guillotine is too merciful for traitors. I would drown them by hundreds—these aristocrats—these rich—these Moderates who have crushed us for ages. If those we smite are not guilty, their fathers were! We must be revenged on the ages."

Then addressing Nicole furiously, he cried: "See here, my girl; if you talk of moderation, you'll go, too!"

There was a moment's silence. Then suddenly, from below, she heard the voice of Dossonville calling:

"Nicole! Ho, Nicole!"

Without was life; within the dim room, martyrdom.

"Then you think," she said, looking down, "that Barabant is guilty?"

"He shall die!"

She was smiling with a deceitful smile as she answered:

"You are perhaps right. Moderation is wrong. We have suffered much."

"Well said!" Javogues cried. "There speaks the patriot."

"Nicole! Nicole, come down!" cried the voice without.

"It is that traitor Dossonville," Nicole said, still smiling. "He does not know that Goursac is to die to-day. Call it down to him. That will enrage him."

With a gleam of joy, Javogues turned to the window; but before he had made two steps, Nicole, bounding forward, buried her dagger between the vast shoulders. The hands went frantically into the air, a hideous sound choked in the throat, and, spinning around, the great bulk tottered and collapsed at her feet. A moment before was martyrdom, now nothing but horror.

Hysterical, panic-stricken, holding out her hand before her,—the hand that bore the curse of blood,—the girl fled from the room, shrieking:

"I have killed him!"

At each flight, shivering as though the specter pursued, she repeated:

"I have killed him! I have killed him!"

She rushed from the doorway into the court, haggard, stretching away the accusing hand, and streaked across the court into the arms of Dossonville, screaming always:

"I have killed him!"

Above, the face of Javogues, purple and choking, appeared a moment at the window, and fell back, crying:

"Help! Help!"

From the four walls the windows put forth frightened heads. Two or three half-dressed figures came tumbling into the court. But Dossonville, seizing the maddened girl, rushed her away through the passage and up the street before the startled lodgers could divine what had happened.

X

UNRELENTING IN DEATH

Placing Nicole in safety in the Maison Talaru, a privileged jail, of which the keeper, Schmidt, was his friend, Dossonville, picking up Le Corbeau and Sans-Chagrin, returned to the court, now packed with excited women. Forcing his way through the press, heedless of questions, he mounted the stairs, to find the room of the Marseillais black with the curious crowd, who shouted advice or sobbed hysterically as they strove forward. Raising his voice, Dossonville thundered:

"Silence!"

There was a lull, and a hasty turning of heads.

"In the name of the Nation I summon all citoyens to depart! The Nation takes possession."

Then followed a ludicrous sidling, shifting rush for the door as each, fearing to be marked for arrest, strove to depart unnoticed. All at once the long arm of Dossonville shot out and barred the way.

"Remain!"

Boudgoust fell back. Again, as Cramoisin sought to escape in the shelter of a fat woman, the prohibition rang out:

"Remain!"

Jambony next presenting himself, the arm of Dossonville again denied the way. In the room there remained at last but the wounded man, unconscious on the bed, a bundle of humanity crouching at the head, a doctor, and the three Tapedures huddling together against the wall.

From the doorway, the solemn face of Le Corbeau peered in, flanked by the mocking smirk of Sans-Chagrin. Dossonville, master of the quiet room, strode up and down in indecision, with glowing eyes fastened on the frightened three, who dared not meet the menace of his glance.

After five minutes of this torture, during which all awaited the order of arrest, Dossonville suddenly halted, extended his hand, and cried:

"Pass out!"

Sans-Chagrin, fearing to misinterpret the command, checked the foremost, asking:

"Citoyen, are we to arrest them?"

"Not now."

Confident that the menace would rid the city of the three, Dossonville turned anxiously to the doctor.

"Well, citoyen, what's your verdict?"

"Nothing to be done."

"Will he regain consciousness?"

"It is possible—probable."

Dossonville frowned.

"How long will he live?"

"Not beyond the day."

Desiring to prevent all communication with the outer world, Dossonville said, with a quick resolve:

"Then I shall be forced to establish a guard. The Citoyen Javogues is under arrest."

Turning to Sans-Chagrin, he gave orders to allow no one to enter—a command which had the desired effect of hastening the departure of the doctor. Approaching the bed, Dossonville became aware of the figure at its side, drooped over an arm of the invalid that hung down.

"Mordieu! what's this?" he cried; and placing his hand on the shoulder, he shook it.

The bundle resolved itself into the wild figure of a girl.

"Geneviève!"

At the next moment the girl, recognizing him, flew at him with a cry of hatred. Avoiding the blind rush, Dossonville caught her by the arm, crying:

"Eh, Le Corbeau, take her! Sans-Chagrin, go to his aid!"

Feeling herself overpowered, the girl became suddenly quiet, calculating, and dissimulating; but from her eyes murder looked out.

"Take her below!"

The wild light died out in the girl, who, bursting into tears, cried:

"No, no! Let me stay! Let me stay!"

"Diable! what a complication!" Dossonville thought. Then, aloud, he cried roughly: "Impossible! She must go!"

Geneviève, breaking away, clasped his knees, imploring pity.

"Let me stay, good, kind Dossonville. See, I kiss your hands. I'll be quiet. Let me stay. I love him. I adore him. Don't take me away from him now. I know he's going to die. I'll be quiet. I'll bless you."

"Stay, then!" Dossonville cried angrily. "I am a fool to do it."

The girl, released, flew to the bed and crouched down, laying her cheek against the shaggy arm, while the big eyes looked up with frightened, thankful appeal.

"Go and eat," Dossonville said, turning to Sans-Chagrin and Le Corbeau. Accompanying them to the hall, he added in a whisper: "Mingle with the crowd; convey the idea of an assault. Nicole was defending herself, you know. Return in an hour."

He shut the door, straddled a chair, and folding his arms on the back, with a glance at Geneviève, who continued motionless, entered on his vigil.

In the room the only sound was from the troubled breathing of the wounded man. The girl did not even shift her head; while on his chair Dossonville, like a statue of melancholy, waited the ebbing of life, musing at this end to their conflict, marveling the while at the strange antipathies that set men at each other's throats from their first glance.

All at once Javogues, raising himself on the bed, opened his eyes and stared at Dossonville, who matched the delirious glance with a quiet gaze. Javogues, without deviating, stared stupidly, then as suddenly fell back into apparent insensibility again; while Geneviève, dragging her body along the floor, wound her arms about the bull-neck and whispered in his ear.

Again the Marseillais rose and fastened his uncomprehending stare upon Dossonville. Suddenly, extending his hand, he cried:

"Who's that?"

Falling back, he almost immediately exclaimed:

"It's Dossonville! Ah, Dossonville! Dossonville! Spy! I have you at last!"

"He is still delirious," Dossonville muttered, drawing breath. "I thought he saw me."

"I know it by the look in his eyes!" Javogues cried from the bed. "I'll not give my hand to a spy! Boudgoust, Cramoisin, Jambony, watch him, follow him! Maillard, if he is acquitted, I swear I'll cut his throat!"

At times he was at the siege of the Tuileries, again in the court of the Abbaye, or again back in the cabaret of the Bonnet Rouge on the night of their first encounter. The flash burned itself out again and he dropped into further insensibility.

A knock was heard on the door. Dossonville, shifting slightly, said:

"Come in."

Le Corbeau and Sans-Chagrin tiptoed in and, at a sign, noiselessly took their places against the wall. Slight as was the interruption, it caught the senses of the wounded man and seemed to clear his vision. He opened his eyes and recognized the room. A moment he remained frowning; then, turning to the girl, he said with a note of tenderness:

"Ah, Geneviève!"

A sob escaped from the girl.

"What's the matter with you?" he cried, but immediately added: "Ah, I remember."

Presently he said roughly:

"Tell me, child; what is it?" Then, as the girl buried her face in the bed to choke the sobs, he answered himself: "It is death."

His eyes fixed themselves on the foot of the bed, and a great breath passed through his body. Presently a movement of Sans-Chagrin's crossed his vision, and he raised his glance to Dossonville.

"You are here to see there's no slip," he said scornfully.

"Javogues," Dossonville said impulsively, "I bear you no hatred."

"But I do!" Javogues cried fiercely. "I have never compromised with you. I'll not do it now." Turning to Geneviève, he regarded her a moment, and then said softly: "Kiss me, mignonne; I know you love me." For a moment pain checked his breathing. "Take my hand. That's it. Don't let go of it."

"Javogues, as a mere formality," Dossonville broke in, "do you wish a priest?"

"A priest! Yes, a priest!" Javogues cried, with a laugh of scorn. "Spy, you would make me out a hypocrite!"

"Man, have you no terror of God?"

"There is no God!" With the cry, the Javogues of the mob rose up, carrying Geneviève to her feet.

"Have you no doubts?"

"Bah!"

"And if there be a God?"

"And if there be a God, I do not fear him!" he cried; and in the Titan the unconquerable revolt of the Jacobin flamed out. "If there be a God, he shall answer to me for what he has done! In the name of the slave and the harlot, I'll accuse him; in the name of the galleys and the prison, in the name of those who grind out their lives with the labor of beasts, in the name of the famished and the leper, in the name of those who groan under kings and aristocrats, in the name of the poor, who fight for breath, for food, for sleep—in the name of all misery, I'll accuse him! If there be a God, he shall answer that!"

The effort exhausted him; he collapsed. The listeners, struck with terror at the audacity of the atheist, composed themselves with long breaths.

Dossonville transferred his glance to Geneviève bending over the hand she never quitted. A half-hour passed without a movement from the girl. It began to grow dark, and on the quieter air the sound of voices reached them.

Suddenly Dossonville, waiting patiently, saw the girl raise her head and begin to rub the hand she held. Then she stopped, sank back, and pressed the hand against her heart.

Presently she raised her head and gazed in perplexity at Javogues. She half rose, and dragging her body forward, seized the head between her hands, calling anxiously:

"Javogues, Javogues!"

Almost immediately she recoiled, bounding to her feet, her hands to her temples, staring aghast, while the cry was torn from her heart:

"He's dead!"

With a scream she rushed past them out of the room, and fled down-stairs. Dossonville, approaching the bed, looked down upon the body that was Javogues's. He looked and looked, forgetting all else, until Sans-Chagrin impatiently touched his arm. Then, with a start, he came to himself and led the way from the empty room.

XI

NICOLE FORGOES THE SACRIFICE

The Maison Talaru, where Dossonville presented himself the next day, was the strangest of all the strange prisons improvised to suit the needs of the Revolution. Crowded with aristocrats, it remained unmolested, thanks to the enormous sums its lodgers paid for their security. In return, the inmates passed the time in agreeable intercourse, gambling, amusing themselves, and eating well. Schmidt, the jailer, not without a touch of humor, replaced the enormous dogs which attended his confrères by a peaceable lamb, whose neck and feet, decorated with pink bows, never failed to reassure the new arrivals.

Placed in his lucrative position by the aid of Dossonville, Schmidt had nothing to refuse his protector; but, as he was at bottom avaricious, he met him with an anxious query as to the probable duration of Nicole's stay.

"What difference can that make to you?" Dossonville replied.

"The fact is, citoyen," Schmidt began cautiously, "the citoyenne has a room to herself, at your request, which brings me in eighteen livres a day, which makes five hundred and forty livres a month, which makes six thousand six hundred livres a year. It's a good sum."

"Mordieu! what gratitude you must bear me, my friend!"

"Yes, yes!" the jailer hastened to say, but with a doubtful inflection. "The ci-devant Marquis of Talaru has only a little office, and he pays that price."

"But he is the proprietor, I thought?"

"He rented the place to the section for six thousand six hundred livres."

"The price you charge him?"

"Yes."

"Good! So he pays you back, for the privilege of remaining a prisoner in his own home, the amount of your rent. Excellent! And they say we republicans are lacking in wit! As for you, citoyen, reassure yourself; the Citoyenne Nicole is here but temporarily."

"Eh, she can stay as long as she wants," Schmidt said hastily, with an eye to future patronage. "I only wanted you to know that I have gratitude."

"And its extent," Dossonville replied with a smile. "Lead the way with your lamb. Did the citoyenne remain quiet? Did she eat anything?"

"A nothing—a sip and a nibble."

Somewhat apprehensive at this symptom, Dossonville approached her room and entered with a hearty "Well, and how goes it?"

Nicole, still exalted and intense, without replying, came forward, questioning him with a glance.

"Reassure yourself, Nicole; everything is for the best," he said. Then, unable to meet the persistent search of her eyes, he admitted grudgingly: "Javogues is dead."

She inclined her head.

"When you kill a man, you know it. There is an intuition. What do they say of me?"

"Everything turned out miraculously," Dossonville answered joyfully. "My men were on guard. No one entered. Javogues did not betray you. The belief is that you stabbed him to save yourself." Without noticing the revolt in her eyes, he continued eagerly: "You are in no danger. I have routed the Tapedures for the present. In a week I'll transfer you to the Madelonnettes, where I have Barabant safely tucked away. There you can wait until the tide sets against the Terrorists, and—"

He stopped, perceiving his blunder, while Nicole, smiling a little at his confusion, said:

"Why do you stop?"

As he began again lamely, she interrupted:

"No, Dossonville, you see as well as I that it cannot be. Why does every one wish to save me?"

"I do not understand."

"Yes, Dossonville, you do, and you see your mistake. You would make me out a murderess. I am not a murderess. I gave my life to the Nation in exchange for Javogues's. I killed him to save Barabant, to save a hundred others who would perish if he had lived. As a patriot, I killed him to deliver the Nation of a monster. Only my life can justify the deed. Don't you see?" She took his hands in hers, saying: "Dear friend, bring me before the tribunal and I will bless you."

"And Barabant?" Dossonville said desperately.

She shook her head. In her present exaltation all that seemed like another life which she had renounced for martyrdom.

"And Barabant?" repeated Dossonville.

"Tell him I did it to save him. He will venerate my memory." She added slowly: "Then I will hold a place in his heart that no woman can ever take. That will be for the best."

"Nicole, listen to me," cried Dossonville. "Listen, for what I say is true. Denounce yourself, and you will drag Barabant to his death. Once admit your reasons for killing Javogues, and Barabant dies as your accomplice."

"Oh, oh!"

Recoiling before this immense, inexorable obstacle to her purpose, Nicole fell to her knees, imploring him with her hands:

"No, no, Dossonville, you are telling me that to save me."

"Yes, to save you; but it is true. Decide for yourself, but your confession sends to the guillotine every friend you have!"

"Dossonville! Dossonville! You are plunging a dagger into my heart!"

"Listen, Nicole; I swear to you it is the truth," he said, raising her from the floor to a chair. "Denounce yourself now, nothing can save him. I say no more; decide for yourself."

Leaving her limp with despair, he departed, well satisfied that the leaven would work and that time and reflection would temper her resolve.

The next day, instead of returning, Dossonville sought out Barabant, obtaining from the frantic lover a letter to Nicole, which he had delivered by the medium of Schmidt. Each day,ignoring the demands the girl sent him by the jailer, Dossonville repeated the same tactics, confident in the power of lovers' logic to sway her finally.One misfortune disturbed his triumph. On the day following Javogues's death, Louison informed him of the execution of Goursac. Dossonville, who from his fruitless efforts to save the Girondin had retained a deep sentiment of admiration for him, was much affected by the news, and yielding to his anger, scoured the city for traces of the three Tapedures. But despite the most diligent search in café, market, and boulevard, not a sign nor an echo could he find of the former despots.

On the ninth day of Nicole's imprisonment, Schmidt handed him a word from the girl, promising to reason over the decision. But Dossonville, though encouraged, divined that she would meet him with fresh arguments, and absented himself, until at the end of a week he received a second message:

"I renounce. Come."

Then, satisfied, he mounted to her room, grumbling to himself:

"Mordieu! one can't talk forever of dying when one is young and is loved!"

To his alarm, she received him without protestations, while her eyes, as they regarded him sadly, conceded the victory, but reproached him for the means.

"I must see him," she said simply. "Take me to him."

"What then?" Dossonville questioned, suspicious of her calm.

"I will do nothing to endanger his life."

"It is a promise?"

"I promise to do nothing that will endanger his life," she repeated carefully.

"She is still determined to sacrifice herself," he thought. "Mordieu! what an idea! Barabant will make her forget."

That night, toward eleven, he conducted the girl to Les Madelonnettes and restored her to Barabant. Only the lantern of the jailer lighted the sleeping halls as Nicole, with a cry, flew to her lover's arms. In their happiness they forgot their protector; but Dossonville, well content, withdrew, drawing after him the guard.

"You seem different," Barabant said at last. "What is it?"

"I have been away from you."

"How could you think of sacrificing yourself?" he said reproachfully.

"I was away from you," she repeated.

"You are here as my wife," he whispered. "Citoyenne Barabant, you understand?"

"Yes."

"But what is the matter? Why do you cry?"

"It is from joy," she said.

Then for the two prisoners began that weary cycle of the prisons, days so incredible that even those who survived looked back to them, doubting their memory. Everything became monotonous; scenes of heart-rending grief, partings of mothers and children, husbands torn from their wives, the experience of every day cloyed in the lassitude that came from too much suffering. Toward six in the afternoon they assembled in the main halls, listening at first with faltering courage, and then with indifference, to the turnkey reading the list of those summoned to the bar of the Revolutionary Tribunal.The accused passed out, sullen, resigned, hoping, trusting to a straw, indifferent, tired, and their names were heard no more until the following day, when a turnkey, with brutal exultation, read the list of those who had perished on the guillotine.

A shriek, a sob, a curse, perhaps, would be heard, a sudden converging where a woman had fallen unconscious; but the rest stolidly, dully, counted the hours to the next summons. New arrivals, the daily papers, an occasional letter, brought them news of the fantastic, heaving outer world. It was Frimaire, with tales of the drownings at Nantes—republican marriages, where man and woman, tied together, were thrown into the river with brutal jests; Ventose, with its incredible news that Hébert, the savage Père Duchesne, and the bull-dogs of the Terror had fallen; Germinal, more amazing than all—Danton the lion and Camille Desmoulins, beloved of all, swept into the common fate. And all the time the prisons were bursting with suspects arriving by hundreds from the sections, faster than the guillotine could serve them.

In Nivôse the names of the Citoyen and Citoyenne Barabant were called, and hand in hand, without a word, they presented themselves. They entered the rolling chariot, seeing again the unfamiliar streets; but it was not to trial that they were borne, but to another prison, the Bénédictins Anglais. In Germinal they were again called, and once more expecting death, were again transferred, this time to the Prison des Quatre Nations, with a glimpse of the sun on the warm waters of the swollen Seine and the breath of the spring that, as in mockery, brought to their laps a shower of petals from the flowering trees. Twice again transferred, they passed through the Hôtel des Fermes and arrived in Fructidor at Les Carmes.

Here new tortures awaited them from the hands of their captors, clamoring for measures that would empty the prisons of this constantly swelling horde of suspects. First, the newspaper was forbidden them, then all communication with the outside world. On pretext that the aristocrats were tempting the guards by bribery, a search was instituted and all money and valuables were seized. Later, another search was ordered, and all knives, forks, razors, and pins were confiscated, until for a woman to keep a hair-pin exposed her to immediate trial.

These tyrannical measures, designed to provoke complaint, failing of their purpose, the jailers had recourse to petty tyranny, to insults and jibes. Families were separated that they might feel the force of punishment due their crimes. Miniatures of loved ones were snatched from their throats, with the brutal declaration that traitors had no right to consolation. The vilest bread, spoiled meat, decayed herring, were put before them, and when still no complaint was heard the turnkey, nonplussed and furious, exclaimed:

"Damned aristocrats! What, we feed you garbage and you won't complain!"

Of the two, Barabant, tired of the long suspense, no longer retained any desire to struggle. Nicole alone upheld his resolution, encouraging, inspiring, invigorating him with her indomitable gaiety.

In the long months, she had gone resolutely and without subterfuge over the problem of their relations. At first, in the new flush of happiness at again possessing him, she had yielded weakly, and, banishing from her mind the inexorable figure of Javogues, she had turned to life and hope. In the ascendancy that her courage took over the limp resolution of Barabant she felt in herself a new power, and in him a new need for her, that tempted her with the bright vision of marriage.

As she began to reason the mood passed. For the first time she saw him in the company of men of intelligence and education, with whom he discoursed on things that were to her a closed book. Then she realized that between Barabant and herself was a gulf of opportunity and interests which she could never bridge. He too, she soon realized, felt insensibly the distance between them: she passed for his wife, but the constant reiteration never suggested to him what it brought to her. To become his wife was to be a drag to his future; to remain as they were was to count the hours of her youth. So, vaguely, in a confused intuition, the girl, struggling to understand what was barred to her, grew to realize the limitations to her life. It was a tragedy whichever way she sought, but the tragedy had begun at the first breath of love that had awakened her. So renouncing the future, she returned to the thought of sacrifice,—to save Barabant and, appeasing the manes of Javogues, to dwell in her lover's heart a bright memory of youth and devotion, that would abide with him through life. Therein she took her courage and all her consolation.

With the arrival of Thermidor, the Terrorists, checked by the passive attitude of the prisoners, introduced, as suspects among the prisons, spies, who, succeeding by malignant imagination where brutality had failed, denounced to the Committee of Safety a conspiracy by which the prisoners were to escape by ropes from the windows, overpower the guards, and assassinate the Convention.

The pretext was found sufficient and elastic, and the hecatombs began. The spies, called moutons, prepared the lists each night that sent troops of twenty-five or more each day into the fatal chariots,—paralytics, men of seventy, feeble women and maidens,—the crimes of all comprised under the heading of intention to assassinate the Convention. As fast as the prisons were emptied the influx arrived, forcing more transfers.

On the 7th of Thermidor, for the fifth time, Nicole and Barabant were placed in the chariots, to be conveyed to another prison. Then Barabant, utterly tired, rebelled and said:

"At last it is too much. I want to end it. I can endure it no longer. Nicole, let me die now and be through with the suspense. We cannot escape. They are guillotining fifty a day. Next month it will be a hundred. Let us be firm and not await another month of torture."

"Then, Barabant, after all I have done," she said reproachfully, "you would send me to the guillotine?"

"You?"

"I follow where you go."

But their companions cried in alarm: "What are you doing?"

"You'll betray us all!"

"For mercy's sake, be silent!"

Barabant, without energy to pursue long any determination, resigned himself wearily to their protests and the appeal of Nicole.

The chariot rolled out into the streets, where the passers-by, weighted down with the prevailing depression, regarded them without hatred and without curiosity. Their journey led them by the gardens of the Luxembourg, resplendent with green and the glisten of cool fountains. In the chariot some one said:

"Pleasant weather!"

"What good does that do us?" grumbled another.

"I played there as a youngster; but what of that?"

"It does not seem different. How curious!"

"Where are we going?"

"To the Porte-Libre."

"I was there in Prairial."

"What's it like?"

"The same as the rest."

The whispered comments ceased as the prison loomed over them. The carts ground on the cobblestones, passing the gate. From somewhere among them a sigh was heard. A voice said, with a low laugh:

"Here's the inn. All down!"

They passed to the office for identification and enrolment, and on through a square into the strange corridor to the hall, where a score of inmates straggled in curiously to see if they recognized any of the new arrivals. There, to her despair, Nicole beheld, in the shadow of a pillar, screened a little from the crowd, the face she had dreaded for months to encounter—the malignant face of Cramoisin, the Tapedure.

XII

THE FATHER OF LOUISON

The turbulent months which devastated the city with the fury of a pest had been to Dossonville an exhilaration. Paths beset with a hundred pitfalls he ran with enjoyment, passing from side to side with agility and alacrity, reveling in intrigues, nourished by entanglements. But the recrudescence of the Terror alarmed him in one way, for it rendered him powerless to aid Barabant and Nicole. He still watched over them, but even he dared not risk a communication, for the moment had arrived when it sufficed no longer to be Jacobin or Moderate. To sleep securely at home one must have been born lucky.

The death of Javogues and the disappearance of Cramoisin, Boudgoust, and Jambony had left the domination of Dossonville undisputed. Geneviève alone remained; but the girl, violently cast into womanhood by the spark of love, had relapsed into childhood. He saw her once or twice struggling under the weight of a bucket of water,—a child again opening its uncomprehending eyes on the world.

Thus left to the liberty of his own pursuits, Dossonville had passed the time running the streets, nose in the wind, smelling out the popular favor, prying, laughing, never abandoning his equanimity, furious and frantic when it was necessary, moderate and smooth of speech when clemency was in the air.

So that the prudent, desiring no more than to agree with the strong, had trimmed their sails by the conduct of Le Corbeau and Sans-Chagrin, who reflected the mood of their inscrutable leader. In Nivôse, when a wave of pity swept over the Convention, nothing could have been more touching than the laments of Sans-Chagrin, while the glance of Le Corbeau was benevolence itself. Their weapons disappeared, replaced by boutonnières, while, lingering behind their leader, they jested with all comers.

With the news of the wholesale drownings at Nantes and the revival of massacres, the two had put forth cutlasses and pistols as a chestnut blossoms overnight, and, stalking abroad with violent gestures and furious speech, struck dismay in all who met their suspicious glances.

But the leader who, with a sign, worked these sudden transformations was always at the head, imperturbable, alert, and impudent, twirling as his only weapon the little ivory wand with which he whipped circles in the air.

Occasionally he saw Louison, when the execution of a Mme. Du Barry or a Maillard drew him to the spectacle of the guillotine. Between the singular girl and himself there developed a curious attraction and repulsion, which impelled or checked his interest as regularly as the ebb and flow of the tides. When he saw her on the boulevards he felt strongly her magnetism, but in the vicinity of the guillotine she caused him a cold, almost repulsive, sensation.

So marked were her habits that a few had even bestowed on her the soubriquet of "the daughter of the guillotine." At the Cabaret de la Guillotine, where at lunch the menu bore the list of those to be executed in the afternoon, she was pointed out as the one who had never missed a performance. When discussions arose as to an execution, it was always Louison who was appealed to to decide.

This development astounded Dossonville, then annoyed him, and finally aroused him to such a pitch of disgust that one day he broke out:

"Louison, it is not right, nor human, nor decent to give way to such a curiosity. You must stop it. It is dangerous. It will become a mania. Already you seem at times inhuman."

"Others are there every day," she protested.

"But not like you. You must stop. What, does it please you to be called the daughter of the guillotine?"

"I don't know. It is always pleasant to be known."

"It is repellent."

"Don't come, then."

For a fortnight he absented himself, angry and disturbed. But in measure as she ceased to appeal to his interest she perplexed his curiosity, and he was impelled more and more to study her, seeking to understand the reasons of her indifference to suffering and the evident absence of emotion. At the end of two weeks, she met him on the boulevards with an amused smile.

"Since you persist in regarding me as a curiosity," she said, "you might try what you can discover. Mama is back."

Dossonville, without waiting to be urged twice, made a trip to the shop of the wig-maker and discovered that la Mère Baudrier had indeed returned from the provinces. So that night, toward eleven o'clock, he led his watch-dogs back, relying on a plan of campaign which he had imagined to force a revelation. Stationing Sans-Chagrin at the door, under which showed a slit of light, he knocked and entered without awaiting permission.

A woman, shading a candle, came precipitately down the stairs, crying:

"Who's there, and what do you want?"

"Are you la Mère Baudrier?"

"Well?"

"Are you?"

"Yes."

"Descend; I wish to speak with you."

She came down slowly, regarding him with alarmed surprise.

"Who are you?"

"The Citoyen Dossonville. I represent the Nation."

Then, while the look changed to one of dismay, she blurted:

"But what has the Nation to do with me?"

"Do not fear, citoyenne, you will have every chance to excuse yourself."

"Then I am to be arrested?"

Dossonville, without replying, said:

"Lead the way to the back; I must speak with you alone."

She obeyed, repeating:

"Am I under arrest? Am I? There's some mistake. I'm the Citoyenne Baudrier. Of what can I be accused?"

"Exactly on that point I am to interrogate you. It may be long; sit down."

La Mère Baudrier, trembling, took a chair, never ceasing her mumbling.

"But what? I don't understand. Why, every one will tell you that I am a patriot."

Dossonville, who had been a moment interested in the resemblance of daughter and mother, seized upon the last word.

"Citoyenne, there's the point: what constitutes a patriot? Do you know the law of suspects?" He tilted back his head and closed his eyes, not so tightly though as to miss the expression of her face. "These are declared suspects:

"All aristocrats.

"All priests.

"All Moderates.

"All those who, although they have done nothing against the Nation, have done nothing for it."

He examined the prisoner carefully as he continued, emphasizing each word:

"All those who correspond with the enemies of the country.

"All who habitually entertain strangers.

"All those who in the past have been associated with the aristocrats, whether as servant, mistress, or friend."

"She does not seem to fear the word aristocrat," Dossonville added to himself. Then aloud: "Citoyenne Baudrier, you are accused of favoring the aristocrats."

A look of amazement overspread the woman's features, which was so complete an answer to the charge that he added quickly:

"Citoyenne, you are said to have been very intimate in the past with the ci-devant nobles."

The blank look of astonishment gave place to one of indignation.

"I? I, the Citoyenne Baudrier? Come, that's a joke!"

"Citoyenne Baudrier, listen to me," Dossonville said, checking the explosion, "you are accused of having a daughter whose parentage you will not reveal, because the father is a ci-devant aristocrat and an enemy of his country."

At this point-blank accusation, to his surprise, she rose and said scornfully, with her hands on her hips:

"Ah, I see this is a trick of Louison's."

For answer he displayed the shield of an agent de sûreté. La Mère Baudrier, overwhelmed, fell back, covering her face with her hands, while a single word escaped her:

"Never!"

"Citoyenne," Dossonville cried sternly, "I warn you that only by proving the parentage of your daughter can you clear yourself. If you refuse, you must answer before the Tribunal to the accusation."

The woman shook her head without looking up.

"Le Corbeau! Sans-Chagrin!" he called.

At the noise of their entrance into the hall she sprang up, crying: "Wait! Wait!"

Giving them an order to halt, Dossonville returned, saying roughly:

"Well, have you decided to speak?"

For a moment the woman remained swaying, babbling to herself; then suddenly she sank back, crying:

"No, no!"

"Undoubtedly it is an aristocrat, and some one formidable," Dossonville thought, seeing the pallor of her face. Then, raising his voice, he called his men.

At their entrance a trembling seized the body of the woman, but at the sight of the mocking face of Sans-Chagrin she recoiled as before a vision, and a scream escaped her.

"The Curé Sans-Souci! The Curé Sans-Souci!"

"Who calls me by that name?" Sans-Chagrin cried, his face assuming a look of amazement. "Tiens! but I know that woman!"

Suddenly he struck his head.

"Of course!" he cried. "Pardi! what is there so terrible about me? I was always a good friend to you, La Glorieuse."

"You knew it, then, all the while?" the woman cried, turning fiercely to Dossonville.

"I know nothing," Dossonville answered; and seeing that chance had come in somehow to his aid, he demanded curtly of Sans-Chagrin: "What do you know of her?"

"A good deal," Sans-Chagrin began, with a smile. "I confessed her when I was a ci-devant curé in the days of fanaticism and error."

La Mère Baudrier, very white, extended her hand for permission to Dossonville, who said encouragingly:

"Allons, you are going to be reasonable now?"

"I will speak." She turned to Sans-Chagrin. "Citoyen Sans-Souci—"

"I am Sans-Chagrin now."

"Citoyen Sans-Chagrin, they accuse me of having a daughter by an aristocrat—Louison, the bouquetière."

"But your little one was called Rose."

"I changed the name afterward." For a moment she was thrown into confusion, but rallying, she continued: "You can say if the father was an aristocrat."

"I should hope so: it was I that baptized her. Come, now, what was he called? La Gloire—la, le—no, Lajoie, Simon Lajoie, that's it."

"Simon Lajoie!"

The thunderclap was Dossonville's, who, thrown off his guard, caught Sans-Chagrin by the shoulder, repeating:

"Simon Lajoie!"

But immediately, by a violent effort, he controlled himself, and dismissing them hurriedly, turned his back on the frightened woman, seeking to regain his composure. When he turned, it was with the calm of intense excitement.

"Is that the Simon Lajoie who used to frequent the Café Procopé?"

The woman remained dumb.

"Is it?"

"Yes."

"Good. Your explanations are sufficient. You are released."

He watched the look of immense relief that spread over her countenance as she rose, with a mumbled thanks, and started for the door.

"By the way, citoyenne," he cried carelessly; "one moment. Come back. Sit down. Could the Citoyen Lajoie have been any one in disguise?"

Terrified and trapped, the woman sprang up.

"For instance, the good Citoyen Charles Sanson?"

Her answer was a shriek and the thud of her body falling in a swoon to the floor.

XIII

DAUGHTER OF THE GUILLOTINE

"Certainly, he is demented," Le Corbeau cried when, after a dozen zigzags, Dossonville continued to plunge furiously ahead up street after street.

"Decidedly so," grumbled Sans-Chagrin. "Here's three times we've passed the Tour St. Jacques."

"What the devil could have happened?"

"You know Lajoie?"

"Why, of course—a little insignificant man."

"It was perhaps his brother."

"He hadn't the look."

"Anyhow, I say it's time to rest."

"My legs are worn out."

"If we suggested a halt?"

"I don't dare."

"Neither do I."

Oblivious to their fatigue, Dossonville wandered on in absurd circles, heedless of his surroundings, while if he passed a corner three times he did not notice it once. Vain and proud in his imperturbability, for the first time he was completely unnerved by this vision of the executioner that rose up at the side of the girl whom he had been on the verge of loving. All at once the mystery of her character was revealed, the insensibility to suffering, the unnatural curiosity, and the sang-froid beyond a woman.

"What an inheritance! What a curse!" he repeated.

Under the broken silhouettes of the housetops across the luminous sky, from out the mysterious, vague corners of the night, there started up, more ghostly and more sinister, the shadowy dynasty of the Sansons, the pariahs accursed, isolated, loathed, flinging themselves in vain against the barriers of prejudice, striving to escape into the obscurity of their fellows, always discovered, always driven back on the fingers of the crowd, that shrank away even as it pursued.

Back of the furtive figure of Sanson appeared the troop of malign ancestors, masked in scarlet or in black, nonchalant in their blood service, while behind hovered the red cloud of victims,—men, women, priests, nuns, children and gray-heads,—in long danse macabre around the ax, the gallows, and the guillotine; and among the Sansons, he saw, calm and uncomprehending, the figure of Louison.

Suddenly above his head rose the twin shafts of the guillotine, dominating the desert of the night. Then trembling, aghast at this sinister menace, Dossonville, with a cry of horror, turned and fled from the inanimate thing that waited there relentlessly the coming of the day.

In the first recoil from his personal association, he had promised himself never again to encounter Louison; but with the morning she seemed so expelled from his past that, yielding to an overpowering desire to study her in the light of his new knowledge, he drifted, almost unconsciously, to the Place de la Revolution.The crowd in which he sheltered himself was loose, not very attentive, nor very large: the spectacle was old; there was not enough variety in the performers. In front, scores of women, seated indolently on their chairs, suspended their knitting at each fall of the ax, counting:

"Twenty."

"Twenty-one."

At each execution a murmur wandered through the crowd—a conventional, listless, slurred cry:

"Vive la Nation!"

Louison, never still, moved among the tricoteuses, nodding and chatting. As each hum announced the arrival of a victim on the scaffold she turned for a momentary, prying glance; then, without interest, wheeling about, she cried her cockades, seeking in the crowd a likely customer.

Absorbed in the girl, marveling at the strange and terrible forces that drew her back to the parent scaffold, Dossonville fell into so deep an abstraction that it cost him his concealment. Before he could retire with the departing crowd, Louison, perceiving him, had hastened to his side.

"What happened last night?" she said, with an imperious gesture. "What did you say to my mother?"

"How do you know I saw her?" he said, unable to control a slight movement of recoil.

"I know it. What happened?" she demanded impatiently. "I was there this morning, but she was gone—gone during the night. What passed between you?"

"You have been misinformed."

"Dossonville, you are deceiving me," she said, looking in his face. "You saw her, and you learned the name of my father."

Without allowing time for denial, she took his arm and led him toward the Cours la Reine, turning among the bypaths of the luxuriant woods. There, amid the joyous gaiety of thespring, under the soft foliage of the chestnuts, she faced him with a peremptory question:

"You saw her?"

"No."

"She told you?"

"No."

Louison examined his face attentively.

"What is the matter with you to-day, and why do you conceal it from me? Did you not promise to tell me?"

"Yes."

"Then?"

"Nothing has happened."

"Dossonville, you are lying lamely," she said; then she added, with a frown: "My father was a great scoundrel, then?"

Dossonville did not reply.

"How stupid you are! You think it would make a difference. How does it affect me? Come, I am not responsible, no matter who it is. Tell me. It cannot affect me."

"It will."

"Then you know," she said instantly.

Dossonville shrugged his shoulders. He desired the appearance of resistance more than to resist, for his curiosity was stronger than his pity. But having thus betrayed himself, he added impressively:

"Do not force me to tell you."

She began to laugh.

"Louison, I warn you, do not demand to know."

"I do demand it. I insist."

"You will curse me."

"No."

"I cannot tell you."

"Who is it?" she cried, with a laugh. "Philippe Egalité, a farmer-general, Bailly, Capet even,—I mention the worst."

"Louison," he said shortly, "they call you the daughter of the guillotine."

She stopped, perplexed.

"You are well named."

"Don't return to that," she said irritably. "It was agreed we were not to mention that. Come, don't keep me waiting. I tell you it will make no difference."

"You absolve me?"

"Of course."

"Even if Sanson were your father?"

Louison burst out laughing, but suddenly she broke off at the sight of his face.

"Is that serious?"

"Yes."

She repeated, "Is that serious?"

"Yes."

"I am the daughter of Sanson?"

Dossonville inclined his head, awaiting the explosion. To his surprise, she remained quiet, withdrawing a little, while her eyes still waited on him, as though expecting a denial.

"How curious!" she said at length. "I never thought of that. Ah, I understand why she hid it. Now tell me all."

Seeing that she did not realize the extent of the revelation, Dossonville quickly related the facts, astonished at her calm, wondering what force was working beneath the surface.

Louison, in fact, unable immediately to comprehend the situation, continued to watch Dossonville, as though to estimate from his behavior the force of the change to her. Remembering his attempted escape on the Place de la Revolution, and alarmed at a new reserve in his manner, she asked herself angrily, albeit anxiously, what difference the knowledge would make in him. To test him, she advanced a step and said, holding out her arms as though to embrace him:

"Thanks, my friend; you have kept your promise."

He withdrew but a step and only for an instant, but that involuntary shrinking was her sentence.

With a cry of despair, she bounded back, transformed with hot, revolting anger, her fingers struggling against the temptation of the dagger, crying to him:

"Go! Go quickly! Go now!"

Then, distrusting the murder in her heart, she fled into the woods; but in a moment, crazed with the cruel injustice of her fate, she came running back, her lips trembling with passion, her breath cut and quick. With his accustomed prudence, Dossonville had retired by another direction, leaving Louison to tire herself out among the fragrant paths in fruitless, maddened rushings.

Gradually among the tricoteuses, the bouquetières, and the clientèle of the Cabaret de la Guillotine it began to be whispered that something extraordinary had happened to Louison. Her manner had changed. She was no longer indifferent, mocking, and careless under the scaffold. Instead, her companions began to be alarmed at the cloud on her brow, the brooding fixity of her glance, the abruptness and the poverty of her speech. Her questions were even stranger than her moods. One day she asked of her companion, thrusting her hand toward the guillotine:"Does that affect you to see them die like that?"

"I dream sometimes at nights," the girl answered.

Then Louison, turning on her an uncomprehending glance, exclaimed:

"True?"

Another time she said:

"Doesn't that make you curious?"

"Of what?"

"Curious to know what you would do."

Those who repeated her remarks exclaimed in apprehension and tapped their foreheads. As a natural consequence, the most extraordinary rumors arose. One declared that she had been seen thrice at midnight prowling about the vicinity of the scaffold. Another affirmed that he on whom she looked with anger would perish. Others, scorning these absurd rumors, gave it as their opinion that her mind was shaken by her unnatural obsession. The girl did not fail to notice the change in the demeanor of her companions, and, in her tortured imagination, ascribed to it a different cause.

"Why do they draw away from me?" she said once.

"It's your imagination."

"Are you superstitious?" she said disjointedly.

"I? A little."

"Why do they call me the daughter of the guillotine? Doesn't that strike you as odd?"

And she threw upon her companion a quick, cunning glance, as though to surprise the momentary confusion that would expose her real knowledge.

Thermidor began with the hecatombs from the pretended Conspiracy of the Prisons, and the transfer of the guillotine to the Barrière du Trône Renversé. The great rolling biers, attended by the scum of the city, bore each day to the scaffold their thirty, forty, sixty victims. Even the Faubourg St. Antoine, satiated and appalled, began to grumble, while from time to time voices broke out in protestation, willing from mere lassitude to end the spectacle by their own sacrifice.

On the 6th of Thermidor, almost at the side of Louison, a bouquetière, her comrade, cried out:

"I am sick of it! Robespierre is a scoundrel. They kill too many people. I want to die."

The next day she was on the scaffold, looking down indifferently, contented to end the fatigue of surfeited disgust.

Louison laughed aloud.

"Why do you laugh?" her neighbor said. "What has she done to you?"

"I do not laugh at her," she answered impatiently. "I laughed because I told her I would go first."

Her companion edged away. The tricoteuses, stopping their needles, counted:

"Forty-eight!"

At that moment Louison beheld Dossonville on the outskirts of the crowd. Seizing the girl nearest to her, a child of fifteen, by the shoulder, she cried, with a furious gesture:

"Jeanneton, do you see that fellow over there? He thinks I can't see him, the fool! As though I cared!"

The child struggled to free herself, but Louison, without relaxing her hold, transferred her look to the scaffold. Twice again the murmur rose:

"Forty-nine!"

"Fifty!"

"Do you know what I am wondering?" Louison said suddenly to the child whimpering in her clutch. "How strange it must feel to be there."

All at once, releasing the frightened Jeanneton, she advanced toward the guillotine, as though irresistibly sucked into the maelstrom, stopped, drew her hand across her forehead, then, facing the crowd, flung away her basket of flowers and shouted:

"Vive le Roi!"

In an instant she was surrounded, while everywhere the cries went up:

"She is mad!"

"She is drunk!"

"We have seen it for weeks."

"She is not responsible."

"She is a patriot."

Others insisted:

"Arrest her!"

"The Nation is insulted!"

"No favor!"

About the fringes of the crowd they questioned excitedly, running to and fro:

"Who is it?"

"Louison."

"Impossible!"

"Yes, Louison."

"She is mad!"

About her the mass struggled and swayed, some crying to her to simulate drunkenness, others clamoring for her arrest. In the center, Louison, alone calm and indifferent, secure in the knowledge of what must follow, continued to regard the silhouette of the guillotine, while about her lips was that curious smile which is seen only on the face of the martyr or the insane.

XIV

THE LAST ON THE LIST

As Nicole, in the hall of the Porte-Libre, stopped aghast at this apparition of their enemy, Cramoisin perceived her, and scuttling hurriedly forward, cried in triumph:

"Bonjour, Nicole. What luck, eh? Well, aren't you going to say good day?"

"Bonjour," she answered hastily.

"And Barabant, too," he cried. "Better still, and so glad to see me! Bonjour, Barabant."

"Ah, it's you, hypocrite!" Barabant answered scornfully.

There was a movement of incredulity and alarm among the prisoners, who hastened to withdraw from them. Cramoisin, as though whipped across the face, fell back, scowling and cursing, while Nicole, seizing Barabant's arm, cried:

"Barabant, what have you done?"

"Nicole," he answered, "do you remember what Goursac said when they arrested him?"

"No."

"'They are liberating me.' Well, I too wish to be free. I have lived like a dog for months. That is ended. I will not cringe before this bully, who will send us to-morrow to the guillotine."

"Then you are determined to die?"

"Yes."

"So be it."

They took their places at the long table, huddling among the famished and the fever-racked, while the scullions brought in pails the revolting food. Anxious to learn the position of Cramoisin, Nicole was about to question her neighbor, an abbé whose kindly look encouraged her, when Cramoisin, suddenly appearing at her shoulder, exclaimed:

"Eh, Nicole, my dear, if you want to know what I am doing here, ask me. I'll tell you. I am the secretary of the Conspiration. I keep a list of all the good conspirators and I see that they are rewarded. I bring good luck. I've been here but a week and we've guillotined forty!"

"You know him?" the priest asked as the bully swaggered down the line, and Nicole perceived the slight movement with which he drew away.

"He is our bitterest enemy."

"Pardon," he murmured, regarding her with compassion.

"We expect death," she answered quietly.

"What he says is true," he added in a whisper. "Since he has been here they have taken forty of us. He makes out the lists every night. We live at his pleasure."

"Does he live among us?" she asked, with a quickened interest.

Again Cramoisin returned, strutting with bombastic gestures, crying to the room:

"I am the friend of Fouquier. Fouquier promised me to-day that in two more weeks we could put out a sign, 'To let.' Isn't he kind to us, though? He's very sympathetic, is Fouquier. And I am his friend—I, Eugène Franz Cramoisin. He honors me with his confidence. Eat in peace. I'll speak to him about you. Don't worry."

He swaggered on, vaunting his intimacy, loudly assuring them he brought good luck.

Nicole anxiously repeated her question.

"He keeps up the farce of being a prisoner," her neighbor answered.

"Where does he lodge?"

"Near you, where the new arrivals are put."

"Sangdieu!" rose again the voice of Cramoisin, who, farther down, had halted at the side of a woman. "The herring is rotten. Do you not see it? Come, you must complain."

"It is all I need," came the faint answer. "I am not hungry."

"Bah, you aristocrats, you haven't the courage of dogs!" He returned to another: "And you, young man, they treat you badly, eh? Shall I complain to Fouquier?"

The youth, who had imprudently met his eye, instantly dropped his head; but Cramoisin, amid the jeers of the turnkeys, with a pretense of listening for his answer, exclaimed:

"What's that you say? Robespierre is a scoundrel?"

"I said nothing!"

"Then you thought it, and thoughts are offenses!"

Arrived opposite Barabant, he planted himself with folded arms and cried:

"Well, Citoyen Barabant, the food's good, eh?"

Pushing back his plate, Barabant likewise folded his arms and answered with a sneer:

"Do you think so?"

"To me it is delicious!"

"That's not astonishing,—it's the food of swine!"

A murmur rumbled over the hall, rising to weak cries of protests:

"No."

"He slanders it."

"We don't think so, citoyen."

Others implored Barabant to be silent, trembling at his rash speech, that would suffice to empty the prison. Under pretense of upbraiding him, they surrounded him, beseeching him to have a thought of their danger. Yielding to their terror, Barabant remained silent; but when, after the meal, they had dispersed to their rooms, he exclaimed:

"Ah, that did me good! I feel I am a man again. Nicole, to-night I shall sleep soundly for the first time in months, knowing that after to-morrow I may sleep more soundly."

Waiting barely long enough to assure herself of his unconsciousness, Nicole withdrew from his side and stole down the corridor, seeking until she found under a door a slit of light.

At her soft entrance Cramoisin started up in alarm from the desk where he had been preparing his list, and placed the chair between them.

"I am not come to harm you," she said disdainfully. Still for a moment he eyed her in doubt, before he was reassured. He grumbled:

"What do you want?"

From where she was she could see the list, and at its head the one name she dreaded to find.

"Read, if you wish," he said indifferently. "It will give you pleasure."

There were ten names in all, Barabant's being the first, and hers was not of the number.

"I have something to ask of you."

"Ask."

"I do not ask that we be sent to the guillotine together," she said, planning cunningly to avoid one danger. "That would be too great a consolation for you to accord us. Exchange my name for Barabant's."

"Nini," he said, watching her with covetous, blinking eyes. "I don't intend to let you go."

"If you will send me instead," she cried; "if you swear it, swear to spare him, I will give you a secret that will earn you the gratitude of Fouquier."

"You are too pretty," he said, with a smirk; "when one is as pretty as that, one is a patriot."

"You will not accept?"

"What, after this evening?"

"Citoyen," she cried, "he is in a delirium! It was the fever."

"Yes, indeed."

"Citoyen, he admitted to me that it was unjust."

"He shall go. You I'll keep."

"Citoyen Cramoisin," Nicole said coldly, "you can never make me belong to you, if that is your purpose. You are not Javogues, and I killed Javogues. Do you understand?"

Before the fire in her eyes Cramoisin shrank away, mumbling:

"You are more difficult than the women of the aristocrats."

"I give you my secret!" Nicole cried in despair. "Use it for your own good. I did not kill Javogues because he pursued me; I killed him to destroy a tyrant. Place my name there instead of Barabant's, and I will affirm it before the Tribunal. You will have the credit of discovering a plot. Fouquier will reward you."

"Is that your secret?" Cramoisin said contemptuously. "Nothing new in that."

"What! You knew," she cried, "and held back my name?"

"Bah! When one is dead, one is no longer a patriot."

"Citoyen Cramoisin, listen. If you will put my name on the list instead of Barabant's, I'll give you all the money I have."

To her joy, he looked up with a sudden interest.

"How much have you?"

"Twenty livres."

At the mention of this amount, which Nicole had managed to preserve, his eye became eloquent; but suddenly controlling himself, he asked:

"Paper?"

"Gold."

"You have it with you?"

"Yes."

"Let's see it."

"When you agree."

"It is right to be merciful," he said at last, with a sigh. "But I cannot spare him more than one day."

"For a week?" she pleaded.

He shook his head.

"Six days—five?"

"Impossible!"

"Cramoisin, for pity's sake, four?"

"Never, never!"

"Cramoisin, by your hope of salvation!"

"I'll give you three; not another hour."

He stretched out his hand.

"No; erase first."

He took off the name of Barabant and substituted, "The woman Nicole."

"What did you write?"

"The woman Nicole."

"Put the Citoyenne Nicole Barabant."

"What! You are his wife?"

"Put it down."

"There! Give me the money."

"And you will keep Barabant's name until the 10th of Thermidor?" she said solemnly.

"Yes."

"Swear it."

"I swear it."

"On your honor."

"There, on my honor, then! Give me the money."

She gave it to him, and suddenly casting herself on her knees, she cried hysterically:

"Thanks, thanks! You have a heart, I know. You will keep your word. You can pity. You can be merciful. Thanks! Thanks!"

Catching the ugly, cruel hands in hers, she covered them with her kisses and her tears. Then, escaping, she fled down the corridor, returning to bed, but not to sleep.

In the morning Barabant awoke, to find her eyes open and the sunlight in the room."How well I slept!" he said, springing up. Going to the window, he spread his hands into the beam of the sun that entered. "That feels good. Tiens, you have a strange look! What is it? You are not afraid?"

"No," she answered, smiling.

"Well, what then?"

"I have something— "

"Why, you're all wrought up," he said, in surprise, as she stopped.

"Barabant, I ask you only because there is no hope of life. Barabant, I— "

"Why, mignonne, what is it? What has happened?"

She threw herself in his arms, sobbing:

"Barabant, I want to be a wife!"

The moments that he held her in stupefaction were moments of agony to her. He put her from him, looking in amazement at the tear-stained face.

"Idiot that I am!" he cried suddenly. "That is what has been tormenting you!"

Waiting only for the accent of his voice, she sprang back, trembling, not daring to look at him.

"Then you will?" she cried, stretching out her hands to him. "Then you will?"

"Of course!"

Into his arms she threw herself, sobbing with the poignant ecstasy of joy, while he listened, still uncomprehending.

"That means so much to you?" he said. "But I always considered you as my wife."

Even in her emotion his simplicity drew from her a smile.

"Since when have you had this idea?"

"From the beginning."

"True?"

"Yes."

"From— "

"From the afternoon of the 10th of August; but I did not realize it then."

The correction summed up all her history.

All at once Barabant, rousing himself from his amazement, said:

"But how are we to be married?"

"Do you remember the abbé next to us?"

"Yes."

"I will ask him."

"Do you think he will do it?" he said doubtfully.

"I know how to convince him."

He kissed her and drew her away from him.

"Shall I go?" she said. "Now?"

"Fly!"

She was away a long time. When she reappeared with the priest she said timidly:"I have taken very long. I wanted to confess. It did me good. Does that annoy you?"

"No," he said smilingly; and looking at the face of her companion, he said to himself: "She has made him cry."

They joined hands, kneeling before the black-robed figure in the warm room, pervaded with the sunlight that the bars on the window could not arrest. He made them man and wife, and blessed them, and, bending, put out his hands to raise the woman. But almost immediately, with a smile that was of the compassionate master, he ceased his attempts and stole from the room.

"Tell me one thing," Barabant asked."What is it?"

"Why did you not ask before?"

"I could not ask. Now it makes no difference."

"But why?"

Again and again, through their solitary afternoon, as they waited, now silent, now questioning each other, he returned to his query without success. At five o'clock, perceiving in her body an involuntary shudder, he said:

"You're not afraid of to-morrow?"

"No. So many others have gone." She had a superstitious idea of God and another world, confused, simple, and sufficient. Thinking of Javogues, she added: "The abbé said I should be saved. Do you believe it?"

"Yes," he answered, respecting her faith. "I shall not fear, either."

"I know," she answered dreamily.

"She does not think of me," he thought. Then wishing to talk of himself, he said:

"It is life that I regret. I ought to have done so much."

"I wanted to give you that," she said at last, feeling in the air the approach of the last hour. "I wanted to die for you. That was my dream. You would have revered my memory and I should have been happy."

"Why do you say that?" he said, frowning. "And what do you mean?"

"I am only an ignorant girl," she said. "I could not long have been your companion."

"You are wrong," he cried vehemently, repeating it several times, "and you do me an injustice."

She yielded, and asked the question that had been on her lips a dozen times:

"Truly, Eugène, you would have married me?"

"Can you doubt it, Nicole?"

"You are good, very good." She smiled, satisfied to bear this promise away with her, but in her heart she was not quite convinced. "You have been very kind."

He was glad at such a moment to own a good action.

"Do you know, it's good to have you," he said slowly, a moment awed by the thought of the morrow. "I do not fear, but I am glad you are to be with me."

"Yes, I know."

All at once she sprang up, trembling from head to foot, crying:

"Do you hear?"

"The bell?"

"It is six."

"What! you are trembling?"

"Kiss me."

She threw herself into his arms, clutching him to her, while he, in bewilderment, said:

"But I don't understand."

"Hold me, Eugène, hold me!" she cried. "Don't let me go!"

She kissed him, holding his head in her hands, and the kiss awakened in him the memory of that first meeting of their lips, in the dark stairway, under the weak torch. He placed his arm about her waist, drawing her gently down the corridor, and believing that her courage at the last had failed her, he whispered as they went:

"Do not fear, little one. I am with you. I'll have courage for us both."

The prisoners assembled in the great hall, listless and dragging their steps, searching among themselves with anxious or mechanical curiosity, seeking to divine the chosen. Soon from the courtyard rumbled the wheels of the arriving cart.

Presently, faint at first, down the distant corridor fell the step of the turnkey, approaching slowly, as though to prolong the cruel suspense. With a crash the gates were flung open, and, flanked by two mastiffs, holding in his hand the fatal roll, the jailer suddenly confronted every eye. Without pause, the monotonous, singing voice opened the long, dreary preamble, finished it, and, rising to a shout, began the list:

"The Citoyenne Nicole Barabant!"

A sigh of relief escaped the girl, and her head fell on the shoulder of Barabant; but her ears, deaf to the cries of sorrow, to the lamentations of mothers and wives, to the screams of astonishment and despair that woke the silent hall, followed anxiously the roll, counting:

"Seven—eight—nine!"

At the tenth she relaxed, and her arms wound about the neck of Barabant in the last long embrace, violent with the pang of parting. Suddenly, with a cry of despair, she tore herself from him,—an eleventh name was being read:

"The Citoyen Eugène—"

Something extraordinary had happened; the jailer had stopped in indecision. Nicole, in the agony of her mind, saw but one face—the mocking face of Cramoisin—against an opposite pillar.

"The Citoyen Eugène Franz Cramoisin!"

The sneer dropped out; the face grew livid. On all sides astounded cries went up:

"Cramoisin?"

"Impossible!"

"Cramoisin arrested!"

Nicole, understanding nothing but that Barabant was saved, hearing only Barabant's voice demanding like a madman to be taken, fell into his arms, crying:

"No, no, it is not a mistake! It is I who have saved you. Barabant! Barabant! It is as I wanted it! Remember me, Barabant! Don't forget me! The abbé will tell you all. Barabant—Barabant!"

They tore her from his arms and swept her away, still stretching out the unavailing fingers, still calling:

"Barabant! Barabant!"

The weeping and the wailing died behind the clashing gates. A woman, catching her in her arms, supported her down the unending corridor, whispering:

"Lean on me. I have no one."

They entered the courtyard and climbed into the chariot, where a few prisoners sadly and indifferently watched their arrival. There presently two turnkeys, laughing boisterously, bore out and dumped beside them the body of Cramoisin, who had fainted.

XV
THE FALL OF THE TERROR

On the 9th of Thermidor Dossonville, who had long foreseen the inevitable conflict of Robespierre and the Convention, resolved on another rapid shift, and, appearing in the Rue Maugout, denounced Robespierre and the Jacobins in such unmeasured terms that he not only sent his listeners galloping off to denounce him, but to his amazement on turning about, found himself deserted even by Sans-Chagrin and Le Corbeau.

According to his custom, he visited the Conciergerie to inspect the prisoners. Already in the streets was the awakening of the great conflict. In the crowds the Jacobins alone raised their voices in furious boasting; but silence predominated, and the silence told of anger and condemnation.

In the first division he found no familiar face among the twenty-odd prisoners until, on the point of turning away, he discovered the abject form of Cramoisin. The downfall of the Terrorists appeared to him as a favorable presage.

He passed to the second division; there the crowd was thicker and more turbulent. Over the uneven field of bobbing heads he saw the judges on the bench, the listless jury, joking among themselves, and the abhorrent figure of Fouquier; while to the right, packed together on the benches, were the score of prisoners who waited, without hope, the mockery of a trial.

Dossonville, taking his place in the stream of those who constantly pressed to the front seeking the face of relative or friend, yielded good-humoredly the right of way to those who sought in sorrow. After some delay he reached the front rank. There a cry was torn from him:

"Oh, mon Dieu!"

At the first glance he had seen Nicole. Drawn by some subtle intelligence, she raised her eyes and saw him.

"What a fatality!" he cried to himself. "She herself has done this!"

A sudden anger filled him, of revolt and resentment against the stubborn sacrifice of this frail girl who had defeated him at the very last. His glance of reproach she met with one of content, which said: "You see, it is as I said."

She smiled seriously, a little sadly, as one who, though not regretting the decision, had not foreseen the cost.

A hand swept him back as others pressed fervently forward. He heard a mother's voice cry at his side:

"They have taken my child, my son."

His glance following dumbly the outstretched hands, he beheld at the side of Nicole the figure of a boy, who searched the crowd with frightened face. The buzz of voices rose about, the mother's mingling with the crowd.

"But it's a mistake. He's sixteen."

"Then don't worry, they can't touch him!"

"Aye, he's safe!"

"They arrested him for his brother, who's twenty-six."

"Calm yourself, la petite mère, any one can see he's a boy."

"They'll release him?"

"Of course—he's under age."

"Aye, any one can see that."

Dossonville but half heard them. He was crushed by the cruel turn of fate that had claimed her at the last, when the morrow would mean life and security. His eyes, yet refusing to believe, had never left Nicole's face. She was pale; but the pallor was of serenity, and gave to her person a certain distinction that seemed to raise her above her class. From time to time a certain pensiveness, whether of melancholy or of regret, gathered in her eyes. She was looking with womanly revolt below her, where, on a litter, exposed to all eyes, lay the unconscious form of a woman. The audience, rebelling against such cruelty, began to murmur:

"Remove her!"

"Take her out!"

"Send her to the hospital!"

The cry was taken up, passing from a murmur in the front ranks to volume and distinctness as it rolled back. The protest became so insistent that several of the jury began to cast anxious glances at the audience, and a judge motioned to Fouquier. There was an expectant lull; but Fouquier cried, with a sneer:

"She'll revive. Call the roll!"

The storm that had subsided in anticipation burst forth anew.

"No! No!"

"Remove her!"

"Justice!"

"Outrage!"

Near Dossonville a blacksmith, with leather apron, was shouting:

"To the hospital!"

A red-haired man in a baker's cap, with clenched fists, added:

"Tyrant!"

Fresh arrivals, bringing tidings of uprisings throughout the city, gave new courage to the protests. Fouquier, impressed at last by the outbursts, rose sullenly and commanded:

"Bear the woman to the witness-room, but the instant she revives bring her back."

The roll-call was begun—the simple attestation of individuality that had replaced the pleas of advocates and the taking of testimony. Encouraged by its first success, the audience began to murmur:

"They say the Quartier St. Antoine is in revolt against Robespierre."

"The Convention will surely declare him under arrest."

"If he falls, the executions will stop."

"I say the trial ought to stop until we see."

"Yes, postpone the trial."

"What! There are traitors, then, in the room!" cried Fouquier, who, the better to see, had mounted a step. Before his threatening glance the movement of clemency died away. Again was heard the monotonous voice of the clerk intoning the roll and the listless responses of the accused. In the stand one of the jury impatiently pulled out a watch, another stifled a yawn.

All at once there was a craning of heads. An interruption had come; the voice of the young boy was protesting:

"Citoyen, the accusation is for my brother. I am not twenty-six. I have done nothing against the Republic. Citoyen, I am sixteen. I have my papers to prove it."

A greffier nodded his head in confirmation, and extended a handful of papers toward the judge, saying:

"Citoyen, he speaks the truth."

Murmurs ran through the crowd:

"It's a mistake!"

"He's a child!"

"Release him!"

On the judges' bench the figure of Dumas arose.

"And if you are only sixteen," he cried brutally, "in the matter of crime you are fully eighty." Then, with a furious gesture, he added: "Pass on, and make haste!"

The murmur of revolt from the audience was overwhelmed in a sudden roar of astonishment. Dumas had been arrested! The counter-revolution had come! Those who had not seen the arrest cried:

"But what has happened?"

"Tell us! Tell us!"

Others answered:

"Dumas!"

"Arrested!"

"The counter-revolution has come!"

A voice cried:

"The quartiers are in arms!"

"True?"

"The tocsin is ringing!"

"They'll make an end of Robespierre?"

"Impossible!"

"It's true! Haven't they arrested Dumas?"

"Suspend the trial!"

"Mercy! Clemency!"

All eyes turned to Fouquier, who answered contemptuously and stubbornly:

"Justice must take its course!"

At Dossonville's side the blacksmith, with the sudden frenzy of prophecy, cried:

"Fouquier, beware! The guillotine is waiting for you!"

While with brawny shoulders he wriggled free of the willing crowd, Dossonville looked for the hundredth time at Nicole. She had not abandoned her calm; only a slight frown told of the havoc the sudden opening and closing of the gates of hope played in her soul.

Another judge replaced Dumas. The roll-call was hurried on. Twice Fouquier sent a physician to report the condition of the woman in the witness-room. A flutter of the eyelids would have meant death. She remained in a stupor, and was at last sent to the hospital. The roll-call ended. The jury, after the farce of declaring that they had heard sufficient evidence, retired to deliberate upon the guilt of the twenty-six. They returned shortly. It was late, and many suffered from the postponement of the luncheon-hour. One man acquitted—Aviot Turot, laborer.

A shudder passed through the body of Dossonville, and a groan escaped his lips. The fatal, inevitable word "Guilty" overwhelmed him. Nicole heard it with a smile—sad, yet satisfied.

Another stir, and a buzz of comments rose as the executioner entered and began to converse with Fouquier. Those in front, who could hear, called back:

"Sanson is remonstrating."

"Sanson wants the execution deferred."

"He says the city is rising."

A last time Fouquier refused to budge, and, crossing his arms, reiterated bluntly, to be heard by all:

"No, no! I say no! Justice must take its course."

The condemned, who had paused as they had risen trembling with hope, filed out, while the crowd in the court-room surged forth to meet the tumbrels.

Dossonville, using his privilege of agent de sûreté, entered the prison, seeking Nicole in the crowd of prisoners massed in the outer hall; threading through anxious groups, who whispered:

"You saw Dumas arrested?"

"They say there is a revolt against Robespierre."

"The people seemed to sympathize with us."

Others, scorning to hang their hopes on desperate chances, waited stoically or reverently the summons to the tumbrels. A young aristocrat was whistling defiantly:

"Oh, Richard, oh, mon roi, L'univers t'abandonne!"

In another group, guarding their enmity to the end, two brothers of the people retorted with the "Marseillaise."

Two women near Dossonville were chatting gaily:

"I am so pale those cursed revolutionists will think that I am afraid."

"You must not give them that satisfaction."

"I do seem pale, then?"

"Yes."

"Ah, then I must rouge!"

Dossonville examined the figure of the graceful woman, who was gaily daubing her cheeks, and recognized the famous Duchess of M— —. At this moment, in the obscurity of the arches, he discovered at last the blue dress and golden hair of Nicole.

"Oh, it is you," she cried joyfully. "I had hoped you could see me."

"Nicole," he said bitterly, "this is your doing."

Her manner changed; she grew serious.

"My friend," she said, "I have but done what I wished. I am happy." She held up her finger with Barabant's ring on it. "You see, I am his wife, and I have saved him."

The outward movement toward the tumbrels had begun. From the doorway the guards repeated:

"Hurry up, there; hurry up, you cursed aristocrats!"

Dossonville kissed her with more feeling than he had believed possible, and said, through the tears that clouded his eyes, "I would have saved you."

"Do not grieve," she said, touched by his sorrow. She took her scarf and put it into his hand, saying: "Give it to him. Tell him that I am happy—that it is best so. Adieu!"

Then, as though fearing to lose her self-control, she pressed his hand and hurried away.

Dossonville, passing out by a side entrance, hastened to meet the slow procession across the river. The city was in uproar; over the roofs the bells were crying the civil strife, while every street seemed to give forth the thunder of drums. Masses of volunteers, without formation or leader, swept the boulevards, while the air was charged with the conflict of shouts:

"Vive la Commune!"

"À bas les Jacobins!"

"Vive Robespierre!"

"Robespierre à la Guillotine!"

The chariots crossed from the gates of the Conciergerie, acclaimed by the hoots and jeers of the daily hordes of mad women who gathered to shriek their foul abuse and frantic revilings. But as the tumbrels passed the river the insults ceased, replaced by murmurs of sympathy.

In the third chariot Dossonville found Nicole. The duchess, with her brilliant cheeks, was on the same bench, and between the two women the boy, his hand in Nicole's.

From the direction of the Convention came wild rumors of Robespierre's defeat. The crowd, increasing, began to cry:

"Enough blood!"

"No more blood!"

"Pity on the condemned!"

Dossonville, hardly daring to hope, noticed that Sanson examined the crowd anxiously—a not unfriendly glance. The demonstration continued, growing bolder, a hundred voices insisting:

"Enough blood!"

"No more victims!"

"Stop the massacre!"

Among the prisoners several, unable to resist the sudden leap of hope to their eyes, stretched out their hands, crying:

"We are innocent!"

In the first chariot Cramoisin, in a frenzy, was shouting:

"Citoyens, do not mistake me. I am a republican. Vive la République! Save me, at least!"

Nicole was speaking to the boy; for the new vision of life had made him tremble. Amid the leaping floods of humanity she remained calm, a certain maternal sweetness and repose enveloping her as she sought to fortify the resolution of her companion. To Dossonville, through the rising storm of sound and swaying of bodies, a lull of peace seemed to surround her and to remove her from the frenzy.

Again the revolt rose in him that she should die thus. Perceiving all at once that the crowd had pressed about the carts until their progress was impeded, he flung himself into the swirl, exhorting and encouraging. The cries redoubled, becoming more threatening:

"Save them!"

"Enough butchery!"

"On, comrades! Save them!"

"Aye, deliver them!"

"Stop the chariots!"

"Unhitch the horses! Unhitch the horses!"

At this last, the cry of Dossonville, the multitude, with a shriek of triumph, surged up against the tumbrels. A hundred hands checked the horses, reaching out for the buckles of the harness, while a dozen voices cried:

"Courage! We'll release you!"

Already the prisoners exclaimed joyfully, already Dossonville stretched out his arms to Nicole, when a cry of fear and despair burst from the rescuers, voiced in the dreaded name:

"Henriot! Henriot!"

Up the street, at the head of his dragoons, sabres flashing in the air, break-a-neck came the wild figure of the Jacobin.

The surge of the fleeing crowd held Dossonville a moment against the tumbrel, where he heard through the confusion a cry of despair from the boy, "I could have borne anything but hope!" Then, as Dossonville was swept away, he saw the child's head fall upon the shoulder of Nicole. The next moment he was buffeted and hurled aside; then a horse struck him and flung him to the ground, where a dozen feet trampled him. Stunned, covered with dirt, and bleeding, he stumbled to his feet. The tumbrels, surrounded by cavalry, were disappearing in the distance, moving swiftly. He ran after them, shaking his helpless fist, and as he turned the corner, a groan burst from him. Over the heads of the people the twin shafts of the guillotine sprang into view.

Numb and half unconscious, seeing only, in the third cart, the distant blot of blue, he limped on, following as best he could into the square. He fought his way to the front, beside the cordon of naked swords that girdled the scaffold, repeating to himself a hundred times:

"I must not stay! I will not stay!"

But still the pitiful hope of a deliverance held him there, to snatch at every message of the air that floated over the distracted city. One after another the condemned mounted the steps and passed across the stage like phantoms, hurried on by the remorseless Jacobin, while those about him cried:

"Oh, for two hours—for one!"

"Cursed Henriot, we could have saved them!"

"Why does the Convention delay?"

"Ah, the monster! He is afraid to lose a single one!"

She came at last, a patch of blue, a white face against the stretch of heads. She saw him not at all, nor any one. The maternal instinct of the woman that had raised her above her companions on the journey was gone, and with it all consciousness of the world and the sorrows and the responsibilities which had so transformed her. Only once did she notice her surroundings, when the bourreau, with impatient hand, bared her throat. Then for a moment her hands went instinctively to cover herself from the multitude. Almost immediately her face became grave and reverent. The assistants advanced to take her to the guillotine. Then with a rapid motion she made the sign of the cross, raising her eyes to the deep sky, as though already she saw beyond the grave,—the timid question of a child who hesitates in wonder before the incomprehensible.

With a sob, Dossonville turned, shrinking from the sight of the mutilating knife, and waited with averted face.

There was a vast moment, then a shock of steel, and a woman who had seen his tears whispered:

"It is over!"

Then, fleeing from the inexorable machine, he plunged, weeping, through the crowd, stumbling aimlessly on into the frantic city, where, too late, every street was echoing to the fear-releasing shrieks of rejoicing:

"Robespierre is fallen!"

"The Terror is ended!"

www.ingramcontent.com/pod-product-compliance
Lightning Source LLC
Chambersburg PA
CBHW080907190726
48294CB00008B/1997
* 9 7 8 1 8 3 5 9 1 3 1 0 9 *